BLACK'S

MUSHROOMS
&TOADSTOOLS
OF BRITAIN AND EUROPE

Andreas Gminder and Tanja Böhning

A&C BLACK
LONDON

Contents

Groups of Fungi

Mushrooms with Pores

Mushrooms with Gills

Other Fungi

How to Use this Book

This book contains information about the habitat, life, biology and edibility of each of the mushrooms listed. Recognition is made easy by the informative illustrations with notes on key features. The large main image also shows each mushroom's typical appearance. Other illustrations highlight key details for identification or similar species. The text and illustrations in the margins provide information about the habitat, key facts to note and a cross-section of the mushroom or, less frequently, an image of the whole mushroom. On pages dedicated to individual mushrooms, a **'Did you know?'** box provides information about amazing and unusual things associated with the mushroom and the **'Caution – Poisonous!'** box provides information about inedible or poisonous similar species. This is especially important with regard to the more popular edible mushrooms.

Common name

Scientific name
Family

Size
(cap diameter)

Season
with normal weather

General information
Provides information
about the species.

Box
For portraits occupying
a whole page, this con-
tains important notes on
poisonous similar species
('Caution – Poisonous!')
or interesting additional
information ('Did You
Know?').

Gy
Cortin
Cap 5–1,

The or
It used
skin-lik

Edibility

shroom

_us_ (mushrooms with gills)
ober

ushroom's common name are unknown.
n a separate genus (_Rozites_) because of the
n its stipe.

d Webcap (_C. armillatus_) has such
s. Although it is eaten by some,
ended because of the substances

Habitat In coniferous forests, especially in heathery spruce forests, on dry, acidic, nutrient-poor soils, rarely under deciduous forests.

> Ring skin-like and solid
> Spores rusty brown
> Common in Europe but declining in many areas
> Similar species other _Cortinarius_ species

Caution!

The Gypsy Mushroom may be confused with many _Cortinarius_ species if the structure of the velum zone is not taken into account. Two such examples are _C. patibilis_ (left) and the hygrophanous _C. malachiu_ (right).

Gills brownish

Flesh pale brownish

Cap ochre-brown with a light violet band in the centre

201

Additional illustrations
This usually shows similar species or varieties and sometimes shows additional characteristics or detailed enlargements.

Key features
Summarised, general information about the species as well as its distribution in Europe. For portraits of edible mushrooms occupying whole pages, this includes the most important poisonous similar species.

Detail Illustrations
Further details about the species, which are not visible on the main illustration, such as a cross section.

Colour code and silhouette
Each of the three main groups is colour coded (page 1).

Main Photo
Shows typical examples of each mushroom in its natural habitat.

Stipe same colour with obvious, longitudinal fibres

5

Mushroom Structure

When people think of mushrooms or pick them, they usually only see the 'fruiting body' on the surface. In reality however, mushrooms represent a network of thin threads growing in the ground known as the mycelium. Although calling these spore carriers 'fruiting bodies' is botanically incorrect (since ovaries are not involved in the production of the 'fruit'), the term will be used in this book for ease of understanding. The sole purpose of the entire fruiting body is to release the tiny spores which are distributed by the wind to (hopefully) land and flourish in a suitable location. These spores are formed in the fruit layer (hymenium). This blankets the exterior of the gills,

hymenial folds or teeth, the interior of pores and tubes, or is simply formed around a more or less unstructured exterior. The fruiting body is generally elevated correspondingly by a stipe so that the released spores can be carried off by the wind. Exceptions to this include puffballs and sac fungi, which actively or passively expel their pores upwards into the air, and polypores, truffles and stinkhorns which rely on animals to distribute their spores.

Gilled mushrooms/boletes

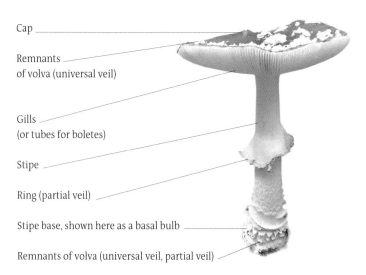

Cap

Remnants
of volva (universal veil)

Gills
(or tubes for boletes)

Stipe

Ring (partial veil)

Stipe base, shown here as a basal bulb

Remnants of volva (universal veil, partial veil)

Structure of Other Fruiting Bodies

Polypores and crust fungi

Polypores and crust fungi generally form bracket-shaped fruiting bodies. The exceptions to this are perennial species, which form a new layer of pores over the previous year's pores. In contrast, the growth of crust fungi is two-dimensional, meaning that only the fruit layer is visible. However, they sometimes form cap rims at their limits, meaning that growth can be both two-dimensional and bracket-shaped.

Upper surface, crust-like here
Flesh (trama)

Tube layer, many tubes here

Coral and antler fungi

Here, the fruit layer is undifferentiated and is on the exterior of the fruiting body, similar to crust fungi.

Branchlet Tip

Branchlets covered by the fruit layer

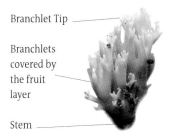

Stem

Puffballs

The fruit layer is formed inside the fruiting body which is more or less globose in shape. It decays quickly, leaving a powdery mass on reaching maturity which is expelled when pressure is applied to the fruiting body.

Fruiting body still closed

Mature, burst fruiting body filled with a powdery spore mass

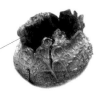

Sac fungi (cup fungi)

The predominant, name-giving form of these fungi is a bowl or cup shape. However, globose, closed fruiting bodies also occur (truffles) as well as species with a head and stipe-type structure (lorels and morels).

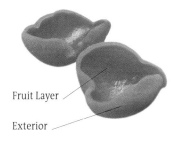

Fruit Layer

Exterior

Structure of Other Fruiting Bodies

The typical fruiting body form of most gilled mushrooms and boletes has a clearly defined structure comprising of a stipe and cap. However, other forms also exist.

shell-shaped

bracket-shaped

crust-like

globose/egg-shaped

coral-like

club-shaped

bulb-like

star-shaped

trumpet-shaped

spinning top-shaped

cup-like

cushion-like

shoot-like

with brain-like lobes

Cap Rim

The cap rim can also display key features.

ribbed, notched

long grooves

short grooves

fringed

Cap Shapes

The caps of most young mushrooms are half globose, changing to a flattened dome when mature. Older examples are often slightly indented with an upturned edge.

domed

conical

indented

upturned

conical peak

humped

lobed

honeycomb-like

funnel-shaped

navel-like

Cap Surface

An important feature, especially if caps are slimy or covered with veil remnants. However, slimy caps can dry and scales and veil remnants can be washed off by the rain. Cap colouring is highly variable and can change due to exposure to the elements.

micaceous

powder covered

slimy

radial fibres

zoned cap

scaled

water-stained cap

with remnants of veil

9

Gills

One of the most important features in the identification of gilled mushrooms is the positioning of the gills, that is, how they are attached to the stipe. For example, this method can be used to identify the *amanita* and *lepiota* genera and those of the button mushroom by their exposed gills.

exposed

ascending, fixed to stipe

descending into a tooth-shape

descending slightly

recessively fixed to stipe

broadly fixed to stipe

descending acutely

Unusually wide gill spacing or compacted gills are particularly noteworthy:

Coloured gill blades, forked or cross-linked gills:

wide spacing

normal

red blade

cross-linked

compacted

forked

Spores

Gill colour often also determines the colour of the spores, but not always. You can find out the actual colour of the spores by pressing the underside of a mushroom cap on to a piece of white paper.

Stipe

Whether or not this has its base in a velum or has a root is determined on one hand by the surface structure and the characteristics of the stipe base on the other. Length and girth are less important since they depend to a large extent on external influences.

slimy · smooth · longitudinal fibres · frosted

belted · flaked · snakeskin-like

Stipe Base

The shape of the stipe base is extremely important, especially with regard to the deadly poisonous species of amanita (see p. 116-125).

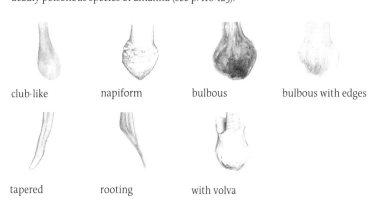

club-like · napiform · bulbous · bulbous with edges

tapered · rooting · with volva

Key factors here are the possible presence of a ring or a fibrous zone.

skin-like ring   fibrous zone   ascending   hanging   complex

Flesh

The flesh of a mushroom can become discoloured when it is cut open. Milk caps and some mycena exude a latex which is sometimes coloured. Smell and taste are also key factors (do not swallow taste samples!). However, odours often only become apparent after some time and may not be detectable in closed containers or when the weather is cold.

blueing   blackening   reddening   turning milky-white

orange milkiness   violet milkiness

Types of Growth

Many mushrooms grow in highly characteristic forms and the most common forms of growth are as follows:

coalescent

shrub-lke   gregarious   ranked   in roof tile form

How to Collect Mushrooms

There are a few simple rules to note which will help you to enjoy success when collecting mushrooms, whilst leaving the natural environment unharmed.

The correct equipment

In addition to clothing suitable for the terrain and weather (especially footwear), your container must be well-ventilated. Ideally, you should use a woven or chip basket. These allow mushrooms to be stored with optimum ventilation without being crushed. Never use a plastic bag as you may find there is nothing left of your mushrooms when you get home but a misshapen, pulpy mass. Consuming decaying mushrooms such as these can lead to food poisoning.

Cutting and extracting

Even though some books recommend one particular method, it is quite unimportant as far as the mushroom is concerned. If you want to identify the mushrooms at home or have someone else identify them, it is important to remove the mushroom in its entirety, including the stipe and any parts of the stipe in the ground. These are often key features for identification (see Amanitaceae, p. 116). The resulting hole left in the ground should, however, be filled in, so as not to dry out the mycenium. Positively identified, edible mushrooms should be cut near to the ground and cleaned off as best as possible to avoid cross-contamination in transit.

Pick mushrooms considerately!

A conservational approach to nature should go without saying. Because mushrooms are a key source of nourishment for many animals, you should never pick more than you can reasonably use and always leave old fruiting bodies as you find them. Rare species should never be picked, even if they are edible, and access to conservation areas may be restricted. Many people do not realise that a number of species of fungi are protected by law in Britain and Europe and may only be picked in small quantities, if at all. These may include well-known edible varieties such as the Cep, Chanterelle and Red-capped Scaber Stalk.

Cleaning mushrooms

You should use a small paintbrush for cleaning and cut away any heavily soiled areas. You should, as far as is possible, avoid washing mushrooms as they quickly soak up moisture like sponges. Hard, woody stipes (*K. mutabilis*, Parasol) should be discarded. It is recommended to remove any slimy layers present on mushrooms. It can lead to stomach upsets and is quite unappetising. The same is true for the tube layer in older boletes. If this layer separates easily then you should remove it.

Mushroom preparation

You can fry the prepared mushrooms in a pan with some butter, salt and pepper. You can add some herbs and spices for variation although they may mask the actual taste of the mushrooms. You should allow enough time for the mushrooms to simmer in the cream if you are making mushroom sauce. Why not experiment with various mushrooms? There are no limits to what you can try. It is important, however, that mushrooms are cooked properly (at least 15 minutes at 70°) since many of them can cause stomach problems if not cooked properly and may even be poisonous if eaten raw (e.g. the Blusher or the Red-Capped Scaber Stalk).

Mushroom storage

Leftover mushrooms can be reheated (up to approx. 1 day later) as long as they have been kept in the fridge in the meantime. Raw and cooked mushrooms can also be frozen. Blanching the mushrooms beforehand is recommended for all but Ceps. This saves space in your freezer.

Mushrooms should be dried quickly and continuously at a moderately warm temperature with good ventilation. If you use an oven to dry mushrooms, the door must be kept open and the temperature must be kept low, otherwise they will burn and the taste will be spoiled. You can powder the dried mushrooms (which rustle like leaves when touched) and store them in airtight jars. This makes an excellent addition to sauces and soups.

Mushroom Poisoning - What to Do?

1. If someone clearly becomes unwell after eating mushrooms, seek medical assistance immediately. The seriousness of poisoning often depends on the length of time that elapses between eating the mushrooms and the start of treatment. It is therefore essential that you dial 999 for an ambulance or take the person to the nearest Accident and Emergency department. Phone 999 (or 112 in mainland Europe) for an ambulance or take the person to the nearest Accident and Emergency department. Always try to provide a sample of the suspected cause of poisoning.

2. Avoid self-treatment. The use of milk or salt water to induce vomiting has no effect and charcoal tablets can have a negative effect. Inducing vomiting by hand will only have an effect if the mushrooms were eaten (at most) 4 hours previously.

3. Secure all of the remaining mushrooms and parts thereof (leftovers, discarded parts, or even vomit if necessary). Even if vomiting occurs soon after eating, possibly indicating a minor stomach upset, there may have been other more poisonous elements in the mushrooms which trigger symptoms later.

Cep

Boletus edulis (mushrooms with pores)

Cap 10–20 cm   July–November

🍴

Habitat In spruce forests and under beech trees on acidic soils, not on chalky soils.

> Pores white when young, changing to yellow-green
> Spores olive-brown
> Common throughout Europe
> Similar species Bitter Bolete

Good locations for Ceps or 'Penny Buns' are often indicated by the presence of Fly Agarics and Peppery Boletes, since these three species often cohabit areas in spruce forests. The Ceps are probably the most popular edible mushrooms. While the species is not protected in the UK, Ceps should only be picked for personal use. Species such as *Boletus aereus* are fully protected on the continent.

Claret-coloured line under skin of cap

Flesh is white and unchanging when exposed to air

18

Cep (left): cap smooth, light to chestnut brown

Boletus aereus (middle): cap leathery, rusty, blackish-brown

Summer Cep (right): cap finely felted, light brown

Cap smooth, slightly uneven with white rim

White reticulum on stipe, relatively smooth, spreads out towards base of stipe

Caution!

Although not poisonous, the Bitter Bolete (p. 19) has an unpleasant, bitter taste and often grows in the same locations as the Cep. Tasting a small amount of the flesh should be enough to distinguish it immediately.

Bitter Bolete

Tylopilus felleus (mushrooms with pores)
Cap 8–15 cm   July–November

One single Bitter Bolete can be enough to ruin any mushroom dish. However, this is easily avoided if you taste a small sample of the flesh (do not swallow it!), an instant indicator that it is not palatable. However, it is non-toxic and can be eaten by people who do not mind the bitterness. The Bitter Bolete is the only European bolete with pale pink spores.

Habitat *In spruce forests and under beech trees on acidic soils, not on chalky soils.*

> *Pores white when young, changing to pale pink*
> *Flesh bitter*
> *Spores pale pink*
> *Common throughout Europe*

Did you know?

Young Bitter Boletes (middle) can have a deceptively similar appearance to Summer Ceps (right) and Bay Boletes (left).

Flesh is white and unchanging when exposed to air

19

Cap suede-like, olive to yellowish-brown

Pore layer pink, curved downwards

Summer Cep 🍴

Boletus reticulatus (mushrooms with pores)
Cap 10–20 cm   June–September

Habitat *In open deciduous woodland under beech and oak trees, on moderately acidic to slightly alkaline soils.*

> Pores white when young, changing to yellowy-green
> Cap often becomes convex with age
> Spores olive-brown
> Common throughout Europe

Flesh is white and unchanging when exposed to air

If you have noticed that some Cep-like mushrooms always appear very early in some locations, then they are probably the Summer Cep. No matter what kind of cep they are, they all taste excellent. However, firmness varies from species to species. The flesh of the Summer Cep is the least firm, whereas *Boletus aereus* has the firmest flesh of all.

Cap finely felted

Most likely to be confused with the Spring King (*Boletus pinophilus*) found under Scots Pines and which has more intense notes of red about it and a less apparent reticulum on its stipe.

Reticulum reaches stipe base

Queen Bolete 🍴

Boletus aereus (mushrooms with pores)
Cap 10–25 cm   July–October

Habitat *In open decid-uous woodland under beech and oak trees on moderately acidic (south) to alkaline soil (north).*

> Pores remain white to cream-coloured for a long time
> Spores olive-brown
> Common throughout southern Europe, rare north of the Alps

Flesh is white and unchanging when exposed to air

Happening upon this warmth-loving species in central Europe is certainly a memorable experience. It usually grows alongside other rare species. The French name for the mushroom 'tête de nègre' (akin to a chocolate tea cake), comes from its dark, blackish brown cap and the almost white pores.

Cap leathery, chestnut brown

The Queen Bolete is one of the most popular mushrooms sold in France, but is rarely found in Britain.

Reticulum brownish, very subtle

Red Foot Bolete

Boletus erythropus (mushrooms with pores)

Cap 10–20 cm   June–October

Many people dislike this mushroom because of its red pores and strong, blue discoloration of its flesh when exposed to the air. It is, however, one of the best edible mushrooms and its characteristics make it easy to identify, even for beginners. The flesh is firmer than that of Ceps and the blue discoloration disappears when cooked.

Very rarely, albino variants with no red colouring can also occur. Although they may look very different, the only real difference is in their yellow colouring.

Habitat In deciduous and coniferous forests, mainly under spruces or beech trees on acidic soils.

> Red tubes and pores
> Pleasant, mushroomy odour
> Spores olive-brown
> Common throughout Europe, mainly in (sub)montane regions in the south

Flesh immediately turns dark blue when exposed to air

Did you know?

The stipe is pustulated rather than reticulated, making confusion with poisonous boletes less likely. The cap is also completely dark brown which distinguishes it from all other species with red pores.

21

Stipe base with olive-yellow felt

Stipe with subtle, red pustules

Cap dark brown, slightly suede-like

Lurid Bolete (❨❬❭❩)

Boletus luridus (mushrooms with pores)
Cap 8–15(20) cm   Late May–October

Habitat *Under decid-
uous trees in parks
and gardens, very rare
in coniferous forests,
prefers chalky soils.*

> Red tubes and pores
> Stipe base interior and
  exterior red
> Spores olive-brown
> Common throughout
  Europe (as far north as
  central Sweden)
> Similar species Devil's
  Bolete

Very occasionally, consuming this mushroom with alcohol
can cause unpleasant side-effects such as increased heart rate,
dizziness and breathlessness, similar to those caused by the
Common Ink Cap (p. 146). Those who wish to try this otherwise
good, edible mushroom should cook it well and abstain from
alcohol 72 hours before and after consuming it. Even one glass of
beer can trigger the aforementioned symptoms.

Cap olive-yellow with slight
hint of orange near the edge

Flesh immediately turns dark
blue when
exposed
to air

Red line
between
tubes and
cap flesh

22

Stipe with rough
reticulum

Red tube base
is a key feature.

Caution!
*The Devil's Bolete
(p. 23) can easily be
distinguished by its
light grey cap, subtle
reticulum, yellow
tube base and its
typical, unpleasant
odour.*

The Devil's Bolete

Boletus satanas (mushrooms with pores)
Cap 10–25 cm   July–October

Dr. Harald Othmar Lenz's experience of eating the Devil's Bolete resulted in what he described as "a fearful and horrible night." He had been poisoned by this mushroom, which had been unknown before 1830, prompting him to name it accordingly. Did the barren, white cap not remind the scientist of a human skull, or was he not repulsed by the carrion odour released by old fruiting bodies? There is a lot of debate about the dangerousness of the Devil's Bolete. Even though some people can eat it without experiencing problems, most people suffer from severe food poisoning, justifying its classification as a poisonous mushroom.

Habitat *In deciduous woodland, parks and embankments, only on chalky soils.*

> *Red tubes and pores*
> *Smells of nappies when young, changing to carrion when older*
> *Spores olive-brown*
> *Patchy distribution throughout southern Europe, rarely found in the north*

Flesh only turns slightly blue when exposed to air

Stipe normally rotund

Did you know?

Devil's Bolete may be confused with Boletus rhodoxanthus *with its crimson reticulum and its chrome yellow flesh, which only turns blue in the cap (left), and the False Devil's Bolete (*Boletus rubrosanguineus*) with a thinner stipe and a claret-coloured cap when mature (right).*

23

Cap thick, cushion-like, white to creamy-grey

Stipe colour ranges from orange to crimson

Pretty-Foot Bolete

Boletus calopus (mushrooms with pores)
Cap 10–20 cm   July–October

Habitat In montane, coniferous forests on acidic soil, rarely under deciduous trees on alkaline, loamy soils.

> Yellow tubes and pores
> Bitter taste
> Spores olive-brown
> Occurs at altitude in central Europe, otherwise rare or absent

Even though it looks deceptively similar to ceps, this mushroom tastes bitter and is also poisonous. Observant mushroom collectors will not confuse it with edible varieties since edible boletes never have reticulated, red stipes. Despite steadily decreasing in number in the last few decades, stocks of the Pretty-Foot Bolete seem to have stablised again.

Upper area of stipe yellow, lower area rhubarb red

Cap thick and cushion-like, stony grey to leather-coloured

Flesh turns blue when exposed to air

Rooting Bolete

Boletus radicans (mushrooms with pores)
Cap 10–25 cm   July–October

Habitat In deciduous woodland, parks and at the side of roads, only on alkaline soil.

> Yellow tubes and pores
> Bitter taste
> Spores olive-brown
> Patchy distribution throughout Europe or absent, occurs as far north as central Sweden

This relatively unknown mushroom has an extraordinary ability to adapt to man-made biotopes. It is not unusual to find it growing at the edge of a road surfaced with limestone chippings, verges and semi-natural forests. Because their large size makes them so obvious, passers-by often pick them, only to find out later that they should not have. Apart from tasting bitter, it is also slightly poisonous.

Boletus fechtneri, flesh in cap is sky blue but is coloured red in the stipe base. Edible, but it is rare and should not be picked.

Stipe primrose yellow, very subtle reticulum of the same colour

Flesh turns blue when exposed to air

Rooting stipe base

Cap thick and cushion-like, grey-white to leather-coloured

Spindle-Stemmed Bolete

Boletus appendiculatus (mushrooms with pores)
Cap 10–20 cm   July–October

All the parts of Ceps that are white are yellow on Spindle-stemmed Boletes. Other than this, they are very similar to each other. Although edible, they are rare and should not be picked.

Habitat In beech, hornbeam and oak forests on neutral to alkaline soils.

> **Vibrantly yellow tubes and pores**
> **Spores olive-brown**
> **Rare in Europe, found as far north as central Sweden**

Cap light to chestnut brown

The rare Iodine Bolete (*Boletus impolitus*) is very similar but it does not have a reticulum (a magnifying glass is required!) and the stipe base has a distinct medicinal smell about it.

Flesh yellow, blue discoloration in places

Stipe pale yellow with a very subtle reticulum of the same colour

Rooting stipe base

25

Royal Bolete

Boletus regius (mushrooms with pores)
Cap 10–20 cm   July–October

The Royal Bolete is perhaps the most attractive of all the boletes. Finding a specimen will be one of the highlights of any mushroom-gathering expedition, but it has become an endangered species. It is protected under schedule 8 of the Wildlife and Countryside Act 1981 and must not be picked for any reason. It is still sold in Dalmatia, where it is most commonly found.

Habitat In beech, hornbeam and oak forests on neutral to alkaline soils.

> **Vibrantly yellow tubes and pores**
> **Spores olive-brown**
> **Very rare in southern and central Europe**

Cap cherry to blood red

Vibrantly yellow stipe with subtle reticulum of the same colour

Flesh yellow, no discoloration

The cap flesh of the equally rare *Boletus fuscoroseus* turns blue when exposed to the air and is less vibrantly coloured.

Birch Bolete 🍴

Leccinum scabrum (mushrooms with pores)
Cap 8–15 cm July–October

Habitat In forests, parks and gardens, consistently under birch trees, prefers dry soils.

> Dirty grey tubes and pores
> Insect fretting marks on stipe turn ochre
> Spores olive-brown
> Common throughout Europe

All boletes with scaly stipes are edible. This simple rule applies to all scaber-stalked boletes (birch boletes and scaber stalks). Species which grow in moisture-rich areas become soft very quickly. Thus, it can sometimes be the case that your carefully picked and stored mushrooms have turned to pulp by the time you get home. However, the flesh of young Birch Boletes is firm.

Cap various colours of brown

The Hornbeam Bolete (*Leccinum carpini*) has a blackish, smooth, uneven cap surface. It only grows under hornbeams.

Flesh whitish, may or may not turn slightly pink

Stipe has blackish scales on a white background

26

Mottled Bolete 🍴

Leccinum variicolor (mushrooms with pores)
Cap 8–15 cm July–October

Habitat On marshland and damp areas, always under birch trees.

> Off-grey tubes and pores
> Stipe base often has blue-green marks on it
> Spores olive-brown
> Patchy distribution in southern and central Europe, more common towards the north

The striking colouring of the flesh only becomes visible after some time. The green discoloration in the stipe only occurs after a few hours. This species is often found growing near to the Yellow Swamp Russula (p. 228).

Cap colours are white and grey-brown with a granite-like appearance

Leccinum nucatum grows in the same biotope and has a white to cream-coloured cap, often with traces of olive-green, unchanging flesh and light stipe scales.

Flesh in cap is pink

Yellowy-green discoloration occurs in the stipe

Stipe with grey-black scales

Orange Birch Bolete

Leccinum versipelle (mushrooms with pores)

Cap 8–15 cm   July–November

All scaber stalks make very good eating if cooked properly, although they can be very poisonous if eaten raw. The blackening of the flesh can be prevented by slicing the mushrooms into lemon juice or vinegar. As they are becoming less common, some species are protected and may only be picked for personal consumption.

Habitat Under birch trees on sandy, acidic soils, also on heath land.

> Pores are white when young, changing to yellowy-grey.
> Stipe base often has blue-green marks on it
> Common throughout Europe, more frequently in northern and eastern parts

Flesh turns pale pink then violet-black within a few minutes of being exposed to air

27

Cap yellow with overhanging rim

Stipe has black pustules on a white background

Did you know?

There are around 5 scaber stalk species and each is associated with particular species of tree: (left) Red-Capped Scaber Stalk (Aspen): stipe scales white when young; (middle) Orange Oak Bolete: stipe scales fox-coloured; (right) Foxy Bolete (Scots Pine): stipe scales smoky grey.

Bay Bolete

Xerocomus badius (mushrooms with pores)

Cap 8–15 cm July–November

Habitat *In coniferous forests on acidic soil, especially under spruces.*

> **Pores greenish-yellow, turning blue when pressed**
> **Spores olive-brown**
> **Common throughout Europe**

Very few boletes vary as much as the Bay Bolete. In high grass, they often have thin stipes and slimy caps, while they are dry and Cep-like when growing on ground covered with pine needles. However, the golden rule also applies here: all smooth-stiped boletes without red pores are edible!

The Chestnut Bolete (*Gyroporus castaneus*) has white pores which do not change colour when pressed and has a hollow stipe.

Flesh pale yellow, turns faintly blue

28

Caution!

Even though there are no poisonous similar species to the Bay Bolete because of its smooth stipe, they should be avoided if Bolete Eater Mould (Hypomyces chrysospermus) is present on them. This mould can cause food poisoning. Affected boletes can usually be recognised by their greenish-grey pores.

Stipe greenish-yellow, smooth

Cap chestnut brown, finely felted when dry, slimy when wet

Red-Cracked Bolete

Xerocomus chrysenteron (mushrooms with pores)

Cap 5–12 cm   June–October

All boletes with yellow pores and no reticulation on the stipe are edible. The subdivisions defined by experts are therefore of less interest to collectors of edible mushrooms. However, it must be noted that all *Xerocomus* species quickly become soft and pulpy and only the younger, firmer specimens should be picked. It is also necessary to check the mushrooms for the onset of mould as this can cause food poisoning (see box on page 28).

Habitat Non-specific, prefers coniferous forests and acidic soils.

> Pores edgeless and yellow when young
> Spores olive-brown
> Common throughout Europe
> Similar species – Pretty Foot Bolete

Caution!
Large specimens (left) must not be confused with the Pretty Foot Bolete (right) which has reticulation on its stipe and bitter flesh (p 24).

Flesh pale yellow, turns slightly blue, rhubarb red in parts of the stipe

29

Cap brown to greyish-brown. Insect fretting marks turn cherry pink

Stipe streaked with red, smooth or slightly postulated

The Sepia Bolete (*X. porosporus*) is a dark, olive-brown colour and only occasionally has a red zone on its stipe.

Matt Bolete

Xerocomus pruinatus (mushrooms with pores)
Cap 5–12 cm   (July)August–November

Habitat In coniferous and deciduous forests, prefers acidic soils.

> **Pores bright yellow when young**
> **Spores olive-brown**
> **Common throughout Europe**

The flesh of the Matt Bolete is considerably firmer and more durable than that of the Red-Cracked Bolete, making it a preferable choice for eating. It is rarely found before September, whereas the growth period of the Red-Cracked Bolete begins to taper off towards the end of September.

The rare, apricot-coloured *Xerocomus armeniacus* prefers warmer areas and moderately acidic, nutrient-poor soils.

Stipe smooth, yellow when young

Cap brown, smooth, uneven

Violet-red rim on cap

Flesh pale yellow, turning slightly blue in the stipe only

Ruby Bolete

Xerocomus rubellus (mushrooms with pores)
Cap 5–12 cm   July–October

Habitat In deciduous forests and parks, often in damp areas.

> **Cap fades to leathery-brown when more mature**
> **Spores olive-brown**
> **Common throughout Europe**

If you look at the pores of a young mushroom with a magnifying glass, you will see that the configuration of most *Xerocomus* species' pore exits is labyrinth-like. This is particularly apparent in the Ruby Bolete.

Cap is blood red to crimson when young

The very similar *Xerocomus communis* is just one pale-capped variety. It also has the typical orange flecks in its stipe-base.

Flesh pale yellow, turns slightly blue

Interior of stipe base has carrot-coloured flecks

Stipe smooth, orange-yellow towards the top changing to crimson towards the bottom.

Downny Bolete

Xerocomus subtomentosus (mushrooms with pores)

Cap 5–12 cm   July–October

There are often ridges and veins on the top of the stipe which are sometimes so intertwined with each other, that they have the appearance of a reticulum. This can make identification more difficult ('none of the *Xerocomus* species have reticulation'), but it is not a real reticulum. It gets its name because of its finely felted cap surface.

Habitat In deciduous and coniferous forests, usually on neutral to alkaline soils.

> Cap colour very variable
> Spores olive-brown
> Common throughout Europe

Did you know?

A similar, edible species is Xerocomus ferrugineus, *with paler flesh, which does not turn blue.*

Flesh is yellow in cap, turning slightly blue, orange-ochre towards stipe base

Stipe pale, brownish-yellow, smooth

31

Cap yellow to olive-brown, suede-like

Parasitic Bolete 🍴

Xerocomus parasiticus (mushrooms with pores)
Cap 3–7 cm   July–October

Habitat In coniferous forests on sandy, acidic, nutrient-poor soils.

> **Grows on earth balls (p. 288)**
> **Spores olive-brown**
> **Patchy distribution throughout Europe, otherwise uncommon**

This is the only native bolete which lives as a parasite on other mushrooms. Almost all other boletes are mycorrhizae, meaning that they obtain their nutrients from tree roots. A large number of tiny fruiting bodies form on the exterior of earth balls, of which only a few actually reach maturity.

Earth balls are affected by parasitic boletes in that they are prevented from forming significant quantities of spores.

Stipe base pale brownish-yellow, smooth

Cap completely yellowy-green, smooth

Pores creamy, dirty yellow

Golden-Gilled Bolete 🍴

Xerocomus pelletieri (mushrooms with pores)
Cap 4–8 cm   July–October

Habitat In coniferous forests on sandy, acidic, nutrient-poor soils.

> **Flesh pale yellow, unchanging**
> **Spores olive-brown**
> **Uncommon in Europe**

Finding a Golden-Gilled Bolete for the first time is usually a confusing experience. From above, it is hard to distinguish it from a Bay Bolete, but, on closer inspection, you will be surprised to find that it has gills instead of pores on its underside. However, the gills are heavily cross-linked, which makes it easier to understand why it is a close relative of other *Xerocomus* species.

Cap completely chestnut red or chestnut brown, finely felted

Ammonia vapour briefly discolours the cap to blue-green, the same occurs with the Downy Bolete and *Xerocomus ferrugineus* (p. 31).

Heavily cross-linked gill structure

Stipe yellow to reddish-brown, smooth

Gilded Bolete

Pulveroboletus gentilis (mushrooms with pores)
Cap 4–8 cm   July–October

Because of its small stature, the rare Gilded Bolete is difficult to spot, despite its lovely colours. Its most obvious feature is its electric yellow pore layer. This is the most intensive colour seen in any of the native boletes. This yellow colouring disappears in lime potash, a characteristic specific to the entire genus.

Habitat *In deciduous forests on slightly acidic to neutral soils, prefers warm conditions.*

> *Cap slimy in wet weather conditions*
> *Stipe smooth*
> *Spores olive-brown*
> *Uncommon in Europe*

Pores luminous, golden yellow, delicate

Cap cherry-blood-brownish red, smooth

Flesh pale, cream-coloured, slightly pink towards exterior of cap flesh, unchanging

Peppery Bolete

Chalciporus piperatus (mushrooms with pores)
Cap 4–8 cm   July–November

Since this mushroom tastes peppery when it is raw, it is usually used as a seasoning and it is often recommended to use it in small quantities in place of pepper. However, this recommendation is quite useless as the peppery taste is lost when the mushroom is cooked. As such, the edibility of the Peppery Bolete is mediocre, similar to the Red-Cracked Bolete.

Habitat *In coniferous forests on acidic soils, often near Ceps and Fly Agaric.*

> *Flesh tastes peppery when raw*
> *Spores olive-brown*
> *Common throughout Europe*

Cap orange to rusty brown, smooth, slimy when wet

Stipe smooth, tapered

Tubes and pores are typically a cinnamon or rusty orange colour

Flesh cream-coloured to orange-ochre in cap

Flesh chrome-yellow in stipe-base

Dark Bolete

🍴

Porphyrellus porphyrosporus (mushrooms with pores)
Cap 6–12 cm   June–October

Habitat *In montane spruce forests on acidic soils.*

> Tubes and pores reddish grey-brown
> Spores porphyry brown
> Common in montane regions in central Europe, otherwise relatively uncommon

The automatic assumption on finding this mushroom is usually that it is a bolete, which is too old to be identified. However, the dark colouration is typical, making the mushroom easy to identify. Although it can be eaten, it does not taste particularly good.

Cap dark olive-brown

The botanical name *porphyrosporus* indicates the porphyry-brown spores, which make the entire pore layer this colour.

Stipe is same colour as cap, smooth

Flesh whitish to cream-coloured, reddening, sometimes turns blue or green

Old Man of the Woods

🍴

Strobilomyces strobilaceus (mushrooms with pores)
Cap 6–12 cm   July–October

Habitat *In deciduous and coniferous forests, usually on acidic soils.*

> Tubes and pores dirty grey
> Spores blackish olive-brown
> Common in montane regions in central Europe, otherwise relatively uncommon

The name of this mushroom almost negates the need for a description. Although it is edible, its appearance, cotton wool-like velum and weak taste make it mediocre.

Cap light grey, covered with dark, protruding, cotton wool-like scales

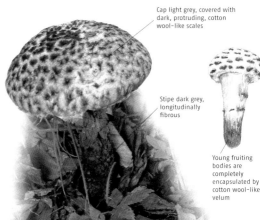

Stipe dark grey, longitudinally fibrous

Flesh orange-red then violet, finally turning blackish

Young fruiting bodies are completely encapsulated by cotton wool-like velum

Blue Staining Bolete

Gyroporus cyanescens (mushrooms with pores)
Cap 6–12 cm   July-October

The tube layer in the Blue Staining Bolete is more integrated with the cap than on most other boletes and so it is more difficult to separate it from the cap flesh. This, together with other anatomical features, is an indicator to researchers that this genus is one of the original boletes.

Habitat *In deciduous and coniferous forests on sandy, acidic soils.*

> *Tubes and pores dirty cream-coloured*
> *Spores straw-coloured*
> *Patchy distribution in Europe, relatively uncommon*

Cap cream to straw-coloured, fibrously felted

Stipe smooth, pale straw yellow, tip off-white

Flesh immediately turns Cornflower blue when exposed to air

The tubes on the *Gyrodon lividus* are even more tightly integrated with the cap and also continue on to the stipe. Some experts associate it with bracket fungi and it does bear some resemblance to the Fringed Polypore (p. 267).

Stipe typically becomes hollow

Dotted–Stalk Slippery Jack

Boletinus cavipes (mushrooms with pores)
Cap 6–12 cm   July-October

The stipe quickly becomes hollow and, while this is a good feature for identification, it also has disadvantages, such as providing nesting space for insects and snails. It is therefore sensible to cut these mushrooms open before cooking them.

Habitat *Consistently under larches, avoids heavily acidic soils.*

> *Flesh yellowish, no discoloration*
> *Spores olive-brown*
> *Patchy distribution in montane regions in Europe, otherwise uncommon*

Cap orange to dark brown, rough to slightly scaly

Stipe brownish, smooth with rings of velum remnants

Pore layer continues on to stipe

The large, irregular pores are in a recognisable, longitudinal configuration and represent a 'crossover point' to gilled mushrooms, this is even more apparent in the Golden-Gilled Bolete (p. 32).

Stipe typically becomes hollow

Larch Bolete

Suillus grevillei (mushrooms with pores)
Cap 6–12 cm   July–October

Habitat *Consistently under larches, usually without preference for particular soil types.*

> All parts of fruiting body golden to yellowy-orange
> Cap skin easy to remove
> Spores olive-brown
> Common throughout Europe

As its name suggests, the Larch Bolete is more frequently found under larches than any other bolete since it has no real soil preferences. Because of its colour, it is not unusual to find the mushroom before the tree. As with all slimy-capped boletes, the slimy layer should be removed before cooking.

Did you know?

*The larch has two other companions which grow primarily on lime-rich soil, the Sticky Bolete (*S. viscidus*) with larger, grey pores and blue-green discoloration in the stipe base (left) and* S. tridentinus, *which prefers warm conditions and also has larger, orange pores (right).*

Flesh pale to orange-yellow, unchanging

Ring skin-like, slimy upper surface

Cap yellow to orange, very slimy

Weeping Bolete (❨❅❩)

Suillus granulatus (mushrooms with pores)
Cap 6–12 cm   June–October

Not everyone can stomach boletes with slimy caps. It is not uncommon for people to experience diarrhoea or mild stomach pains, even if the skin was removed from the cap before it was cooked. Personal tolerance should therefore be tested by eating small quantities to begin with.

Habitat *Consistently under Scots pines on neutral to alkaline soils.*

> **Milky deposits from pores and stipe tip**
> **Cap skin can be removed easily**
> **Spores olive-brown**
> **Common throughout Europe**

Cap orange-brown, very slimy

The Ringless Pine Bolete (*S. collnitus*), with pink base mycelium and clear liquid deposits, also grows under Scots Pines, but only on chalky soil.

Flesh pale yellow, un-changing

Stipe has no ring, glands at tip

Slippery Jack (❨❅❩)

Suillus luteus (mushrooms with pores)
Cap 6–12 cm   July–October

Together with the Scots Pine, the Slippery Jack has been distributed to the far corners of the globe and can now even be found in Southern and Eastern Africa. However, native Africans treat it with suspicion and do not eat it. In Europe, it is seen as a good, edible mushroom. However, caution should be exercised since it causes stomach upsets in some people.

Habitat *Consistently under Scots Pines, no soil preferences.*

> **Cap skin can be removed easily**
> **Spores olive-brown**
> **Common throughout Europe**

Cap chocolatey brown, very slimy

The tube layer is covered by a white velum layer when young. As the cap widens, this tears and is left as a ring on the stipe.

Flesh pale yellow, un-changing

Suillus variegatus

No common name (mushrooms with pores)
Cap 6–15 cm   July–October

🍴

Habitat Consistently under Scots Pines on nutrient-poor soils.

> **Tubes and pores olive-brown**
> **Thin tube layer**
> **Spores olive-brown**
> **Common throughout Europe**

Flesh orange–ochre, turns slightly blue above the tubes and in the stipe tip

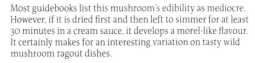

Most guidebooks list this mushroom's edibility as mediocre. However, if it is dried first and then left to simmer for at least 30 minutes in a cream sauce, it develops a morel-like flavour. It certainly makes for an interesting variation on tasty wild mushroom ragout dishes.

Did you know?

The flaky, loose cap surface distinguishes it from the otherwise very similar Bovine Bolete.

Cap yellow to orange–brown, becomes scabby

Stipe thick, same colour as cap

Bovine Bolete

Suillus bovinus (mushrooms with pores)
Cap 4–8 cm   July–October

The Bovine Bolete usually grows in large clumps which one might think would make them worth picking. However, they do not taste particularly good and older specimens almost have the consistency of rubber. If they are cooked, they turn a surprisingly intense violet colour.

Habitat *Consistently under Scots Pines on nutrient-poor, relatively dry soils.*

> Tubes and pores olive-brown
> Thin tube layer
> Spores olive-brown
> Common throughout Europe

Cap yellow to orange-brown, smooth, slightly sticky

The Rosy Spike (*Gomphidius roseus*) only grows in close proximity to the Bovine Bolete, but they do not always produce fruiting bodies at the same time.

Flesh pale ochre, unchanging

Stipe relatively thin, same colour as cap

39

Rosy Spike

Gomphidius roseus (mushrooms with gills)
Cap 4–8 cm   July–October

For a long time it was unknown why the Rosy Spike and the Bovine Bolete were found growing together so often. It is now known that the Rosy Spike is a mycorrhizal parasite. This means that it taps into the root connecting the Bovine Bolete with the Scots Pine, thereby supplementing its supply of nutrients at the cost of the Bovine Bolete.

Habitat *Consistently under Scots Pines on nutrient-poor soils together with the Bovine Bolete.*

> Gills soft, separable
> Spores greyish-black
> Patchy distribution throughout Europe

Cap pink to blood red, slimy

Stipe completely white

Flesh whitish, pale pink towards stipe base

Sometimes the Rosy Spike and Bovine Bolete grow in such close proximity that they appear to be fused together.

Slimy Spike

Gomphidius glutinosus (mushrooms with gills)

Cap 4–12 cm   July–October

🍴

Habitat In coniferous forests, particularly under firs on relatively acidic soils.

> Gills soft, separable
> Spores greyish–black
> Common to patchy distribution throughout Europe

Flesh white, unchanging

Interior of stipe base chrome yellow

The Slimy Spike is prized among many collectors who value it because of its delicate aroma. However, its flesh is very soft which makes drying it quite problematic. It often grows in the same locations as Ceps, but is often left untouched because it is less widely known, often compensating the person who arrived too late to pick the Ceps!

Did you know?

Young Slimy Spikes are totally encapsulated by a slimy velum. This should be removed before cooking as it does not look appetising and can cause stomach upsets in some people.

Cap grey-brown, with black flecks and a thick slimy layer

Stipe slimy

Spotted Spike (¶¶)

Gomphidius maculatus (mushrooms with gills)
Cap 4–8 cm   July–October

The Spotted Spike is considerably less solid than the Slimy Spike and is very uncommon in non-mountainous regions. Its flesh is just as soft as the Slimy Spike's but is less aromatic. It is not a recommended edible mushroom as it may cause stomach upsets, as with all other spike mushrooms.

Habitat Only under larches, prefers alkaline soils, very uncommon on flat land.

> *Gills soft, separable*
> *Spores greyish-black*
> *Patchy distribution throughout Europe*

Cap beige, with a thick, slimy layer

Although it is beige-brown all over when young, it can develop wine brown to black spots when touched or when mature.

Stipe has red flecks

Flesh reddens equally

Copper Spike ¶¶

Chroogomphus rutilus (mushrooms with gills)
Cap 4–10 cm   July–November

Since the Copper Spike often grows in large numbers, it is worth getting to know this edible mushroom. If you do cook it, do not be put off by the fact that it turns a deep violet colour like the Bovine Bolete (p. 39).

Habitat Consistently under Scots Pines, prefers alkaline soils.

> *Cap slightly fibrous when young, smooth when mature*
> *Spores greyish-black*
> *Common throughout Europe*

The Copper Spike must not be confused with the deadly poisonous Deadly Webcap (p. 191).

Cap copper to brownish-red

Gills widely spaced, continuing down towards stipe

Flesh orange-ochre, yellowish-ochre in the stipe base

Brown Roll-Rim

Paxillus involutus (mushrooms with gills)
Cap 5–15 cm   July–November

Habitat *Under deciduous and coniferous trees, in parks and gardens.*

> *Cap brownish, finely felted to smooth*
> *Spores olive-brown*
> *Common throughout Europe*

As late as 50 years ago, this mushroom was still being recommended as an edible variety. It is now known that it only loses its toxicity once it has been thoroughly cooked. If consumed on a regular basis, it can cause the destruction of the red blood cells, which can be fatal. It is therefore strongly recommended that you avoid eating this mushroom, even though it is still sold at markets in eastern Europe.

Flesh ochre with reddish-brown discoloration

The more brightly coloured *Paxillus filamentosus* grows under alders and its cap usually becomes slightly flaky.

Cap rim turned under outer edge of gills

Gills close together, continuing down towards stipe

Did you know?

As with the tube layer on boletes, the gills on the Brown Roll-Rim can easily be separated from the cap flesh.

Velvet Roll-Rim

Tapinella atrotomentosa (mushrooms with gills)
Cap 5–20 cm   July–October

The appearance of the Velvet Roll-Rim's velvety cap from above fools many mushroom collectors into thinking they have found a Bay Bolete. While this fruitful and delicious looking mushroom is not poisonous, it has such an unpleasant earthy, bitter taste that it cannot be eaten. All attempts to make it edible by methods such as boiling have failed.

Habitat On rotting pine tree stumps in all types of coniferous woodland.

> **Cap shell-like or kidney-shaped**
> **Spores olive-brown**
> **Common throughout Europe**

Did you know?

*The smaller Stalkless Paxillus (*T. panuoides*), which has almost no stipe, grows on pine fittings such as supporting beams and has even been found on supports deep inside mines.*

Gills white, continuing down towards stipe

Stipe off-centre

Cap brown, velvety

43

Stipe dark brown, plushy

False Chanterelle

Hygrophoropsis aurantiaca (mushrooms with gills)
Cap 4–8 cm   July–November

Habitat In coniferous
and mixed woodland
on acidic to alkaline
soils.

> Fruiting body elastic
> Spores white
> Common throughout
>   Europe.
> Similar species Jack o'
>   Lantern Mushroom

The False Chanterelle can easily be mistaken for an actual
Chanterelle. However, the mistake would be a harmless one
to make as both are edible. It is distinguishable by its soft,
almost elastic flesh, richer colours and tightly packed gills. The
Chanterelle's thick hymenial folds and its peppery taste when
raw also give it away.

Caution!
*The highly poisonous Jack
o' Lantern Mushroom (p. 45)
looks very similar. However,
it (normally) always grows
in clumps on wood. It is very
uncommon north of the Alps
and only occurs in warm
locations.*

Flesh
yellowish

Gills con-
tinuing
down
towards
stipe

In addition to pale varieties, there is also a variety
with dark brown felt on the cap, which looks like a
Xerocomus species from above.

Gills close together,
occasionally forked

Cap and stipe
both equally
yellowish–orange

44

Jack o' Lantern Mushroom ☠

Omphalotus olearius (mushrooms with gills)

Cap 4–10 cm   July–December

This attractive species is seldom seen in Central Europe. However, since individual specimens may be confused with the Chanterelle, it is worth being able to identify, especially if you are looking for mushrooms in the Mediterranean region.

Habitat On living and dead deciduous wood, usually on tree stumps, particularly on olive trees, chestnut trees and oaks.

> **Flesh firm**
> **Spores white**
> **Patchy distribution in southern Europe**

This mushroom, which occurs individually and primarily on buried wood, is sometimes seen as being a species in its own right (*O. illudens*). It is easy to confuse with Chanterelles, making it quite dangerous.

Gills continuing down on to stipe, orange

45

Cap vibrant yellowish-orange

Stipe compact, firm

Did you know?

The Jack o' Lantern Mushroom's gills glow in the dark! A clump of them produces enough light to read a newspaper by.

Witch's Hat

Hygrocybe conica (mushrooms with gills)
Cap 2–8 cm   June–November

Habitat *On all kinds of lightly or non-fertilised grassland, less common in open woodland.*

> Old fruiting bodies are completely black
> Spores white
> Common throughout Europe

This mushroom is the most common of the hygrocybes. It is slightly less sensitive to the nitrogen enrichment of soil and can therefore occur on ornamental lawns, waysides and similar biotopes. The shape, size and colour of its cap vary considerably.

One of the similar species, which does not turn so black is *Hygrocybe subglobispora* that grows in similar locations but is far less common.

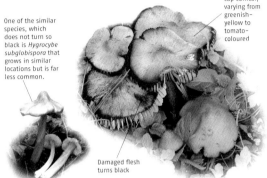

Cap conical, varying from greenish-yellow to tomato-coloured

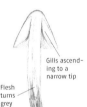

Gills ascending to a narrow tip

Flesh turns grey

Damaged flesh turns black

Parrot Waxcap

Hygrocybe psittacina (mushrooms with gills)
Cap 2–5 cm   August–November

Habitat *On all kinds of lightly or non-fertilised grassland, less common in open woodland.*

> Cap and stipe very slimy
> Spores white
> Common throughout Europe

Apart from being very colourful, the Parrot Waxcap is also particularly slimy. In wet weather, it is almost impossible to pull it out of the ground by hand. Its appearance varies just as much as that of the Witch's Hat, but it is slightly less common.

The Slimy Waxcap (*H. irrigata*) also has a very slimy cap and stipe but is either greyish-beige to brownish-grey.

Cap green, pinkish-violet or ochre-yellow

Gills ascending, tooth-like towards stipe

Stipe tip green

Scarlet Hood (🍴)

Hygrocybe coccinea (mushrooms with gills)
Cap 2–6 cm   August–November

Once autumn arrives and the wild flowers on rough pastures begin to die away, they are replaced by the equally colourful Scarlet Hood and other colourful hygrocybes. The Scarlet Hood is one of the most obvious because of its vivid, red colour and relatively large fruiting bodies. They are rare and should not be picked.

The Crimson Waxcap (*Hygrocybe punicea*) grows up to 12cm tall, has a fibrous stipe and whitish flesh.

Cap cherry red

Habitat On unfertilised meadows and grassland, no soil preference.

> **Cap and stipe dry, smooth**
> **Spores white**
> **Uncommon in Europe, patchy distribution in Alpine regions**

Flesh in cap reddish-yellow

Gills widely spaced

egg-yolk yellow

Vermilion Waxcap (🍴)

Hygrocybe miniata (mushrooms with gills)
Cap 1–3 cm   August–November

The Vermilion Waxcap is one of the smallest hygrocybes. Despite the bright colour, they are easy to overlook because their caps are easily mistaken for fallen rowan berries strewn in the grass.

Cap vermilion to reddish-orange with delicate scales

The Bitter Waxcap (*H. mucronella*) is, as its name suggests, recognisable by its taste.

Habitat On nutrient-poor meadows and heaths on acidic soils, rarely in woodland.

> **Cap and stipe dry**
> **Spores white**
> **Uncommon in Europe, patchy distribution in Alpine regions**

Gills ascending, tooth-like towards stipe

Buffcap (¶¶)

Hygrocybe pratensis (mushrooms with gills)
Cap 4–10 cm   August–November

Habitat *On nutrient-poor meadows and heaths, no soil preference.*

> *Cap and stipe dry*
> *Spores white*
> *Rare to patchy distribution throughout Europe, still common in Alpine regions*

Since the Buffcap can become rather large with thick flesh, it is well known as an edible mushroom in areas where it occurs frequently. However, it has become exceptionally rare outside Alpine regions and is protected in some parts of Europe.

Cap apricot to brownish-orange

Gills broad, descending

The rare Yellow-Foot Waxcap (*H. flavipes*), with its violet-grey cap and yellow stipe base, can be found growing in the same locations.

Snowy Waxcap (¶¶)

Hygrocybe niveus (mushrooms with gills)
Cap 2–8 cm   August–November

Habitat *On nutrient-poor meadows and heaths, no soil preference.*

> *Cap and stipe dry*
> *Spores white*
> *Common to patchy distribution throughout Europe*

Although it is edible, two reasons for not picking this mushroom are that it is rare and that it is easily confused with the poisonous Fool's Funnel (p. 56).

Cap milky white, slightly water-absorbent

Flesh white

Gills broad, descending

The Cedarwood Waxcap (*H. russocoriacea*) can be identified by its characteristic aroma of cigar boxes or leather

Yellowing Woodwax

Hygrophorus discoxanthus (mushrooms with gills)

Cap 4–10 cm   August–November

This mushroom, occurring in late autumn, is characterised by its unique odour which is reminiscent of mandarin zest. Butterfly/moth enthusiasts may know this smell which is the same as that of the Goat Moth caterpillar. This mushroom is edible and is easy to identify because of its slimy cap, colour and odour. However, as with other slimy woodwaxes, it does not taste good and is therefore not recommended.

Habitat *Consistently under beeches, no soil preference.*

> *Odour aromatic and tart*
> *Spores white*
> *Common to patchy distribution throughout Europe*

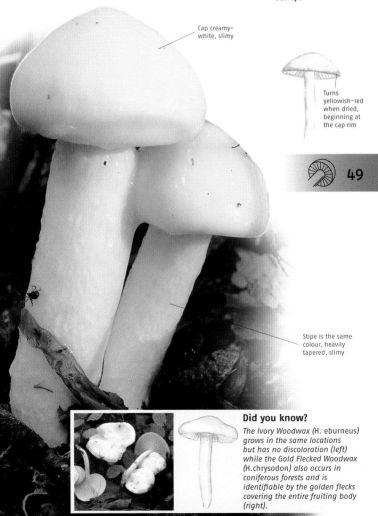

Cap creamy-white, slimy

Turns yellowish-red when dried, beginning at the cap rim

49

Stipe is the same colour, heavily tapered, slimy

Did you know?

*The Ivory Woodwax (*H. eburneus*) grows in the same locations but has no discoloration (left) while the Gold Flecked Woodwax (*H.chrysodon*) also occurs in coniferous forests and is identifiable by the golden flecks covering the entire fruiting body (right).*

Almond Woodwax 🍴

Hygrophorus agathosmus (mushrooms with gills)
Cap 4–10 cm   August–November

Habitat *In montane coniferous forests, particularly on alkaline soils.*

> Odour of marzipan
> White pustules on stipe tip
> Spores white
> Patchy distribution outside low mountain regions in Europe

The Almond Woodwax got its name because of its bitter almond odour. It tastes as good as it smells and normally grows in rows and rings, meaning that it does not take long to pick enough for a meal.

Cap white to grey, greasy

Gills widely spaced, arching down towards stipe

Hygrophorus pustulatus differs from the Almond Woodwax in that it has black pustules on its stipe. It is also edible.

Stipe white to light grey, dry

Brown Waxcap 🍴

Hygrophorus discoideus (mushrooms with gills)
Cap 4–8 cm   August–November

Habitat *In montane coniferous forests, particularly on alkaline soils.*

> Odour faint, mushroomy
> Spores white
> Patchy distribution outside low mountain regions in Europe

This little known and rare mushroom can easily be confused with the slightly poisonous *Hebeloma bruchetii* (p. 182). However, if you take the rust-brown spores, the dry cap, the gill configuration and the fibrous velum into account, confusion is far less likely.

Stipe pale brown, slimy

Cap slimy with a brown disc

Hygrophorus roseodiscoideus only occurs in the Mediterranean region and always grows under evergreen oaks

Gills creamy-brown, widely spaced, continuing down towards stipe

Slimy layer on stipe tip in the form of a bulging ring

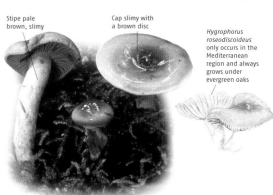

Olive Waxcap

Hygrophorus olivaceoalbus (mushrooms with gills)

Cap 3–6 cm   July–November

It is usually not worth picking this mushroom. Nevertheless, it can sometimes be found in larger quantities, often while it is dry in summer when hardly any other edible mushrooms are to be found. Its flesh is quite soft and the slimy layer on the cap and the stipe should be removed before cooking.

Habitat Under spruces in coniferous forests on acidic soils.

> Odour faint, mushroomy
> Stipe thin, cylindrical, tapered
> Spores white
> Patchy distribution outside low mountain regions in Europe

Cap grey-brown, slimy

The much larger *Hygrophorus latitabundus* grows under Scots Pines on lime soil.

Snakeskin-like, grey-brown, slimy layer

March Waxcap

Hygrophorus marzuolus (mushrooms with gills)

Size 5–12 cm   February–April

It is difficult to find these mushrooms and finding one is an unforgettable moment for mushroom enthusiasts. They remain hidden, almost under the surface for a long time. It is best to search for them when it is rainy and the foliage is weighed down, leaving small, protruding lumps where these mushrooms may be.

It is unique because of the time of year at which it occurs. However, at a glance, it may be confused with the Blackening Russula (p. 223).

Habitat In coniferous and mixed woodlands, on acidic to alkaline soils.

> Appears after snow has thawed
> Fruiting bodies compact
> Spores white
> Common throughout Europe, but especially rare in mountainous regions

Gills white when young, changing to grey

Cap grey-brown to blackish-brown, areas not exposed to sunlight remain white

Gills very thick and widely spaced

Stipe tip relatively flaky

Blotched Woodwax

Hygrophorus erubescens (mushrooms with gills)
Size 5–10 cm   August–November

Habitat *In coniferous (spruce) forests, on alkaline soils.*

> *Flesh bitter*
> *Spores white*
> *Rare in Europe, found in mountainous regions*

None of the woodwaxes are poisonous, but some do not taste good. However, with a bit of experience, you will learn to distinguish them by their widely spaced, thick, waxy and brittle gills. The name 'Woodwax' stems from the fact that many of them have waxy or greasy caps, with a quality reminiscent of silvery snail trails.

Cap flesh dusky pink to orange-pink, yellowy in places

Flesh whitish, turns slightly yellow

The Pinkmottle Woodwax (*H. russula*) has very thick flesh and its gills do not continue down towards the stipe. It is a prized edible mushroom in southern Europe.

Rosy Woodwax

Hygrophorus pudorinus (mushrooms with gills)
Size 5–12 cm   August–November

Habitat *Consistently under white firs in coniferous forests, on alkaline soils.*

> *Smells and tastes slightly of turpentine*
> *Flesh whitish*
> *Spores white*
> *Uncommon in central and southern Europe, found in mountainous regions*

Many people do not even smell the turpentine-like odour emitted by this mushroom, which allegedly becomes more apparent when cooked. A better identifying feature is the orange-pink cap and the yellow stipe base. Apart from being rare, this mushroom does not taste good and should not be picked.

Cap yellowy–orange to salmon pink, cushion–like

Hygrophorus unicolor is like a miniature version of the Rosy Woodwax but grows under beeches

Stipe base yellowish

Stipe whitish, sturdy

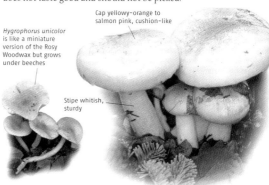

Herald of the Winter

Hygrophorus hypothejus (mushrooms with gills)
Size 4–8 cm   October–December

The Herald of the Winter is a prized edible mushroom because it usually grows in large clumps at a time when it is hard to find other mushrooms. This species is a great addition to any Christmas dinner.

The Larch Waxcap (*H. speciosus*) is distinguishable by its bright orange cap and grows under larches in mountainous regions.

Habitat Consistently under Scots Pines on nutrient-poor, sandy soils.

> Only occurs after first frosts
> Spores white
> Found throughout Europe, very common in some parts.
> Similar species Clitocybe radicellata

Caution!

If you do not identify the greasy cap surface and the yellow gills, it is easy to confuse it with Clitocybe radicellata (p. 59), which is thought to be poisonous.

Gills continuing down towards stipe

53

Cap yellow to olive-brown, dark centre, concave when old

Gills yellow

Omphalina gerardiana

No common name (mushrooms with gills)

Size 2–5 cm   July–October

Habitat *Only in hill bogs, consistently in sphagnum moss.*

> Spores white
> Patchy distribution throughout Europe (Scandinavia) to uncommon (southern Europe).

Omphelinas are small to medium-sized, gilled mushrooms. Their gills continue on quite far down the stipe and they have funnel-shaped caps with a deep indentation in the centre. They are not edible, but many of them are considered by ecologists as indicators of natural balance.

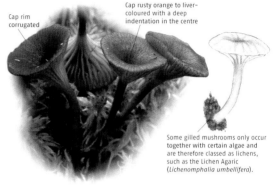

Cap rim corrugated

Cap rusty orange to liver-coloured with a deep indentation in the centre

Gills descend far down the stipe

Some gilled mushrooms only occur together with certain algae and are therefore classed as lichens, such as the Lichen Agaric (*Lichenomphalia umbellifera*).

Orange Mosscap

Rickenella fibula (mushrooms with gills)

Size 1–2 cm   March–December

Habitat *In mosses on the ground or on moss-covered wood, no biotope preference.*

> Stipe and cap covered with a very fine fuzz (use a magnifying glass)
> Spores white
> Common throughout Europe

Although this mushroom is often overlooked, on closer inspection, it can be found on almost all boggy grasslands. Because of its small size, it is not considered an edible mushroom.

Cap yellow to reddish-orange with an indentation in the centre

Cap rim corrugated

Gills descend far down the stipe

The Collared Mosscap (*R. swartzii*) grows in similar locations and is distinguishable by its different colouring.

Amethyst Deceiver 🍴

Laccaria amethystina (mushrooms with gills)

Size 2–6 cm   July–November

The Amethyst Deceiver often occurs in large numbers, often in hundreds. Despite their small size, this makes them worth picking. If left to soak in vinegar, the most interesting colours are produced, especially if they are soaked together with orange milk caps. It may lose most of its colour and become almost totally white.

Habitat *On deciduous and coniferous forest floors with no soil or forest preference.*

> *Odour faint, unspecific*
> *Spores white*
> *Common throughout Europe.*

Whole mushroom equally purple in colour

Gills thick, widely spaced, descending to some extent down stipe

It may be confused with the poisonous Lilac Bonnet (p. 98) whose thinner gills are a lighter shade of purple and more tightly packed. It also smells of radish.

Deceiver 🍴

Laccaria laccata (mushrooms with gills)

Size 2–5 cm   July–November

There are a few similar species between which there is little difference. All deceivers are edible although they taste of very little. They are small, but they often grow in large numbers.

Habitat *On deciduous and coniferous forest floors with no soil or forest preference.*

> *Odour faint, unspecific*
> *Spores white*
> *Common throughout Europe.*

Whole mushroom equally pink in colour, flesh can be brick red

Gills thick, widely spaced, descending to some extent down stipe

The Bicoloured Deceiver (*L. bicolor*) can be identified by the small scales on its cap and its violet basal mycelium.

Bearded Seamine ✗

Ripartites tricholoma (mushrooms with gills)
Size 2–6 cm   July–November

Habitat *On deciduous and coniferous forest floors with no soil or forest preference.*

> Whole fruiting body is flesh-brown
> Spores earthy brown
> Common throughout Europe.

It is not certain whether the Bearded Seamine is edible or poisonous. Nevertheless, eating it is not advised as it is very similar to some of the poisonous *Clitocybe* species. Its earthy brown spores are atypical for mushrooms with gills, which normally all have white to cream-coloured spores.

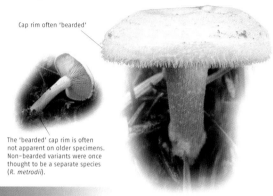

Cap rim often 'bearded'

Gills earthy brown, continuing down on to stipe

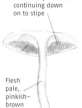

Flesh pale, pinkish-brown

The 'bearded' cap rim is often not apparent on older specimens. Non-bearded variants were once thought to be a separate species (*R. metrodii*).

Fool's Funnel ☠

Clitocybe rivulosa (mushrooms with gills)
Size 4–8 cm   July–November

Habitat *In deciduous woodland in ruderal locations, also on grassland.*

> Flesh pale, pinkish-brown
> Spores creamy white
> Common in central Europe, patchy distribution in southern Europe

All small *Clitocybe* species are poisonous or are thought to be poisonous and some contain large quantities of the toxin muscarine. They are easily confused with edible mushrooms such as the Fairy Ring Mushroom (p. 90) or the Sweetbread Mushroom (p. 106). Mushroom collectors are therefore advised to avoid this mushroom and similar species unless they are absolutely certain that they can identify them as edible.

Clitocybe agrestis is just as poisonous and grows on pastures and heaths.

Cap pruinose on a pinkish-brown base

Stipe smooth, pale, pinkish-brown

Gills continuing down on to stipe, pinkish-brown

Frosty Funnel

Clitocybe phyllophila (mushrooms with gills)

Size 5–12 cm   July–November

The size of the Frosty Funnel is extremely variable and it may therefore be confused with a range of edible mushrooms, such as the Sweetbread Mushroom (p. 106) or the Clouded Agaric (p. 64). Another very similar species not shown here is the more solid Flowery Blewit (*Lepista irina*) which smells strongly of flowers and whose gills can be removed with the finger tips.

Cap with chalk white frosty layer on a creamy-grey base

Habitat In deciduous or coniferous forests without any particular preference.

> *Odour is musty-sweet to aromatic*
> *Spores creamy white to creamy-pink*
> *Common throughout Europe*

Gills stretched out horizontally from stipe, cream-coloured with pink highlights

Flesh pale, pinkish-brown

 57

Stipe smooth, creamy-white

Caution!

All clitocybes with a frosty or glassy-looking cap surface are poisonous.

Trooping Funnel

#F

Clitocybe geotropa (mushrooms with gills)
Size 12–25 cm   July–November

Habitat In deciduous
or coniferous forests
without any particular
preferences.

> Odour is musty-sweet to
  aromatic
> Spores creamy-white
> Common throughout
  Europe
> Similar species Frosty
  Funnel

The Trooping Funnel is a prized and fruitful edible mushroom.
Since their stipes have a relatively hard rind on them and the
stipe interiors are like cotton wool, experts only use
the caps of very young specimens. The
characteristic hump on the cap is
almost always present. However,
it can sometimes be hard to see,
so it is better to feel for it with
your finger.

Alexander's Funnel (*C. alexandri*) only
grows in chalky soils, usually under
spruces.

Cap funnel-
shaped with
hump in
centre

Gills con-
tinuing
down on
to stipe

Caution!
*The Frosty Funnel is smaller, it
has a thinner stipe and does
not have a concave cap with
a hump in the centre. This
clitocybe contains the neuro-
toxin muscarine which is also
present in some inocybes.*

Cap cream or leather-coloured,
no frosty layer

Stipe 2–4cm thick,
same colour as cap

Clitocybe sinopica (❣)

No common name (mushrooms with gills)
Size 3–8 cm   May–August

This little-known mushroom displays beautifully contrasting white gills and a rusty orange cap and stipe. It usually grows in spring and early summer and seldom in autumn. Although it is edible, it does not taste particularly good. Many people also find the strong odour off-putting.

Habitat Under coniferous trees, especially Scots Pines on sandy soils and on burnt areas of ground.

> Odour is flour-like
> Spores creamy-white
> Patchy distribution throughout Europe

Cap brick to brownish-orange, dry

Gills continue down on to stipe, white

Another clitocybe with root threads, but with a greyish-blue cap is *Clitocybe radicellata*. It grows in coniferous forests between February and April.

Stipe base with white root threads

59

Chicken Run Funnel ☠

Clitocybe phaeophthalma (mushrooms with gills)
Size 3–6 cm   July–October

It is very difficult to distinguish between the many small *Clitocybe* species. The Chicken Run Funnel has a unique, rancid-sweetish odour which is hard to describe, but which is easily remembered. It is thought to be poisonous since some of its close relatives are extremely poisonous.

Habitat In deciduous forests on mildly acidic soils, usually in amongst dead leaves.

> Flesh slightly bitter, astringent
> Spores creamy-white
> Common in central Europe, less so in southern Europe

Cap whitish, smooth, funnel-shaped

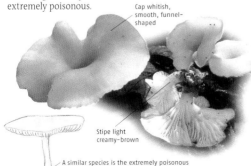

Gills continue down on to stipe, creamy-white

Stipe light creamy-brown

A similar species is the extremely poisonous *Clitocybe candicans*, which is smaller and normally has a bend in its stipe base.

Aniseed Funnel 🍴

Clitocybe odora (mushrooms with gills)
Size 3–6 cm   July–October

Habitat *In deciduous and coniferous forests on clay soils.*

> **Strong aniseed odour**
> **Spores pink**
> **Found throughout Europe**

The combination of its blue-green colour and its strong aniseed odour is unique in the world of mushrooms, making it easily identifiable. However, the greenish colour is not always intense and can fade completely if exposed to direct sunlight. Faded fruiting bodies are therefore very difficult to identify.

Flesh pale blue-green

Gills continue down on to stipe, creamy-white

Cap blue to blue-green when young

Stipe similar greenish colour

The Verdigris Agaric (p. 162) displays the same colours but can be distinguished by its brown spores among other things.

Fragrant Funnel ☠

Clitocybe fragrans (mushrooms with gills)
Size 3–6 cm   May–November

Habitat *In deciduous and coniferous forests, prefers clay soils, less common in deciduous forests.*

> **Aniseed odour**
> **Spores cream-coloured**
> **Common throughout Europe**

Although this species has a pleasant aniseed odour like the edible Aniseed Funnel, it is poisonous. It is essential that odour alone is never used to identify mushrooms, even if they smell edible! This clitocybe often occurs in spring, but also in mild winter periods.

Another clitocybe with a characteristic smell is the inedible *Clitocybe foetens*. When it dries out, it begins to smell of sweaty feet!

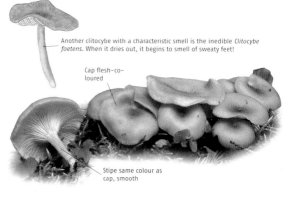

Cap flesh-coloured

Gills broad at stipe, tapering out towards cap rim

Flesh pale, creamy-brown

Stipe same colour as cap, smooth

Mealy Frosted Funnel

☠

Clitocybe ditopa (mushrooms with gills)
Size 2–5 cm   September–December

Once the small-spored Mealy Frosted Funnel has appeared, the end of the edible mushroom season is in sight. It is one of the latest occurring species together with the Clouded Funnel (p. 64) and the Field Blewit (p. 66). This species also occurs under spruces.

Habitat *In coniferous forests in amongst fallen spruce needles on at least moderately nutrient rich soils.*

> **Strong odour of cucumber skin**
> **Spores whitish**
> **Common throughout Europe**

Cap whitish when young, frosted

The Club Foot (*C. clavipes*), which is poisonous when consumed with alcohol, has a bulbous stipe base with spongy flesh.

Cap moist, dark greyish-brown

Stipe greyish-brown with satiny, white covering

Stipe has white fuzz on base

Grey-Brown Funnel Cap

☠

Clitocybe metachroa (mushrooms with gills)
Size 2–6 cm   September–November

The cap of this mushroom looks as though it has had dust sprinkled over it. As with all small clitocybes, this mushroom is thought to be poisonous. It always grows in large groups, sometimes in hundreds.

Habitat *In various types of woodland, normally among fallen pine needles, infrequently in amongst fallen leaves, no soil preference.*

> **Spores whitish**
> **Common throughout Europe**

Stipe grey-brown, base is dark

The number of small species of *Clitocybe* which change colour when dried is amazing. This species is dark brown when moist (left) and creamy-white when dried (right).

Cap dark grey-brown when moist, dehydrates rapidly

Gills continue slightly down on to stipe

Flesh whitish, darker in the stipe

Common Funnel

Clitocybe gibba (mushrooms with gills)

Size 2–6 cm   June–November

Habitat In various deciduous forests and spruce forests on clay, alkaline soils and also on old piles of bark.

> Slight odour of bitter almond
> Spores whitish
> Common throughout Europe
> Similar species other clitocybes

Key features for identifying this clitocybe are its non-water absorbent cap with a small hump in its centre, its pleasant odour of bitter almond and its slightly ochre colour. It is extremely common but is seldom picked because it is not always easy to identify, despite the aforementioned characteristics. Only young specimens should be picked as mature specimens taste insipid.

Clitocybe costata can be distinguished by its dark stipe and wavy cap rim.

Caution!

Other clitocybes which are thought to be poisonous can look very similar, especially the Leather-Coloured Clitocybe (C. diatreta). Its gills only slightly continue down on to the stipe.

Gills heavily integrated with stipe

Flesh pale cream-coloured

62

Cap ochre with a small hump in the centre

Stipe whitish lighter than the cap

Tawny Funnel

Lepista flaccida (mushrooms with gills)

Size 4–10 cm   July–November

This species combines the typical characteristics of the clitocybes (cap shape, gills integrated with the stipe) with those of the lepistas (warty spores, moveable gills). For this reason, this mushroom is sometimes referred to as a clitocybe.

Young specimens are normally lighter in colour, more solid and have typical water marks on the cap rim. The equal brown colouring of the cap only develops gradually with the effect of the elements. The former name for older specimens with water marks was *Lepista gilva*.

Habitat *In various deciduous woodlands and in spruce forests, no real soil preferences, but avoids nutrient-poor soils.*

> **Gills moveable**
> **Spores cream-coloured with a hint of orange-pink**
> **Common throughout Europe**
> **Similar species** Clitocybe amoenolens

Caution!

While the highly poisonous Clitocybe amoenolens has only ever been found in northern Africa and southern France, it is possible that it also grows in warm parts of central Europe. Almost the only difference is its odour.

Gills heavily integrated with stipe

Flesh pale cream-coloured

63

Stipe short, lighter colouring

Cap equally orange-brown

Clouded Funnel
Lepista nebularis (mushrooms with gills)
Size 10–20 cm   September–December

Habitat In all types of woodland, particularly in beech forests with many fallen leaves, absent from nutrient-poor, very moist soils.

> **Odour sweetish-rancid, strong**
> **Spores creamy-white**
> **Common throughout Europe**
> **Similar species Livid Pinkgill**

This species is one of the best-known edible mushrooms, but it is the subject of some controversy. While some people enjoy eating it and it is even sold in some shops, some people think it tastes awful and it causes stomach upsets in others. It should therefore be eaten in moderation when trying it for the first time to gauge whether you like the taste and whether it agrees with you.

If you are very lucky, you might see the parasitic Piggyback Rosegill on decaying Clouded Funnel caps.

Flesh whitish

Stipe base slightly club-like

Caution!
The highly poisonous Livid Pinkgill (p. 107) can grow to be just as large and solid as the Clouded Funnel. It can be distinguished by its pink spores and its strong floury odour.

Gills cream-coloured, continuing down on to stipe

Cap grey to brownish-grey

Wood Blewit

Lepista nuda (mushrooms with gills)
Size 6–12 cm   September–December

The Wood Blewit occurs at a time when there are few other edible mushrooms available. Since its colour, characteristic, sweet odour and spore colour make it easy to recognise, it has become very popular. It can be pickled in vinegar and retains its beautiful colour.

Cortinarius variecolor (p. 195) can look similar

Habitat *In all types of woodland, particularly in beech forests with many fallen leaves, absent from nutrient-poor, very moist soils.*

> **Odour sweetish, perfumed**
> **Spores pale pink**
> **Common throughout Europe**
> **Similar species violet webcaps**

Caution Poisonous!

The web-like veil and the rust brown spores must be clearly identified to avoid confusion with highly poisonous Cortinarius species such as the Bruising Webcap (Cortinarius purpurascens).

Flesh violet, slightly mottled

Gills ascending

65

Cap violet to lilac

Stipe same colour with a white layer of fibres

Field Blewit
Lepista saeva (mushrooms with gills)
Size 6–12 cm   October–December

🍴

Habitat *In orchards, gardens and hedgerows on alkaline soils.*

> **Odour is subtle**
> **Spores light pink**
> **Patchy distribution in central Europe**

While the other lepistas are autumn species, the Field Blewit occurs even later. It often grows in November, even after the first frost. It is the best tasting lepista and is easily identified by the contrasting colours of its violet stipe and horn grey cap.

The completely violet, lavender-coloured *Lepista glaucocona* occurs on chalky soils in montane regions. Although not poisonous, it has an unpleasant taste.

Cap horn grey to bluish-grey, smooth

Stipe violet

Gills ascending

Flesh pale grey, slightly mottled

Lepista luscina
No common name (mushrooms with gills)
Size 6–15 cm   September–November

🍴

Habitat *On neglected grassland and meadows and only on alkaline soils.*

> **Odour slightly floury**
> **Spores light pink**
> **Patchy distribution in central Europe**

As with many lepistas, this species usually grows in what are called 'fairy rings'. These rings can be best observed on open grassland where regular, circular mycelium growth is unhindered.

Cap occasionally has water marks

Cap horn grey to brownish-grey, smooth

Stipe whitish

Flesh pale grey, slightly mottled

St. George's Mushroom

Calocybe gambosa (mushrooms with gills)
Size 5–10 cm   April–May(June)

Opinions on the taste of this mushroom vary from 'one of the best' to 'terrible.' What is certain is that it is definitely edible and occurs at a time when it is hard to find other edible mushrooms. It can even be found in high grass because the grass is dark green and longer where the mushroom grows.

Habitat On all types of grassland, in open, deciduous forests, in spruce forests on former meadows, prefers alkaline soils.

Young St. George's mushrooms (left) may be confused with young Deadly Fibrecaps (right, p. 178) which have not yet developed their colour fully.

> Strong odour of cucumber or flour
> Spores white
> Common throughout Europe
> Similar species Deadly Fibrecap

Caution!

The extremely poisonous Deadly Fibrecap (p. 178) occurs at the same time although it begins to redden after some time. Both species may occur very close to each other in open deciduous forests and parks.

Flesh white, firm

Gills with moat

67

Stipe same colour

Cap off-white to leather-coloured, smooth

Pink Domecap

Calocybe carnea (mushrooms with gills)
Size 2–6 cm   August–October

🍴

Habitat On moderately fertilised to non-fertilised grasslands and meadows, usually on the boundaries of woodlands.

> Odour weak, not floury
> Spores white
> Patchy distribution throughout Europe

Although the Pink Domecap is generally regarded as edible, it is not particularly fruitful. In addition, it is easily confused with a number of poisonous clitocybes (p. 56–62). It must also be noted that cap colour may fade due to the influence of sunlight, especially on mushrooms growing on open grassland, which may make identification more difficult.

Cap pink to skin-coloured, smooth

Gills white, contrasting

Gills with moat

Flesh white, firm

Other colourful domecaps are the Yellow Domecap (*C. chrysenteron*) which grows in coniferous forests and the Violet Domecap (*C. ionides*) which grows on alkaline soils in deciduous forests. Both are rare and inedible.

Stipe skin-coloured

Plums and Custard

Tricholomopsis rutilans (mushrooms with gills)
Size 4–12 cm   June–November

🍴

Habitat On rotting coniferous wood in all types of forest, no soil preference.

> Taste earthy, bitter
> Spores white
> Common throughout Europe

A huge specimen with a cap diameter of 56 cm was once shown at a mushroom exhibition in Italy. Almost all mushrooms can develop unusually large or unusually small fruiting bodies under certain conditions. Abnormal exceptions such as these are not taken into account in the size information in mushroom guidebooks. While this species can be eaten, it does not taste particularly good.

Prunes and Custard (*T. decora*) only occurs in damp, coniferous forests in montane regions. Its yellow cap has blackish scales on it.

Stipe firm with skin-coloured streaks

Cap with purple fuzz on a yellow base

Flesh pale to deep yellow

Grey Knight

Tricholoma terreum (mushrooms with gills)

Size 4–8 cm   August–October

The knights are a large group of species, recognisable by their grey to blackish colour. Odour, taste and flesh colour are key factors for identification. The Grey Knight can be identified by its odourless non-discolouring flesh and the surface of its cap, which has longitudinal fibres instead of scales.

Habitat *Consistently under Scots pines on sandy, alkaline soils, often in large numbers.*

> *Subtle odour, not floury*
> *Spores white*
> *Common throughout Europe*
> *Similar species Ashen Knight*

Caution!

Apart from possible confusion with the quite dissimilar Tiger Tricholoma (left, p. 70), the real danger is confusion with the Ashen Knight (right, p. 71). Both species can be distinguished by their taste.

Flesh white, stipe becomes hollow

Gills white with moat

69

Cap dark grey, stringy with longitudinal fibres

Stipe white

Tiger Tricholoma

Tricholoma pardalotum (mushrooms with gills)
Size 6–12 cm   August–October

Habitat In coniferous forests under spruces and white firs and in deciduous forests under beeches, always on alkaline soils.

> Odour is distinctly floury
> Spores white
> Patchy distribution in Europe, otherwise uncommon

Since the Tiger Tricholoma only occurs on chalky soils, it is unknown in some regions. However, collectors in those regions should know how to identify it as it does grow on forest paths with chalky gravel on them, even if the soil underneath is acidic. Small quantities can cause severe poisoning of the stomach and digestive tract although there are no lasting effects.

The Yellowing Knight (p. 71) can look very similar but is less solid and turns yellowish when older.

Gills recessed

Stipe tip with clear droplets

Did you know?

Typically, the Tiger Tricholoma has a scaly cap. However, there is a variant with more of a felted cap surface (var. filamentosum) which is just as poisonous as the scaly variety.

70

Concentric scales on creamy–white base on cap

Stipe white, solid

Yellowing Knight

Tricholoma argyraceum (mushrooms with gills)

Size 4–8 cm   June–October

Older specimens in particular can be clearly identified by their yellow parts and their strong floury taste. It usually occurs in large numbers which would normally make it worth picking. As with St. George's Mushroom, however, the floury taste does not appeal to everyone.

The Girdled Knight (*T. cingulatum*), which turns just as yellow, has a ring. It consistently occurs on meadows.

Habitat In parks, avenues and under single trees, less common in deciduous forests, prefers clay soil which is not too acidic.

> *Strong floury odour and taste*
> *Spores white*
> *Common throughout Europe*

Cap has dark scales on a white base

Cap turns yellow in places

Stipe becomes yellowish with age

Gills white, turning yellow in places

71

Ashen Knight

Tricholoma virgatum (mushrooms with gills)

Size 4–8 cm   August–October

A few of the knights are slightly bitter or hot-tasting. As taste is a key characteristic for identification, a sample of any mushroom from this group should be tasted. The sample must always be spat out again and never swallowed. Warning! Mild-tasting flesh is not indicative of edibility.

Habitat In coniferous forests on acidic soils, particularly under spruces.

> *Hot taste*
> *Spores white*
> *Common throughout Europe*

Cap flossy with a metallic sheen

The Fleck-Gill Knight Cap (*T. sciodes*) occurs in warmer deciduous forests. It has a less pronounced hump on its cap. When chewed, its hot taste only becomes apparent after 20–30 seconds.

Stipe base often broadened

Cap conical with a hump in the centre

Flesh white

Scaly Knight

Tricholoma vaccinum (mushrooms with gills)
Size 4–8 cm   August–October

Habitat *In coniferous forests on slightly acidic to alkaline soils, particularly under spruces in mountainous regions.*

> **Tastes slightly bitter**
> **Spores white**
> **Patchy distribution throughout Europe**

The woolly, web-like veil between the cap rim and stipe on young mushrooms is unusual for *Tricholoma* species. However, it is normal on *Cortinarius* species (p. 188) which have rust-coloured rather than white spores. The Scaly Knight usually grows in fairly large numbers.

Cap surface wool-like with scales, red-brown

Stipe hollow

Flesh has a slight reddish-brown tarnish

Stipe red-brown

The most distinct identifying feature of this species is the thick, wool-like curtain on the cap rim which gradually dissipates with age.

Burnt Knight

Tricholoma ustale (mushrooms with gills)
Size 4–10 cm   August–October

Habitat *In deciduous forests on slightly acidic to alkaline soils, almost always under beeches.*

> **Tastes slightly bitter**
> **Cap greasy when moist**
> **Spores white**
> **Patchy distribution throughout Europe**

It can be difficult to identify brown tricholomas. They are often of little value to collectors anyway due to the fact that all of them are slightly poisonous or inedible because of their bitter taste. Only the Poplar Knight is picked in some areas.

Cap orange to rusty brown with a hint of olive

Stipe pale orange-brown

The Poplar Knight (*T. populinum*) is considered an edible mushroom in some areas, despite its relatively bitter taste. It is alleged that it aids the treatment of rheumatism, although this has not been proven.

Tricholoma fracticum

No common name (mushrooms with gills)

Size 6–12 cm   September–November

This mushroom is often stuck well into the ground and is only slightly taller than the surrounding grass. For this reason, it is not always easy to spot, even in short grass and despite its actual size. The reason for its absence in parts of Europe are its three special biotope requirements, which must all be present: Scots Pines, warmth and shell limestone.

Habitat In open Scots Pine forests and on heaths, always under Scots Pines on shell limestone soils.

> **Taste** bitter
> **Odour** floury
> **Spores** white
> **Regional distribution in central and southern Europe**

Cap brown, smooth, slightly greasy

Stipe pale brown, tip white

The completely orange Orange Knight (*T. aurantium*) grows under spruces. Its stipe has a distinct snakeskin-like surface. With age, the cap colour oxidises to become green.

Ring zone slightly raised, skin-like

Stipe base tapered

73

Matsutake

Tricholoma matsutake (mushrooms with gills)

Size 8–20 cm   August–November

The Matsutake is the most highly prized edible mushroom in Japan. The highest quality Matsutakes with closed caps command prices of up to a few thousand pounds per kilo. Some American mushroom collectors have been known to fight and even kill each other over Matsutake 'territory'. However, it is less sought-after in Europe.

Habitat In open spruce forests and on heaths, consistently under Scots pines on shell limestone soils.

> **Taste** mild
> **Odour** sweetish
> **Spores** white
> **Very rare in northern and central Europe**

Cap brown with scales

The Eastern Matsutake (*T. caligatum*), with darker scales, is often found in the Mediterranean region under Scots Pines. It tastes bitter and is therefore inedible.

Stipe light brown, with a slightly snakeskin-like surface

Flesh whitish, unchanging

Ring ascending, skin-like

Golden Tricholoma

Tricholoma auratum (mushrooms with gills)
Size 6–12 cm   September–November

☠

Habitat In sandy, nutrient-poor pine forests, a related species occurs under aspens.

> *Odour floury*
> *Spores white*
> *Patchy distribution throughout Europe, common in some regions*
> *Similar species Splendid Webcap*

A few years ago, it was discovered that the Golden Tricholoma is highly likely to cause amyotrophia (muscle wastage). This can occur after regularly consuming relatively large quantities. It is therefore not advisable to eat this mushroom. It is also rare and should not be picked for this reason alone.

The hot-tasting *Tricholoma aestuans* grows in similar locations and is inedible.

Flesh pale yellow, more intense at the edge

Gills recessed

Caution!

The deadly poisonous Splendid Webcap (p. 196) displays the same colours. When young, it has a veil between the cap rim and stipe and has a different odour.

Cap yellow, rusty yellow towards centre, greasy when moist

Stipe yellow

Sulphur Knight

Tricholoma sulphureum (mushrooms with gills)
Size 5–10 cm   August–November

Despite the Sulphur Knight's very unpleasant odour of rotten eggs, some people have actually eaten it in the past. It is therefore known that apart from smelling bad, it causes severe poisoning of the stomach and digestive tract.

Habitat *In mildly acidic soils in deciduous and coniferous forests, has no particular preferences.*

Tricholoma bufonium is exactly the same as the Sulphur Knight in all respects apart from its purple cap, which means that it is often just seen as a variant.

> **Pungent odour of rotten eggs**
> **Spores white**
> **Common throughout Europe**

Cap sulphur yellow, dry

Gills thick and widely spaced

Stipe sulphur yellow, tapered

Flesh sulphur yellow

Deceiving Knight

Tricholoma sejunctum (mushrooms with gills)
Size 5–12 cm   August–November

The Deceiving Knight's ingrown, fibrous cap with its various shades of green makes it easy to confuse it with the Deathcap (p. 116) if viewed from above. However, *Tricholoma* species do not have a ring, volva or exposed gills. Regardless of differences in appearance, the Deceiving Knight is also poisonous and should not be picked.

Habitat *Under beeches in deciduous forests and under spruces in coniferous forests, only on alkaline soils.*

> **Slight floury odour**
> **Spores white**
> **Patchy distribution throughout Europe**

When growing in coniferous forests, it is a warmer colour of orange and often turns reddish-brown when it oxidises.

Cap green to orange-yellow

Gills white, recessed

Ingrown cap with longitudinal fibres

Soapy Knight

Tricholoma saponaceum (mushrooms with gills)

Size 5–12 cm   August–November

☠

Habitat *Under beeches in deciduous forests and under spruces in coniferous forests, only on alkaline soils.*

> *Odour of soap*
> *Spores white*
> *Patchy distribution throughout Europe*

'Nomen est Omen' is certainly the case for the Soapy Knight! Its unique soapy odour reminds people of launderettes, soap and floor cloths. Because the species varies so much in appearance, it can often only be identified by someone with a great deal of experience. Some frustrated mushroom-enthusiasts have even gone as far as to say 'if you can't identify it, then it's a Soapy Knight.'

Did you know?

The Soapy Knight has the most varying appearance of any of the tricholomas, so much so that it is hard to believe that all of the variations can be of the same species. (from the left: var. saponaceum, *var.* squamulosum, *var.* boudieri). *They all have the same odour and have the tendency to turn red.*

Gills white, recessed

Stipe base reddens

Cap smooth, often olive-grey

Stipe white, solid

Grey and Yellow Knight Cap

Tricholoma portentosum (mushrooms with gills)

Size 5–12 cm   September–November

This mushroom is one of many species which is being negatively affected by increasing nitrogen enrichment in forests. It is often found in the same locations as the Golden Tricholoma (p. 74) and both are in steady decline. It should only be picked in very small quantities or not at all.

Habitat In Scots Pine or spruce forests on acidic, dry, nutrient-poor, sandy soils, almost always under Scots Pines.

> *Slight floury odour*
> *Spores white*
> *Patchy distribution throughout Europe, common in some regions*

Cap deep blackish, ingrown, fibrous

Gills white turning slightly yellow with age

Stipe white with yellowy flecks and flakes

Aromatic Knight

Tricholoma lascivum (mushrooms with gills)

Cap 5–10 cm   August–October

Generally, odours play an important role in the identification of mushrooms. The floury smell is particularly important when identifying some tricholomas. There is also a range of species with a very unpleasant odour of sulphur or gas. The Aromatic Knight only has a mild odour when young but gradually develops an increasingly pungent sweetish, dusty smell.

Habitat On moderately acidic to slightly alkaline soils in deciduous forests, usually under beeches or oaks.

> *Odour sweetish-dusty*
> *Spores white*
> *Found throughout Europe*

Tricholoma inamoenum has an equally unpleasant odour and grows in coniferous forests in montane regions. It is less solid and has very widely spaced gills.

Gills creamy-white, tightly packed

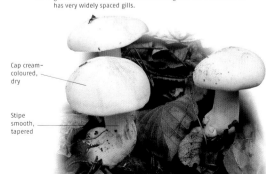

Cap cream-coloured, dry

Stipe smooth, tapered

Flesh pale, cream-coloured

Dark Honey Fungus

Armillaria ostoyae (mushrooms with gills)
Cap 5–10 cm   August–November

¶¶

Habitat In Spruce forests on relatively acidic soils, also on spruce tree stumps in other forest habitats.

> Grows in clumps
> Spores white
> Very common throughout Europe
> Similar species Shaggy Scalycap

The Dark Honey Fungus often grows in large groups in spruce forests in the late autumn. In some forests, you will often find that each tree stump has a thick covering of fruiting bodies. It is a highly edible mushroom but it must be cooked at 60° for at least 15 minutes. The mushrooms should be fried rather than boiled as boiling makes them slimy.

The Dark Honey Fungus uses its thick rhizomorphs to find dead wood on which to grow, and can do so over fairly long distances.

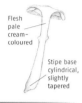

Flesh pale cream-coloured

Stipe base cylindrical, slightly tapered

78

Caution!

The bitter-tasting and inedible Shaggy Scalycap (p. 170) can be easily distinguished by its scaly stipe. While it is not poisonous, it can cause indigestion.

Cap pinkish-brown with dark scales up to rim

Rings skin-like with a brownish rim

Honey Fungus (¶¶)

Armillaria mellea (mushrooms with gills)

Cap 5–10 cm   July–November

Some people have reported stomach upsets after eating Honey Fungus. It should be tried in small quantities to begin with to find out if it causes stomach problems and, of course, it should always be thoroughly cooked.

Habitat In all forest types, in parks, gardens and orchards, on deciduous tree stumps or at the foot of living deciduous trees.

> Grows in thick clumps
> Spores creamy-white
> Found throughout Europe

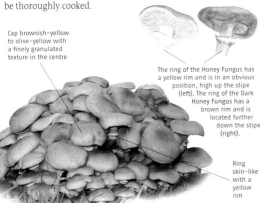

Cap brownish-yellow to olive-yellow with a finely granulated texture in the centre

The ring of the Honey Fungus has a yellow rim and is in an obvious position, high up the stipe (left). The ring of the Dark Honey Fungus has a brown rim and is located further down the stipe (right).

Ring skin-like with a yellow rim

Flesh pale cream-coloured

Stipe long, thin, tapered

Angel's Wings ☠

Phyllotus porrigens (mushrooms with gills)

Cap 3–7 cm   August–October

Until recently, this mushroom was considered edible or at least harmless. The Japanese have since discovered that it can cause serious poisoning. The exact details have not yet been researched, although poisoning has only occurred in people with kidney problems. It is now necessary to list this mushroom as poisonous.

Habitat In humid spruce forests in montane regions, also in lower locations in northern Europe, always on very rotten pine wood.

> Grows in clumps or in small groups
> Spores creamy-white
> Uncommon in southern Europe, otherwise patchy distribution

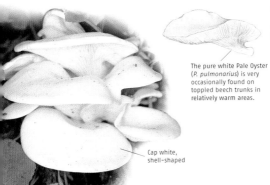

The pure white Pale Oyster (*P. pulmonarius*) is very occasionally found on toppled beech trunks in relatively warm areas.

Cap white, shell-shaped

Narrow gills

Stipe short, rudimentary or absent

Goblet

Pseudoclitocybe cyathiformis (mushrooms with gills)
Cap 4–10 cm   September–November

Habitat In all types of deciduous forest, on nutrient-rich soils, rare in coniferous forests.

> Odour mild, mushroomy
> Spores white
> Found throughout Europe

This mushroom gets its name from its goblet-shaped cap. While it is edible, it can be confused with similar looking, poisonous clitocybes.

Gills descending

Flesh moist, brownish-grey

Stipe normally longer than breadth of cap

Key identifying characteristics are the long stipe in relation to the cap and the forked gills.

Cap chocolate to coffee-coloured

Giant Funnel

Leucopaxillus giganteus (mushrooms with gills)
Cap 15–30 cm   August–November

Habitat In clearings, on forest boundaries and orchards, uncommon inside forests, prefers nutrient-rich soils.

> Slight bitter almond odour
> Spores whitish
> Common throughout Europe

This species usually grows in 'fairy rings' on a huge scale. Diameters of 30–40 metres are not uncommon. The actual fruiting bodies grow in a zone up to 1 metre wide within which any grass will die. Very lush, strong vegetation grows on the fringes of these zones.

Gills descending

Flesh off-white

Other funnels are smaller, often bitter and therefore inedible, especially the rare *Leucopaxillus gentianeus*.

Cap flat, funnel-shaped, creamy-white

Cap short, robust

Imperial Mushroom

Catathelasma imperiale (mushrooms with gills)

Cap 10–20 cm   August–October

A remarkable feature of this mushroom is that its stipe is so deeply embedded in the soil that its cap rim is usually just above the surface, which means that it has to be practically dug out. Pickling it in vinegar used to be popular because of its firm flesh, but many people found its strong taste of gherkins disagreeable. It has now become so rare that it should not be picked at all.

Habitat *In open Scots Pine forests and in montane coniferous forests under spruces and Scots Pines, always on chalky soil.*

> **Strong gherkin-like odour**
> **Flesh white, very firm**
> **Spores whitish**
> **Uncommon in Europe, patchy distribution in Alpine regions**

When young, the gills are covered by the skin-like membrane which forms after the upper ring becomes detached.

Gills tightly packed, descending

Cap grey-brown with flecks of velum remnants

Cap rim heavily rolled-in

Stipe with double ring

Spring Cavalier

Melanoleuca cognata (mushrooms with gills)

Cap 6–15 cm   May–June (November)

As its name might suggest, it is one of the first gilled mushrooms to appear early in the year. However, it also occurs in autumn although much less frequently. Its saffron and ochre gills are unique. Although edible, it does not taste particularly good.

Habitat *On waysides, chaff or in ruderal locations in various forest types, prefers acidic soils.*

> **Odour insignificant**
> **Spores rich creamy-yellow**
> **Found throughout Europe**

Gills saffron to ochre

Confusion is very occasionally caused by exceptionally dark fruiting bodies.

Cap warm brown, rim frosted when young

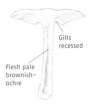

Gills recessed

Flesh pale brownish-ochre

Common Cavalier 🍴

Melanoleuca melaleuca (mushrooms with gills)
Cap 6–15 cm   July–October

Habitat On waysides and forest boundaries on chaff, or ruderal locations in various types of forest.

> Mild, mushroomy odour
> Spores whitish
> Common throughout Europe

Apart from a few exceptions, even specialists find it difficult to identify *Melanoleuca* species positively. However, mushroom collectors may find comfort in the fact that they are all edible, although they do not taste particularly good.

Cap usually has a small hump in the centre

Flesh creamy-white, turning brown in the stipe

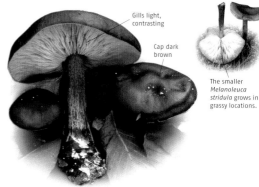

Gills light, contrasting

Cap dark brown

The smaller *Melanoleuca stridula* grows in grassy locations.

Warty Stem 🍴

Melanoleuca verrucipes (mushrooms with gills)
Cap 6–15 cm   July–October

Habitat On chaff, bark mulch and old brushwood piles and occasionally on other plant debris.

> Mild, mushroomy odour
> Spores whitish
> Uncommon in Europe, but on the increase

This species can easily be identified by the rough, flaky surface of the stipe. It has therefore been easy to follow its development over the last 30 years. Because of the increasing number of biotopes available, this formerly rare mushroom has prevailed. Nevertheless, it is still relatively rare and finding one is certainly a memorable experience.

Gills recessed

Stipe scaly

Cap chalk white

The very rare and small *M. subpulverulenta* is easily recognised by its chalk white colour and frosted cap.

Clustered Domecap

Lyophyllum decastes (mushrooms with gills)

Cap 3–7 cm   August–November

The Clustered Domecap is a good edible mushroom which occurs late in the year, remains firm when cooked and usually grows in large quantities. It is not uncommon to find clumps stretching dozens of metres along grassy waysides. Individual specimens also occasionally grow in early summer.

Habitat In various forests, on bark mulch or along paths, nutrient indicator.

> *Usually grows in large clumps*
> *Spores white*
> *Common throughout Europe*

Young *Entoloma lividoalbum* specimens look very similar. However, they have light pink spores.

Cap dark brown, smooth, slightly gristly

Stipe white, smooth

Gills whitish, upturned

Flesh whitish

83

White Domecap

Lyophyllum connatum (mushrooms with gills)

Cap 3–8 cm   August–November

While this species was once considered edible, it is now known that it contains a substance known as lyophillin which is thought to trigger changes in genetic makeup. It is often difficult to distinguish it from poisonous clitocybes anyway and should be avoided.

Habitat Along paths, nutrient indicator.

> *Grows in large clumps*
> *Odour of corydalis*
> *Spores white*
> *Common throughout Europe*

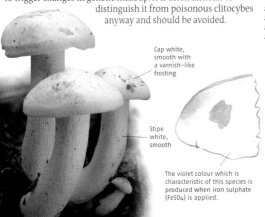

Cap white, smooth with a varnish-like frosting

Stipe white, smooth

The violet colour which is characteristic of this species is produced when iron sulphate (FeSO4) is applied.

Flesh white

Gills white, ascending

Lyophyllum anthracophilum ✕

No common name (mushrooms with gills)
Cap 2–4 cm   June–October

Habitat *Always on areas which were burnt 6–24 months previously.*

> *Odour floury*
> *Spores white*
> *Common throughout Europe*

Burnt areas of ground have a fungal world of their own. These species quickly occupy burnt areas which have been sterilised by heat. However, they are poor competitors and usually disappear after one or two years. This species is one of the most common inhabitants of burnt areas and is not edible.

Cap dark brown

Stipe also dark brown, smooth

Flesh white

Gills white, ascending

The Stalked Bonfire Cup (*Geopyxis carbonaria*) often grows in unison with this species.

Sphagnum Greyling ✕

Lyophyllum palustris (mushrooms with gills)
Cap 1–3 cm   June–October

Habitat *On flat land and hill bogs on sphagnum moss.*

> *Strong floury odour*
> *White spores*
> *Common throughout Europe*

Although this small, inconspicuous mushroom is inedible, it is ecologically interesting as it only ever grows in a bed of sphagnum moss, thereby indicating healthy bog formation. It is easily distinguished from many other similar brownish-grey species by its location and strong odour.

Cap yellow to grey-brown with a translucent rim

Cranberries (*Vaccinium oxycoccos*) are often found growing in unison with the Sphagnum Greyling.

Gills creamy-brown

Stipe same colour as cap, smooth

Lyophyllum inolens

No common name (mushrooms with gills)

Cap 2–4 cm   August–November

This species, which is hardly known, but common in some regions, may be confused with the edible Butter Cap. It is not known whether this could be dangerous since no one knows much about the edibility of this mushroom. It is therefore best to avoid eating it.

Habitat In mountain spruce forests among fallen needles, less common in beech forests under scattered spruces.

> *Odour slightly rancid when fresh*
> *Spores white*
> *Patchy distribution throughout Europe*

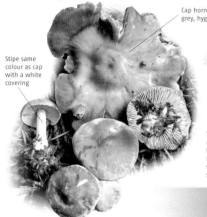

Cap horn to brownish-grey, hygrophane

Stipe same colour as cap with a white covering

Flesh pale grey-brown

Gills ascending, crowded

The best way of distinguishing it from the Butter Cap is to look for the white flakes on its stipe tip.

Butter Cap

Rhodocollybia butyracea var. *asema* (mushrooms with gills)

Cap 2–5 cm   August–November

The Butter Cap gets its name from its unique, shiny cap surface which actually looks as though it has been smeared with butter, although it has a mediocre taste. Since it often grows in large numbers, it is picked by many people although the gristly, tough stipes should be discarded.

Habitat In coniferous forests with a large number of fallen needles, less common in deciduous forests, prefers acidic soils.

> *Stipe surface harder than stipe flesh*
> *Spores creamy-pink*
> *Common throughout Europe*

R. butyracea var. *butyracea* can be distinguished by the warm, red-brown colour of its cap. It prefers neutral to alkaline soils.

Stipe base spongy, thickened

Cap horn to brownish-grey with an oily sheen

Flesh soft, watery grey-brown

Gills whitish, crowded

Spotted Toughshank

Rhodocollybia maculata (mushrooms with gills)

Cap 3–7(12) cm   August–November

Habitat *Primarily in coniferous forests on soils with at least an acidic surface, uncommon in deciduous forests.*

> Odour of freshly cut wood
> Tastes very bitter
> Spores creamy-pink
> Common throughout Europe

The Butter Cap, Spotted Toughshank and *Rhodocollybia distorta* are part of a group whose method of obtaining nutrients differs from other *Rhodocollybia* species. They form a root symbiosis with trees (mycorrhiza) while the other species grow on dead material. The members of this small group have creamy-pink spores and their gill blades are saw-like.

Cap milky-white, becoming increasingly covered with rust-coloured spots

Rust-coloured spots appear on parts of flesh

Gills tightly packed

While it is rare to find *Rhodocollybia* species with distorted stipes, this is a distinguishing feature of *R. prolixa*.

Stipe longitudinally fibrous, tapered base

Spindle Toughshank

Collybia fusipes (mushrooms with gills)

Cap 3–6(8) cm   July–October

Habitat *In oak woodland, parks or other woodland with oak trees, prefers slightly warmer conditions.*

> Stipe flesh very tough
> Tastes slightly bitter
> Spores white
> Common throughout Europe but absent to the north of central Sweden

The Spindle Toughshank has very tough flesh which decomposes very slowly. Fruit bodies often last for weeks and can be seen well into winter. A distinguishing feature of this species is that it grows in thick clumps beneath old oak trees.

The Spindle Toughshank is often thought of as a ground-dwelling mushroom because it usually has its base on the main underground roots of a host tree.

Cap dry, brownish-yellow

Stipe becomes increasingly corky and dark towards base

Gills ascending

Stipe with spindle-like root

Russet Toughshank (Ⱡ)

Gymnopus dryophilus (mushrooms with gills)

Cap 3–7cm   (May) June–October

Opinions on the edibility of the Russet Toughshank differ. While some people advise against eating it altogether, others think it is definitely edible. This is probably down to individual tolerance of the mushroom and so it is advisable to only eat it in small quantities at first.

Habitat *Among fallen leaves or needles in various forest types, also on bark mulch or along paths, nutrient indicator.*

Did you know?

Gymnopus hariolorum looks very similar to the Russet Toughshank but it only grows in deciduous forests, it has felting on its stipe and has a disgusting odour of rotting cabbage.

> Flesh watery brown, thin
> Spores white
> Found throughout Europe

Gills whitish, moderately crowded

Cap ochre-brown, water-absorbent

Stipe smooth

Clustered Toughshank

Gymnopus confluens (mushrooms with gills)

Cap 3–6 cm   July–October

☠

Habitat *Among fallen leaves or needles in various forest types, also on bark mulch or along paths, nutrient indicator.*

> **Flesh watery brown, mild**
> **Spores white**
> **Found throughout Europe**

This mushroom grows in clumps with many fruiting bodies. They are normally found in rows or full circles with large numbers (even hundreds) of fruiting bodies occurring in one location.

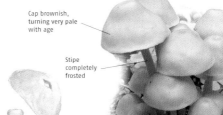

Cap brownish, turning very pale with age

Stipe completely frosted

Gills very crowded

This mushroom gets its name from the huge clumps in which it grows.

Wood Woollyfoot

Gymnopus peronatus (mushrooms with gills)

Cap 4–8 cm   July–October

Habitat *Among fallen leaves, less commonly among fallen needles, in various forest types, prefers acidic soils.*

> **Spores white**
> **Flesh burningly hot**
> **Common throughout Europe**

Typical examples are distinguished by their hot taste when raw, which only becomes noticeable after half a minute of chewing. If the sample is swallowed, it causes a very unpleasant feeling of rawness in the throat which takes a long time to go away.

Gills typically brown-yellow

The edible Fairy Ring Champignon (p. 90) can look similar but has a mild taste and a smooth stipe base.

Stipe base yellow, felted

Cap with ingrown fibres, brownish

Cabbage Parachute

Gymnopus brassicolens (mushrooms with gills)

Cap 1–3 cm   April–June

The variety of odours in the world of mushrooms is fascinating. Some species are characterised by their disgusting odour of rotting cabbage. Amazingly, if you chew a small piece of this mushroom it not only tastes of raw cabbage, but can also cause the same side effects as cabbage, such as bloatedness and wind.

The darkest European Gymnopus is *G. fuscopurpureus* which has a moist, blackish–purple to reddish–brown cap. This dark pigmentation turns green in brine.

Cap pinkish–
brown,
hygrophanous

Habitat *In deciduous forests among fallen leaves on loamy soils and on small pieces of wood, uncommon among fallen needles on chalky soils.*

> **Odour of rotting cabbage**
> **Spores white**
> **Patchy distribution throughout Europe**

Gills whitish,
widely spaced

Stipe black,
finely frosted

Pearly Parachute

Marasmius wynnei (mushrooms with gills)

Cap 2–5 cm   August–November

This species is easily recognised by its light violet to pearl-coloured cap and very tough stipe. Unfortunately, the stipe colour fades rapidly, leaving it a beige-grey to leather colour which makes it harder to identify.

The smaller *Marasmius cohaerens* is also common to the same locations.

Cap violet-grey
to pearly, frosted

Gills
whitish,
very widely
spaced

Habitat *In deciduous forests on humus–rich, loamy soils, usually deep among fallen leaves.*

> **Grows in clumps**
> **Spores white**
> **Common to patchy distribution throughout Europe**

Stipe white
at the top,
turning from
rusty yellow to
red-brown, very
tough

Fairy Ring Champignon

Marasmius oreades (mushrooms with gills)
Cap 2–5 cm   August–November

Habitat *On moderately fertilised meadows and extensively farmed grasslands, always in rings.*

> Slight odour of prussic acid
> Spores white
> Common to patchy distribution throughout Europe
> Similar species Clitocybe agrestis

Marasmius species shrink when it is dry and are rehydrated each time it rains. This can happen a number of times without the mushroom being damaged. The Fairy Ring Champignon is a popular edible mushroom which is particularly suited for making soups. The best way to pick it is to just cut the cap off with scissors or a knife since the stipes are too tough.

The Fairy Ring Champignon usually grows in large circles known as fairy rings. The age of these rings can be determined by their annual increase in size. Some are a few hundred years old.

Gills whitish, very widely spaced

Stipe white, tough

Caution!
The extremely poisonous Clitocybe agrestis (p. 56) also grows on meadows. It can be identified by its more tightly packed gills, its brittle stipe and a slightly glazed layer on the cap surface.

Cap rim slightly ribbed

Cap pinkish-brown to leather-coloured, beige

Garlic Parachute

Marasmius alliaceus (mushrooms with gills)
Cap 1–3 cm   July–October

✕ (fork and knife symbol)

Although this mushroom smells just as garlicky as its little brother (see below), it tastes unpleasant and is not suitable for cooking. The mycelium in the wood has just as strong an odour as the fruiting body.

Habitat *In deciduous forests on humus-rich, loamy soils, grows on fallen, relatively thin Beech branches.*

> **Strong odour of garlic**
> **Spores white**
> **Common throughout Europe, less so in southern Europe**

Cap leathery-grey, smooth, finely frosted

Stipe very tough

Gills pale grey

Stipe completely black

Marasmius querceus grows on oak leaves and is also inedible.

Garlic Mushroom

Marasmius scorodonius (mushrooms with gills)
Cap 1–2 cm   July–October

❙❙ (fork and knife symbol)

One would be mistaken to think that it is not worth picking such a small mushroom, but only a few caps are required for seasoning because it has such an intense garlicky flavour. Known in France as the 'Mousseron', it is a much sought-after mushroom and is sold in dried form for good money per gram. They are almost as expensive to buy as black truffles!

Habitat *In coniferous forests among fallen needles, prefers slightly acidic soils.*

> **Strong, garlicky odour**
> **Spores white**
> **Patchy distribution throughout Europe**

Cap pinkish-brown, cream-coloured towards rim

The smaller Stinking Parachute (*Micromphale perforans*), which has an odour of rotting cabbage, grows individually among fallen needles. It is inedible.

Stipe dark red-brown, tough

Gills white, cross-linked

Collared Parachute (❌🍴)

Marasmius rotula (mushrooms with gills)
Cap 0.5–1 cm   May– October

Habitat *No biotope preferences, occurs on dead wood, prefers deciduous wood.*

> **Odour insignificant**
> **Spores white**
> **Common throughout Europe**

This mushroom's caps look very much like small parachutes. Its very widely spaced gills, which come to an end before reaching the stipe and merge to form a collar, make this likeness is even more apparent. Of all the gilled mushrooms, only a few *Marasmius* species have a collar like this.

Cap whitish, becoming increasingly brownish with age

The Horsehair Parachute *(M. androsaceus)* also grows on small pieces of wood but has more tightly packed gills. It often forms threadlike, false stipes which have the appearance of horsehair.

Gills white, very widely spaced with a collar

Stipe white at the top, becoming blackish-brown towards the bottom

---

Bitter Oysterling (❌🍴)

Panellus stypticus (mushrooms with gills)
Cap 1–3 cm   May–November

Habitat *On dead deciduous wood, particularly on oak tree stumps, no biotope preference.*

> **Tastes slightly bitter, astringent**
> **Spores white**
> **Common throughout Europe**

Many Bitter Oysterling cultures display highly fluorescent gill layers, similar to the Jack o' Lantern (p. 45). However, this has never been observed in the wild and not all strains seem to have this characteristic.

Cap pinkish-brown, shell-like

Gills brownish

Stipe located to the side

Stipe very short or almost absent, beige

There are other small species with shell-like fruiting bodies with very short stipes. One of the most common among these is *Resupinatus trichotis*, which, at 0.5 cm tall, is often overlooked.

Olive Oysterling

☠️

Sarcomyxa serotina (mushrooms with gills)

Cap 2–6 cm October–February(March)

The Olive Oysterling is often confused with the delicious Oyster Mushroom which also grows in winter. Although it only has a mild bitter taste and is not usually considered poisonous, new research shows that it contains many potentially harmful substances including carcinogens. It therefore makes sense to regard it as a poisonous mushroom.

Habitat *On dead beech wood on the ground, usually on thick trunks or branches, rarely on other deciduous wood, no biotope preference.*

> *Tastes slightly bitter, astringent*
> *Spores white*
> *Common throughout Europe*

Cap bottle green to brownish-grey, shell-like

Grows laterally on wood

The short, yellow velvety stipe distinguishes it from the Oyster Mushroom (p. 105).

Flesh watery yellow

Gills yellow, integrated with stipe

Porcelain Fungus

🍴

Oudemansiella mucida (mushrooms with gills)

Cap 3–8 cm August–December

If you happen upon a beech branch lying in a dark gorge, covered with a thick layer of shiny, white Porcelain Fungi, it automatically feels like you are in a fairytale! If you hold the mushroom up to the light, you will see that cap layer directly above the gills is transparent because it is so thin.

Habitat *In humid deciduous forests, often in gorges on large pieces of beech wood lying on the ground.*

> *Whole fruiting body extremely slimy*
> *Spores white*
> *Common throughout central Europe, less common in the south and north.*

The flesh of this species is so thin that the cap is practically transparent.

Cap white to ivory-coloured, very slimy

Grows in small clumps

Stipe ringed

Gills white, widely spaced

Whitelaced Shank (𝗬𝗜)

Megacollybia platyphylla (mushrooms with gills)
Cap 5–12 cm   April–November

Habitat In all types
of forest and on very
rotten deciduous and
coniferous wood, often
appears to be growing
out of the ground.

> **Slight radish-like or
earthy odour**
> **Spores white**
> **Common throughout
Europe**

When nothing else seems to be growing in the forest, you can
almost be sure of finding a few Whitelaced Shanks. It is often
picked to be cooked together with other mushrooms although
some people eat young specimens on their own. There has at times
been suspicion that this mushroom may cause stomach upsets but
there is no real evidence to suggest this. A few specimens mixed in
with other mushrooms would, in any case, be completely harmless.

Did you know?
*The fruiting bodies
do not usually grow
directly on wood but
are connected to it
by their long, strong
mycelium threads
which can grow to
lengths in excess of
30 cm.*

Gills white, widely spaced,
remarkably broad

Stipe
base
with root
threads

Cap grey,
longitudinally fibrous

94

The rare *Clitocybe lacerata*
usually grows in thick clumps
on coniferous wood in
mountainous regions.

Stipe white

Rooting Shank
Xerula radicata (mushrooms with gills)
Cap 3–10 cm   June–November

The remarkable thing about this species is its long root. It is usually the case that the root embedded in decaying substrate is as long as the portion of the stipe visible above ground. Since the stipe can often be longer than 20 cm, specimens with a total length of half a metre cannot be ruled out. This makes it one of the tallest native mushrooms, although it is certainly not the heaviest.

Habitat In all types of forest on rotten tree stumps or on buried wood, making it appear as though it is growing out of the ground.

> **Tastes slightly bitter, astringent**
> **Spores white**
> **Common throughout Europe**

Cap bottle green to brownish–grey, shell–like

It can be distinguished by its very long stipe and root.

Flesh watery yellow

Gills yellow, integrated with stipe

Hydropus subalpinus
No common name (mushrooms with gills)
Cap 2–6 cm   April–June

At first glance, *Hydropus subalpinus* may be mistaken for a small Porcelain Fungus (p. 93) and then perhaps one of the species of *Pluteus*. However, unlike the Porcelain Fungus, it has a dry cap and unlike *Pluteus* species, it has white spores. The name *Hydropus* comes from the fact that the stipe produces a watery fluid when pressed.

Habitat In all types of Beech forest on relatively thin, fallen beech branches lying on the ground or partially buried.

> **Stipe fragile**
> **Spores white**
> **Found throughout central Europe, less common in the south and north**

Although only around 10 *Hydropus* species can be found in Europe, approximately 140 can be found in tropical and subtropical regions. It is sometimes possible to see some of these species in tropical greenhouses, such as this South American species growing out of an Orchid hanging basket.

Cap brass-coloured with a small hump

Stipe white

Gills white

Sprucecone Cap

Strobilurus esculentus (mushrooms with gills)
Cap1-3 cm   December-April

Habitat *In spruce forests and mixed forests with spruces, consistently on old spruce cones.*

> *Stipe flexible*
> *Spores white*
> *Found throughout Europe*
> *Similar species* Mycena strobilicola

This small mushroom is great to have in any kitchen, especially since it grows during a time when very few other mushrooms are available. Although picking a sufficient number of caps can take a long time, they usually grow in large numbers. The rewarding taste of a Sprucecone Cap omelette makes it all worthwhile.

Pinecone Caps (*S.tenacellus*) grow on pine cones but taste so bitter that they cannot be eaten.

Stipe white at top, becoming orange-brown towards the bottom

Gills white

Cap domed, flat when mature, no hump

Cap maroon to grey-brown, sometimes white

96

Caution!

Mycena strobilicola *is extremely similar, but it can be distinguished by its odour of chlorine and its fragile, white stipe. It is not known whether this species is poisonous or edible.*

Conifercone Cap

Baeospora myosurus (mushrooms with gills)
Cap 1–3 cm   June–October

This mushroom's stipe has a hairy root and looks almost like a mouse's tail. It usually grows on spruce cones in such a way that this end of the stipe protrudes out from beneath the cone. Although it is thought to be harmless, very little is actually known about its edibility.

Habitat In all types of forest, on fallen or partially buried spruce cones.

> *Mild taste*
> *Spores white*
> *Found throughout central Europe, less common in the south and north*

Stipe has a white, powdery covering

Cap beige to pinkish-brown

The very rare *Baeospora myriadophylla* grows in winter and has attractively coloured, violet-pink gills.

Gills white, tightly packed

Hemimycena cucullata

No common name (mushrooms with gills)
Cap 1–2 cm   July–October

All *Hemimycena* species are small, completely white mushrooms whose cap diameters are rarely larger than 3 cm. Because they are so small, nothing is known about their edibility.

Habitat In all types of coniferous forest in fallen leaves or needles, usually in groups.

> *Mild taste*
> *Spores white*
> *Found throughout Europe*

The large number of similarly white species includes *Delicatula integrella* which can be distinguished by its scant, venous gills and the presence of a veil on young specimens.

Cap pure white

Stipe pure white

Gills white, tightly packed

Lilac Bonnet
Mycena pura (mushrooms with gills)
Cap 1–3 cm   June–November

Habitat In all types of forest, often among fallen needles but also among fallen leaves.

> Strong radish-like odour
> Spores white
> Found throughout Europe

The Lilac Bonnet is the only *Mycena* species which is known to be poisonous. However, very little is known about the edibility of many of the other species since they are usually too small to be worth picking. The cap colour of the Lilac Bonnet varies considerably and can also be steel blue, ochre, white or a mixture of colours.

The Blackedge Bonnet (*M. pelianthina*) is easily recognised by its black gill blades.

Gills pale violet

Flesh white, violet on stipe exterior

Caution!

The Rosy Bonnet (M. rosea, li.) is much more poisonous than the Lilac Bonnet and contains muscarine. Large quantities can trigger symptoms such as severe nausea, blurred vision and abdominal pain to name but a few.

98

Caps typically blue-violet

Stipe violet, slightly glassy appearance

Milking Bonnet

Mycena galopus (mushrooms with gills)

Cap 1–3 cm   June–November

Apart from the *Lactarius* species (p. 206), only certain *Mycena* species produce milky fluid. However, this white, orange or red fluid often only becomes apparent on close inspection. Once seen, identification is easy since each species produces a differently coloured fluid.

Cap grey, grooved

Stipe dark grey, smooth

The Saffrondrop Bonnet (*M. crocata*) is easy to identify by its saffron-coloured milky fluid and is typical dweller in nutrient-rich beech forests.

Habitat In all types of forest, often among fallen needles or in mossy patches, also in deciduous forests, rare on burnt ground.

> Mild mushroomy odour
> Spores white
> Common throughout Europe

Leaks milky, white fluid when damaged

Burgundydrop Bonnet

Mycena haematopus (mushrooms with gills)

Cap 2–4 cm   July–November

This mushroom gets its name from the brownish-red, blood-like fluid it produces when damaged. This becomes most apparent when the stipe is severed.

Cap light pink to pinkish-red

A further, typical characteristic is the overhanging, skirt-like cap rim.

Stipe has a covering of fine powder

Habitat In all types of forest with adequate humidity, consistently on fallen parts of deciduous trees.

> Mild mushroomy odour
> Spores white
> Common throughout Europe

Leaks milky, brown-red fluid when damaged

Yellowleg Bonnet

Mycena epipterygia (mushrooms with gills)

Cap 1–3 cm   July–November

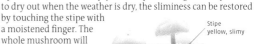

Habitat In all types of forest, particularly in spruce and pine forests, often on rotting wood.

> Cap white, yellow, grey or brown
> Spores white
> Common throughout Europe

This mushroom is easy to identify because it is the only species of *Mycena* which has a slimy, yellow stipe. Although the stipe tends to dry out when the weather is dry, the sliminess can be restored by touching the stipe with a moistened finger. The whole mushroom will then stick to this finger!

Stipe yellow, slimy

Cap yellowish with a lighter rim

Gills white, ascending into a bow-shape

The upper cap layer is tough and very flexible

Common Bonnet

Mycena galericulata (mushrooms with gills)

Cap 2–5 cm   May–November

Habitat In all types of forest, particularly in breaks in alder forests and in oak/hornbeam forests, always on rotting, deciduous wood.

> Odour and taste often slightly floury
> Spores white
> Common throughout Europe

The gills on older specimens of this species usually turn slightly pink. Once this happens, the Common Bonnet may be mistaken for an *Entoloma* species (p. 107) or a *Pluteus* species (p. 114), although the spores of these species are pinkish. The Common Bonnet has white spores, despite the colour of its gills.

Cap grey, dome/bell-shaped

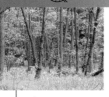

Gills ascending, dog tooth-shaped

This mushroom can be distinguished from other *Mycena* species with grey caps by its cross-linked gills.

Stipe pale grey, tough

Clustered Bonnet

Mycena inclinata (mushrooms with gills)

Cap 1–3 cm   August–November

Mycena species occur in various habitats such as on the ground, among fallen leaves or needles and on wood. Some have no particular preferences and decompose various types of wood and others are restricted to one type of tree. This species is always found on oak wood.

The completely grey *Mycena abramsii* usually occurs in spring.

Habitat *Primarily in oak/hornbeam forests, always on Oak tree stumps.*

> *Flesh watery grey*
> *Odour slightly floury*
> *Common throughout Europe except northern Europe*

Did you know?

The Beautiful Bonnet (M. renati) can be identified by its yellow stipe and nitrous odour. It only grows in humid beech forests, particularly where there are gorges.

Stipe with colour gradient from white to orange-brown

101

Cap grey, grooved

Cap rim slightly toothed

Red Edge Bonnet

Mycena rubromarginata (mushrooms with gills)

Cap 1–3 cm   July–November

Habitat On acidic soils in coniferous forests among fallen needles, branches or coniferous wood (normally from spruces).

> Flesh watery grey
> Odour non-specific, slightly mushroomy
> Common throughout Europe

Coloured gill blades are an important factor for identifying individual bonnets. The gill blades on some species can be red, purple, brown, black, green, orange or yellow. While most species can have red gill blades, the other colours are all attributable to particular species.

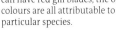

Cap pinkish-grey, grooved

Gills with red edges

Stipe grey, smooth

Despite its name, the Green Edge Bonnet (*M. viridimarginata*) only occasionally has greenish gill blades. However, it is characterised by its olive-yellow colour and nitrous odour.

Pink Bonnet

Mycena rosella (mushrooms with gills)

Cap 0.5–1 cm   August–November

Habitat On acidic soils in coniferous forests, always among fallen needles, particularly those of spruce trees.

> Flesh pale pink
> Grows in large numbers
> Common throughout Europe

The Pink Bonnet always grows in strikingly large numbers. The forest floor can be carpeted with a pink blanket of hundreds of fruiting bodies. Although other bonnets also grow in large numbers, this one is easily recognised by its colour.

Cap pink, grooved

The Orange Edge Bonnet (*M. aurantirmarginata*) grows in the same locations. It can be easily recognised by its luminous orange gill blades.

Gills pinkish-red

Stipe pink, smooth

Cap bell-shaped, never flattens

Mycena zephirus

No common name (mushrooms with gills)

Cap 1–3 cm   August–November

It is not uncommon to find this species growing in mossy coniferous forests in late autumn since it often grows in such large numbers that it is the predominant species.

Habitat *In various types of coniferous and mixed forest, primarily among fallen spruce needles, prefers acidic soils.*

Cap light pink with a lighter rim

Cap bell-shaped, often with a hump in the centre

> **Rust-coloured flecks appear on cap and stipe with time**
> **Mild odour of radish**
> **Common throughout Europe**

Bonnet species are often affected by Bonnet Mould (*Spinellus fusiger*)

Cap bell-shaped, often with a hump in the centre

Gills white, with rust-coloured flecks after some time

Stipe grey with silver longitudinal fibres

Golden Trumpets

Xeromphalina campanella (mushrooms with gills)

Cap 1–2 cm   June–November

Mushrooms of this species always grow in very close proximity to each other, although never in clumps. There are often hundreds of fruiting bodies which can cover entire tree stumps. It is very common, even in dry areas.

Habitat *In coniferous forests on rotting tree stumps in the late stages of rotting, prefers spruce wood.*

Xeromphalina fellea has a long stipe, grows among fallen needles and can be distinguished by its bitter taste.

> **Grows in large numbers**
> **Taste is mild but slightly astringent**
> **Common throughout Europe, particularly in higher areas**

Cap orange-brown, grooved, bell-shaped

Small papilla in centre of cap

Gills heavily cross-linked

Stipe red to dark brown

Velvet Shank

Flammulina velutipes (mushrooms with gills)
Cap 2–5 cm   (September) November–March

🍴

Habitat In lowland forests along the banks of streams, primarily on willows or fallen willow branches, also in wet beech forests.

> *Cap surface moist and slimy*
> *Flesh mild, whitish-yellow*
> *Spores white*
> *Common throughout Central and Northern Europe, less common in the south*

The Velvet Shank is one of the few edible mushrooms that occurs during the winter period and is therefore highly sought-after by collectors. The mushroom is frost-resistant in that it stops growing temporarily until the next mild spell. Its characteristics and the unusual time at which it occurs mean that it is very easy to identify.

Velvet shanks are most commonly found alongside banks of streams with old willow trees.

Stipe black-brown, velvety

Gills widely spaced

Caution!

Poisonous Funeral Bells (p. 204) can occur in the same locations during mild winter periods. However, they can be clearly identified by their stipes which have silvery fibres instead of velvety brown fibres like the Velvet Shank.

Gills cream-coloured

Cap brown-orange with short grooves, hygrophanous

Oyster Mushroom

Pleurotus ostreatus (mushrooms with gills)

Cap 3–8 cm   (September) November–March

The Oyster Mushroom tastes even better than the Velvet Shank (p. 104) and also occurs during the winter period. When hunting for this mushroom, it is advisable to look up rather than down since they usually grow a few metres above the ground on the trunks of damaged trees.

Habitat *Primarily in beech forests on standing beeches with lightning damage, also on fallen beech trees.*

> **Flesh white, mild**
> **Spores white**
> **Patchy distribution throughout central and northern Europe, less common in the south**
> **Similar species Olive Oysterling**

The Oyster Mushroom is easily cultivated and it is now the second most prolific mushroom on the market after the white mushroom.

Gills descending far down stipe

Cap colour varies greatly, mostly blue-grey

Stipe short, white, offset

Caution!

Although it occurs at the same time, the Olive Oysterling (p. 93) only grows on fallen parts of trees. It can also be identified by its yellow stipe.

The Miller 🍴

Clitopilus prunulus (mushrooms with gills)

Cap 2–10 cm   July–November

Habitat In various deciduous and coniferous forests, prefers acidic soils.

> **Strong floury odour**
> **Spores pale pink**
> **Common throughout Europe**
> **Similar species Frosty Funnel**

The Miller is very often found growing in the same locations as Ceps. However, a lot of experience is required to be able to distinguish it clearly from poisonous *Clitocybe* species. Key features for identifying the Miller are its floury odour and its pink spores.

The rare *Rhodocybe fallax* can be distinguished by its cap, which becomes depressed, and the absence of any floury odour. It tastes too bitter to be eaten.

Gills turn pink, descending steeply down on to stipe

Flesh white

Caution !

Young Frosty Funnels (p. 57) look particularly similar and can only be distinguished by the absence of any floury odour.

Cap chalky white, cushion-like

Stipe usually short, white, often slightly off-centre

Livid Pinkgill

Entoloma sinuatum (mushrooms with gills)
Cap 8–15(20) cm   July–October

It is easy to mistake this, the largest of all the entolomas, for a *Tricholoma* (p. 70) species if the pale pink spores are not taken into account. Eating this mushroom can cause serious poisoning of the stomach and digestive tract and can even cause circulatory collapse in some people.

The gills on young specimens often have a unique salmon-pink tinge to them

Habitat In various types of deciduous forest, particularly in oak and hornbeam forests on alkaline, clay soils.

> Floury odour
> Spores pale pink
> Patchy distribution in Europe, otherwise uncommon

Did you know?
One of the few Entoloma *species that can grow to a similar size is* Entoloma lividoalbum. *It is also poisonous and also grows in deciduous forests, usually beneath oak trees.*

Gills turn pink, ascending

Flesh whitish

107

Cap beige-grey with thick flesh

Stipe solid, white

Shield Pinkgill

🍴

Entoloma clypeatum (mushrooms with gills)
Cap 5–12 cm   April–May (June)

Habitat *Always beneath members of the rose family, in hedges, orchards, gardens and on forest boundaries on chalky soils.*

> **Floury odour**
> **Spores pale pink**
> **Regional distribution throughout Europe**

This mushroom and a few of its close relatives have a noticeable relationship with the rose family, in particular, the hawthorn, the blackthorn and other types of plum tree. Shield Pinkgills are also very occasionally found growing around ornamental trees such as the Japanese Cherry, cultivated Serviceberry trees and peach trees.

Gills turn pink, ascending

Flesh whitish

Cap beige-grey with a stubby hump

The Sloe Pinkgill (*E. sepium*) is closely related and can be identified by its reddish-yellow flesh and insect fretting marks.

Stipe white

Wood Pinkgill

☠️

Entoloma rhodopolium (mushrooms with gills)
Cap 3–8(10) cm   July–October

Habitat *In moderately dry deciduous forests, primarily under beeches, no particular soil preference.*

> **Insignificant floury odour**
> **Spores pale pink**
> **Common throughout Europe**

While Wood Pinkgills typically have almost no odour, some specimens have a clear odour of chlorine about them. The latter usually grow on chalky soils on flat lands while the former grow on neutral, clay soils.

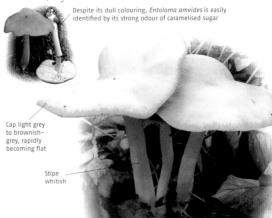

Despite its dull colouring, *Entoloma ameides* is easily identified by its strong odour of caramelised sugar

Flesh whitish

Gills turn pink, ascending

Cap light grey to brownish-grey, rapidly becoming flat

Stipe whitish

Honey Pinkgill

Entoloma cetratum (mushrooms with gills)
Cap 2–4 cm June–October

The approximately 300 *Entoloma* species in Europe vary hugely in stature and colour. However, they all have pink spores, their gills are all attached to the stipe and their spores are uniquely angular.

Stipe silvery-grey

Cap brownish-ochre, grooved

The poisonous *Entoloma hirtipes* grows in spring and can be identified by its codliver oil–like odour.

Habitat *In damp coniferous forests, usually grows in moss and prefers acidic soils.*

> Very fragile fruiting bodies
> Spores pale pink
> Common throughout Europe

Gills turn pink, ascending

Flesh pale, brownish

Mousepee Pinkgill

Entoloma incanum (mushrooms with gills)
Cap 1–3 cm June–October

Most species of *Entoloma* are very difficult to identify without using a microscope. The Mousepee Pinkgill, however, is an exception. It can easily be identified by its garish, greenish-yellow stipe, its turquoise-green discoloration and its unique odour.

The pale pink spores released by taller specimens can sometimes be seen on the caps of smaller specimens.

Habitat *On large expanses of grazing land, juniper heaths and other unfertilised grassland, occasionally on verges, always on chalky soils.*

> Odour of burnt horn, rubber brake pads
> Spores pale pink
> Patchy distribution throughout Europe in areas with chalky soils

Cap olive-yellow with blackish-olive scales

Stipe intensely greenish-yellow

Stipe base turns turquoise-green when touched

Gills turn pink, ascending

Silky Pinkgill
Entoloma sericeum (mushrooms with gills)
Cap 2–5 cm   July–October

☠

Habitat On well-used, non-fertilised pastures, no other preferences.

> **Spores pale pink**
> **Odour rancid, floury**
> **Patchy distribution throughout Europe**

The Silky Pinkgill gets its name from the silky sheen of its cap surface. Not much is known about the edibility of this mushroom, although it has been proven that its close relatives are poisonous. It is therefore advisable to avoid eating this mushroom.

The extremely poisonous *Entoloma vernum* only grows in spring.

Gills off-white

Flesh brownish

Gills ascending

Cap grey-brown, highly hygrophanous

Rosy Pinkgill
Entoloma roseum (mushrooms with gills)
Cap 2–4 cm   July–October

⚔

Habitat On large expanses of grazing land, juniper heaths and other unfertilised grassland, occasionally in open, grassy forests.

> **Spores pale pink**
> **Very rare in Europe**

Rosy Pinkgills grow on meadows, are often brightly coloured and are also very rare. They are as sensitive as orchids to fertilisation.

Cap pink

Stipe smooth, pale pink

Gills turn pink, ascending

Another endangered *Entoloma* species is the Felted Pinkgill (*E. griseocyaneum*) which has a violet-grey stipe and a grey cap with small scales.

Indigo Entoloma

Entoloma nitidum (mushrooms with gills)

Cap 2–5 cm   July–October

Only experts can tell the difference between the many blue species of *Entoloma*. The Indigo Entoloma is an exception because of its ecological preferences. It is the only one of them that grows in acidic soils in coniferous forests.

The violet *Entoloma euchroum* is easily identified because it typically grows on rotting wood.

Habitat In damp coniferous forests on acidic soils, primarily under spruces, also on the fringes of bogs, usually at altitude.

> Spores pale pink
> Patchy distribution throughout Europe

Did you know?

The largest of the blue species of Entoloma *is the Big Blue Pinkgill (*E. bloxamii*). It grows on neglected grassland on chalky soils and is one of the most endangered species of mushroom.*

Flesh white

Stipe tapered

111

Cap blue

Stipe grey-blue, longitudinally fibrous

Rhodocybe gemina

No common name (mushrooms with gills)

Cap 5–12 cm   July–October

Habitat In spruce forests, deciduous and mixed forests, on forest boundaries on alkaline to mildly acidic soils

> **Spores pale pink**
> **Rare in Europe**

There are very few species of *Rhodocybe* and they are relatively unknown. The only edible species is *Rhodocybe gemina* which is highly sought-after because of its fleshy fruiting body and the fact that it grows in groups.

Flesh cream-coloured to pale pinkish-brown

Cap pale pinkish-brown, smooth

Gills turn pink, broad at base

Stipe light beige

Rhodocybe popinalis can be identified by its dark fruiting bodies with black flecks and their strong floury odour.

Rhodocybe nitellina

No common name (mushrooms with gills)

Cap 2–4 cm   July–October

Habitat In spruce forests and other types of coniferous forest, less common in deciduous forests, prefers alkaline soils.

> **Spores pale pink**
> **Floury odour**
> **Rare in Europe**

At a glance, this species might be mistaken for a Russet Tough-shank (p. 87). However, it is easily distinguished from other species because of its clear floury odour and its pale pink spores.

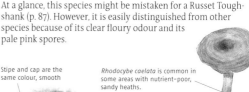

Stipe and cap are the same colour, smooth

Rhodocybe caelata is common in some areas with nutrient-poor, sandy heaths.

Cap orange-brown, smooth, becoming flat

Flesh watery orange-brown

Gills broad at base

Stubble Rosegill

Volavariella gloiocephala (mushrooms with gills)
Cap 10–20 cm   May–October

Like all *Volavariella* species, the Stubble Rosegill is edible, although it has a radish-like taste which does not appeal to everyone. It is necessary to check that the gills turn pink to avoid confusing it with species such as the Deathcap (p. 116).

Habitat In nutrient-rich, ruderal locations, in fields, crops and grazing land.

> Radish-like odour
> Spores pink
> Patchy distribution throughout Europe

Cap white, smooth

Stipe thin without a ring

Amazingly, the cap colour of this mushroom changes from white in spring and summer to olive green in autumn. The reason for this change is unknown.

Gills unattached, becoming pink

Stipe base with a skin-like volva

Silky Rosegill

Volavariella bombycina (mushrooms with gills)
Cap 10–25 cm   June–October

Volavariella species can be identified by their unattached gills, pink spores and the presence of a volva. Although they are all edible, the only one that tastes good is the Paddy Straw Mushroom which is cultivated in China.

Habitat On living deciduous trees and dead wood in the early stages of rotting, prefers warm conditions.

> Gills unattached
> Spores pink
> Patchy distribution throughout Europe, particularly in the south

Cap white with silky hairs

The young fruiting bodies emerge from an egg-like shell, similar to the Amanitas.

The Silky Rosegill can be distinguished from all other *Volavariella* species by its skin-like volva with brown scales and its size.

Deer Shield 🍴

Pluteus cervinus (mushrooms with gills)
Cap 5–15 cm   May–October

Habitat On dead deciduous or coniferous wood and also on bark mulch and saw dust.

> **Radish-like odour**
> **Spores pink**
> **Found throughout Europe**

With the exception of the Willow Shield, none of the *Pluteus* species are known to be poisonous, although none of them are particularly good to eat. While it is often difficult to identify the individual species, their unattached gills and pink spores make them recognisable as *Pluteus* species.

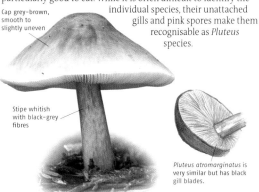

Cap grey-brown, smooth to slightly uneven

Stipe whitish with black-grey fibres

Gills unattached, pink

Flesh white

Pluteus atromarginatus is very similar but has black gill blades.

Willow Shield ✂

Pluteus salicinus (mushrooms with gills)
Cap 4–10 cm   May–October

Habitat In damp locations on dead wood, particularly on willow.

> **Gills unattached**
> **Spores pink**
> **Common to patchy distribution throughout Europe**

The Willow Shield stands out from the other *Pluteus* species because of the substances it contains. It contains small quantities of psychoactive substances (psilocybin, psilocin) which are also found in Liberty Caps (p. 165). It is therefore not advisable to eat this mushroom.

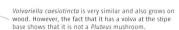

Volvariella caesiotincta is very similar and also grows on wood. However, the fact that it has a volva at the stipe base shows that it is not a *Pluteus* mushroom.

Flesh white

Stipe base slightly thickened

Stipe white

Cap grey to greenish-grey, smooth

Lion Shield

🍴

Pluteus leoninus (mushrooms with gills)
Cap 4–8 cm   June–October

Most species of *Pluteus* are 'loners.' The Lion Shield is no exception and is rarely found in groups of more than three. The Lion Shield's vibrantly yellow, velvety cap makes it easy to identify. However, it is rare and should not be picked.

Habitat *On dead wood, particularly on fallen, moderately thick branches.*

Cap vibrantly yellow to olive-yellow, velvety

Stipe yellowish, smooth

> Gills unattached
> Flesh whitish
> Spores pink
> Patchy distribution throughout Europe, rare in some regions

The white-capped *Pluteus semibulbosus* also grows individually on deciduous wood.

Gills turning pink

🌀 **115**

Wrinkled Shield

🍴

Pluteus phlebophorus (mushrooms with gills)
Cap 3–6 cm   June–October

Wrinkles on caps are a key feature when identifying *Pluteus* species. They are often not obvious on the Wrinkled Shield since they can be flat and subtle. However, some specimens have very prominent, obvious wrinkles.

Habitat *On dead deciduous wood (beech, hornbeam), primarily on thick, fallen branches.*

Stipe whitish, shiny, smooth

Cap brown, slightly wrinkled in the centre

> Slight radish-like odour
> Spores pink
> Common throughout Europe

The Goldleaf Shield (*P. romellii*) can be identified by its yellow stipe. While it often grows between pieces of wood, it often seems as though it is growing out of the ground.

Cap wrinkly, venous, one colour

Deathcap

Amanita phalloides (mushrooms with gills)
Cap 8–15 cm July–October

Habitat In warmer deciduous forests on acidic to neutral soils, particularly beneath oak trees.

> Gills unattached, always white
> Spores white
> Odour of artificial honey when young, foul when old
> Cap skin removable
> Common in central and southern Europe, less common towards the east

The Deathcap is one of the most dangerous poisonous mushrooms because it takes such a long time (6-48 hours) for any symptoms of poisoning to appear. Eating a mere 50 grams of this mushroom would be fatal without medical treatment. Its deadliness was also known in the ancient world when it was sometimes used as a murder weapon. The most famous case is the murder of the Roman Emperor Claudius (AD54) by his wife Agrippina to assist her son's succession to the throne.

Did you know?

When young, Deathcaps are encapsulated in a universal veil which gradually disintegrates. At this stage, it is easy to confuse them with edible puffballs (pages 286/287). However, once they are cut open, the cap colour becomes visible as a yellow line.

Stipe base round with separated volva

Cap fibres ingrown, yellow-olive green, usually without remnants of volva

Pure white, albino Deathcaps also occur very occasionally

Stipe surface snakeskin-like, same colour as the cap

Destroying Angel

Amanita virosa (mushrooms with gills)
Cap 8–15 cm   July–October

This little-known amanita is just as deadly as the Deathcap. However, poisoning rarely occurs because edible mushrooms are seldom found in the same biotopes and it requires nutrient-poor soils, which are becoming less and less common in central Europe. Its name comes from its pure white 'angelic' appearance combined with its deadliness.

Habitat *In damp coniferous forests and under beeches, always on highly acidic soils.*

> *Gills unattached, always white*
> *Spores white*
> *Cap skin removable*
> *Patchy distribution to uncommon in central and southern Europe, more common in northern Europe*

Cap pure white, slightly greasy

Stipe base round with a tightly integrated volva

Cap rim looks like a horizontal eight

Stipe covered with flaky shreds of velum remnants

Did you know?

Very occasionally, the cap is dome-shaped rather than bell-shaped, which makes it easy to mistake it for common, white mushrooms.

False Deathcap

Amanita citrina (mushrooms with gills)
Cap 8–15 cm   July–October

Habitat *In deciduous
and coniferous forests,
prefers acidic soils.*

> **Strong odour of
sprouting potatoes**
> **Gills unattached, always
white**
> **Spores white**
> **Common throughout
Europe**

For a long time it was thought that the False Deathcap was also
deadly poisonous. It is now known that it is, at most, only slightly
poisonous and probably harmless. Traditionally, it is picked in
some eastern countries such as Russia. Since the
similar Deathcap (p. 116) is unknown in these
parts, mushroom collectors from these countries have often ended up poisoning themselves
when picking mushrooms in central Europe.

Caution!

*It is easy to confuse the False
Deathcap with the slightly
poisonous Jewelled Amanita
(A. gemmata) as well as
the Deathcap (p. 116). The
Jewelled Amanita has a
grooved cap rim, a bulging
stipe base and white velum
remnants.*

Pure white, albino
False Deathcaps are not
uncommon. The shreds
of velum remnants and
the round basal bulb
distinguish it from other
albino amanitas.

Stipe base
bulbous with
a defined
edge

118

Ring white,
hanging

Cap lemon-coloured
with brown velum
remnants

Panthercap

Amanita pantherina (mushrooms with gills)

Cap 8–15 cm   July–October

The Panthercap is the main cause of mushroom poisoning in the regions where it is most commonly found. It is frequently mistaken for the Blusher (p. 122) and the Grey Spotted Amanita (p. 123) which both have a smooth cap rim, a hanging, grooved ring and a differently shaped basal bulb. Although poisoning is relatively commonplace and serious, it is, thankfully, rarely fatal.

Habitat *Primarily under oaks on neutral clay or sandy soils with one variant occurring under spruces on acidic soils.*

> *Gills white, unattached*
> *Flesh white*
> *Common throughout Europe*

Did you know?

The abietina variant, which occurs in coniferous forests in the mountains, does not have a grooved cap rim and its cap is dark brown. Caution: it looks similar to the edible Grey Spotted Amanita.

The slightly poisonous Grey Veiled Amanita (*A. porphyrea*) also looks similar but has a violet-brown stipe and ring, round basal bulb and a strong radish-like odour.

Basal bulb round with a bulging rim

119

Cap brown with a grooved rim

Ring white, not grooved, meagre

Velum remnants pure white

Fly Agaric

Amanita muscaria (mushrooms with gills)

Cap 10–20 cm   July–November

Habitat *Under spruces and birches, rarely under any other trees, on acidic soils.*

> **Gills white, unattached**
> **Flesh white**
> **Common throughout Europe**

The poisons and ibotenic acid contained in Fly Agarics can have psychoactive effects. Some cultures therefore use it for religious or cult practices, as seen in parts of Siberia and South America for example. The central Europeans, on the other hand, used to mix pieces of Fly Agaric into a bowl of milk which would then be placed on a windowsill. This attracted flies which would die once they came into contact with the mixture. This is also where the mushroom gets its name.

Basal bulb round with regular bands of warts

The slightly more poisonous Brown Fly Agaric (*A. regalis*) has yellow velum remnants and a nut brown cap. It occurs in heavily forested areas in Europe.

Cap orange to red with white velum remnants

Ring white, hanging

Did you know?

Heavy rain can wash all of the velum remnants away. Fly Agarics may then resemble russulas, although these have fragile flesh and their gills are attached.

Caesar's Mushroom

Amanita caesarea (mushrooms with gills)

Cap 10–20 cm   July–October (December)

Caesar's Mushroom was a popular edible mushroom with the Romans. It may even have been the most popular of all the mushrooms if the name is anything to go by. It is regarded as a delicacy when it is still encased in its universal veil. This is, however, a risky delicacy since it has not infrequently been confused with closed deathcaps. The Romans may well have brought Caesar's Mushroom with them to central Europe since it is most common in areas that were heavily occupied by them.

Habitat *In deciduous forests, primarily on relatively acidic soils, usually under oaks and chestnuts, prefers warmer conditions.*

> **Gills unattached, always white**
> **Spores white**
> **Patchy distribution in southern Europe, very rare north of the Alps**
> **Similar species Fly Agaric**

Caution!

It is easy to mistake Fly Agarics (p. 120) for Caesar's Mushrooms if heavy rain has washed the velum remnants off their caps. However, Caesar's Mushrooms always have yellow stipes and gills!

Stipe yellow

Stipe base bulbous with detached volva

121

Cap orange-red, no velum remnants

Caesar's Mushrooms are most highly sought-after in this form. Size and shape are roughly equivalent to a goose egg.

Ring yellow, hanging

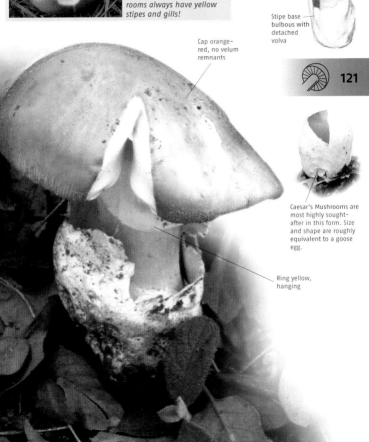

Blusher
Amanita rubescens (mushrooms with gills)
Cap 8–15 cm   June–October

Habitat In deciduous and coniferous forests, no particular preferences.

> **Gills unattached, always white**
> **Spores white**
> **Ring grooved**
> **Found throughout Europe**
> **Similar species Panthercap**

Blushers are easy to identify if they display all the characteristics typical of the species. The fruiting body always has characteristic pink discolorations which are sometimes visible under the cap skin or around insect fretting marks, but are usually found in the basal bulb and around maggot burrows. This distinguishes it from the Fly Agaric and the Panthercap.

Amanita franchetii is very similar and only grows on alkaline soils under deciduous trees. It can be distinguished by its yellow, defined velum remnants and it is also thought to be poisonous.

Stipe base root-like with a few volva remnants

Caution!
The Panthercap (right, p. 119) can be distinguished from the Blusher (left) by its collar with no grooves, its lack of pink discoloration and its differently shaped basal bulb.

Cap whitish to pale pink, usually mottled

Velumn remnants patchy, flaky, whitish

Grey Spotted Amanita

Amanita spissa (mushrooms with gills)
Cap 8–15 cm   June–October

It is easy to mistake Grey Spotted Amanitas for Panthercaps and vice versa, especially since both grow on acidic soils under coniferous trees. The stipe base is the key to positive identification, so care must be taken when extracting the mushroom to ensure that it remains intact. This does not just apply to amanitas, but to all mushrooms that are difficult to identify. The Grey Spotted Amanita can be eaten, but it tastes dull and earthy.

Habitat In deciduous and coniferous forests, no particular preferences.

> Gills unattached, always white
> Spores white
> Ring grooved
> Found throughout Europe
> Similar species Panthercap

Caution!

The Panthercap (right, p.119) can be distinguished from the Grey Spotted Amanita (left) by its collar with no grooves, the absence of a strong radish-like odour and its differently shaped stipe base.

Stipe base root-like with a few volva remnants

Cap brown–grey with no grooves on the rim

123

Velum remnants patchy, flaky, white–grey to grey

Ring hanging, grooved with a grey–brown rim

Warted Amanita

Amanita strobiliformis (mushrooms with gills)
Cap 10–25 cm   June–October

Habitat *Under deciduous trees on alkaline soils, often in parks and gardens, prefers warmer conditions.*

> *Gills attached*
> *Odour and taste slightly radish-like*
> *Spores white*
> *Most common in southern Europe, distribution otherwise patchy to rare*
> *Similar species (albino) Deathcap*

There has been a noticeable increase in Warted Amanita numbers over the past few years, particularly in built-up areas. This increase can be attributed to the general increase in climate temperature. Although it is edible, all of its key characteristics (particularly the whole stipe base) must be identified before it is eaten. There are many other white *Amanita* species in southern Europe and while some of them are edible, most are poisonous.

Stipe base root-like, tapered with flaky velum remnants

Caution!
Albino Deathcaps (p. 116) can be distinguished by the sac-like volva on the stipe base, the different appearance of its velum remnants and its different odour.

The European Solitary Lepidella (*A. solitaria*) is very similar, but can be distinguished by the pyramidal, regular appearance of its velum remnants.

Cap whitish to creamy-grey

Velum remnants flaky, soft, almost cream-like

Tawny Grisette

Amanita fulva (mushrooms with gills)
Cap 6–15 cm   June–October

Tawny Grisettes are characterised by their highly grooved cap rims, the sac-like volva and the absence of any ring. Although all grisettes are edible, care must be taken when identifying them since some poisonous amanitas lose their rings due to the effects of the weather.

Habitat Under coniferous and deciduous trees on acidic soils, also on the fringes of bogs.

> *Gills unattached, always white*
> *Spores white*
> *Common throughout Europe*

Cap orange-brown, no velum remnants

Stipe whitish, smooth

The Orange Grisette (*A. crocea*) is larger, the surface of its stipe is snakeskin-like and does not have rust brown flecks on its volva. It is most commonly found growing beneath birches.

Volva sac-like, attached, with rust brown flecks

Grey Amanita

Amanita submembranacea (mushrooms with gills)
Cap 6–15 cm   June–September

The Grey Amanita is very common in some regions of Europe. It often grows in large numbers at the beginning of summer when very few other mushrooms are available and so it is worth picking. They are, however, very brittle and spoil quickly.

Habitat In coniferous forests in mountainous regions on acidic soils.

> *Gills unattached, always white*
> *Spores white*
> *Common in the mountainous regions of Europe*

Cap grey-brown to olive-grey

Amanita battarae has a dark zone on its cap, its volva has rust-coloured flecks on it and it also has black gill blades.

Stipe surface has a subtle to prominent snakeskin-like appearance

Volva sac-like, attached, becoming grey from the inside

Stinking Dapperling

Lepiota cristata (mushrooms with gills)
Cap 3–6 cm   July-October

Habitat On waysides and in ruderal locations, no particular biotope or soil preferences.

> **Typically strong, un-pleasant metallic odour**
> **Gills unattached, always white**
> **Spores white**
> **Common throughout Europe**

Flesh white, reddish-brown on the stipe surface

Stipe becomes hollow

126

There are hundreds of species of *Lepiota* around the world and each one of them is either poisonous or is thought to be poisonous. Some species contain phallotoxins (like the Deathcap) which are fatal if ingested. The common Stinking Dapperling is only slightly poisonous and can be identified by its relatively solid ring.

Caution!

Very occasionally, other Lepiota *species grow in the same locations which sometimes include deadly poisonous species.* Lepiota lilacea *is thought to be one of these and can be identified by its grey–violet ring and scaly cap.*

Ring skin–like, relatively firm, ascending

Cap brown–red in the centre, becoming increasingly scaly towards the rim

Chestnut Dapperling

Lepiota castanea (mushrooms with gills)

Cap 3–6 cm   August–October

Around 200 species of *Lepiota* occur in Europe and the differences between some of them are often microscopic. The overwhelming majority of them are rare and they are often only found in very specific biotopes (sand dunes, lowland forests). The Chestnut Dapperling is one of the most common species.

Habitat *In deciduous forests, waysides and in ruderal locations, prefers clay soils.*

> **Gills unattached, always white**
> **Spores white**
> **Common throughout Europe**

Cap brown-red in the centre, becoming increasingly scaly towards the rim

One of the few varieties among the *Lepiota* species to grow among fallen needles is *L. felina*. It has a slight odour of cedar wood.

Flesh pale brownish-orange

Stipe becomes hollow

Stipe has brown scales towards the base

Green Dapperling

Lepiota grangei (mushrooms with gills)

Cap 3–6 cm   August–October

The Green Dapperling has the most impressive colours of all the *Lepiota* species. However, the bluish-green colour of young fruiting bodies does change after some time. They usually occur in groups and it is not uncommon to find other rare *Lepiota* species growing in the same locations.

Habitat *On nutrient-rich soils in deciduous forests, prefers warm conditions.*

Cap bluish-green when young

> **Gills unattached, always white**
> **Spores white**
> **Rare in Europe**

Stipe has bluish-green scales at the base

Older specimens are darker and the bluish-green colour oxidises to orange.

Flesh whitish, orange-brown from bottom of stipe upwards

Fatal Dapperling

Lepiota subincarnata (mushrooms with gills)

Cap 3–6 cm   August–October

☠

Habitat In nutrient-rich, alkaline soils in deciduous forests, beneath pines in the south and under cypress trees on the Atlantic coast.

> **Gills unattached, always white**
> **Spores white**
> **Patchy distribution in southern Europe, less common towards the north**

Extreme caution is advised for all small, pink or flesh-coloured lepiotas. They are all deadly poisonous and just as fatal as the Deathcap. Most of these species can also occur in flower beds, greenhouses and flowerpots.

The Deadly Dapperling (*L. brunneoincarnata*) is also deadly poisonous and occurs from time to time in parks, gardens and on verges. Certain varieties have no pink colouring whatsoever.

Caution!

The deadly poisonous Star Dapperling (*L. helveola*) occurs mainly in Mediterranean regions and is characterised by the segregated, concentric scales in its cap. It is very rarely seen in parks and gardens north of the Alps.

Flesh pale, flesh-coloured

Cap pink to flesh-coloured, becoming increasingly scaly towards the rim

Stipe creamy-white with a subtle band of pink

Shield Dapperling

Lepiota clypeolaria (mushrooms with gills)
Cap 5–10 cm   August–October

This species and its relatives can sometimes grow to such a size that they could be mistaken for small parasol species. The unpleasant consequences of such a mistake can be avoided by checking for the cotton wool-like velum flakes on its stipe. In contrast, parasols (p. 130/131) have a movable, skin-like ring.

Habitat In deciduous and coniferous forests, normally without any particular soil preference, although it is absent from highly acidic soils.

Did you know?

The Orange-Girdled Parasol (L. ignivolvata) with its orange-brown ring zone (left) and the Orange-Scaled Parasol (L. magnispora) with its brightly coloured velum remnants (right) are both very similar and both grow in the same locations.

> *Gills unattached, always white*
> *Odour strong, unpleasant*
> *Spores white*
> *Found throughout Europe*

Flesh whitish

Cap ochre in the centre, becoming increasingly flaky towards the rim

Stipe covered in cotton wool-like, whitish velum remnants

Parasol ❚❚

Macrolepiota procera (mushrooms with gills)
Cap 15–25 cm   August–October

Habitat In deciduous and coniferous forests, no particular soil preference although it is absent from highly acidic soils.

> Gills unattached, always white
> Flesh unchanging
> Spores white
> Found throughout Europe
> Similar species Green Spored Lepiota

The Parasol is justifiably one of the most popular edible mushrooms. Apart from being very easy to identify, it can also be cooked in a variety of ways. Large caps can be fried whole in breadcrumbs. Although the stipes quickly become tough, they can be dried and and added to sauces in powdered form. Young specimens can be added to dishes or steamed/fried and eaten on their own.

Ring doubled, grooved, movable

Caution!
Macrolepiota *species with reddening flesh without snakeskin-like stipe surfaces may be poisonous (p. 131-132). The Parasol's flesh never changes colour and the stipe surface has a snakeskin-like appearance.*

Cap centre nut brown with a hump

Stipe surface snakeskin-like

Scales on cap become smaller towards rim

At first, only the caps of very young Parasol specimens protrude from the huge-looking basal bulb. The stipe only appears gradually.

The Slender Parasol (*M. mastoidea*) is also edible. It is always smaller, its cap has a nipple-like hump in the centre and its stipe can either be smooth or have the appearance of snakeskin.

Shaggy Parasol

Macrolepiota rhacodes (mushrooms with gills)

Cap 10–15 cm   August–October

(⚒)

The Shaggy Parasol was once generally considered to be a good edible mushroom which was easy to recognise because of the discolouration of its flesh. However, it was not uncommon for specimens from gardens and compost heaps to cause stomach problems and some very close relatives are also known to be poisonous. It is therefore advisable to try a small amount of this mushroom at first to check personal tolerance. Any varieties growing in gardens should be avoided.

Habitat *Primarily among fallen needles in spruce forests, less common in deciduous forests, also occurs under planted hedgerows (e.g. thuja), no soil preference.*

> **Gills unattached, always white**
> **Spores white**
> **Found throughout Europe**

Cap scales rough, almost tile-like

Stipe whitish, smooth

The *hortensis* variety grows on over-fertilised areas and has rough scales on its cap. Its edibility is still under discussion so it is best to avoid picking these mushrooms!

Flesh turns saffron orange as soon as it is touched

Stipe base bulbous

Macrolepiota venenata

☠

No common name (mushrooms with gills)

Cap 6–15 cm   August–October

This mushroom was declared a new species a mere 30 years ago after a case of poisoning in France. Today, it is still not certain as to whether this mushroom really is highly poisonous or whether it only affects certain people. This is similar to the case of the Yellow Stainer, which can be eaten by some people without any problems, but which causes serious stomach problems in others.

Habitat *Has only been known to occur in green-houses and flowerpots in central Europe, occurs on open ground and in flower beds in southern Europe.*

Cap scales extend outwards from violet-brown centre to the rim, forming a star-like pattern

> **Gills unattached, always white**
> **Spores white**
> **Very rare in Europe**

Flesh orange at first with cloudy, claret-coloured discoloration

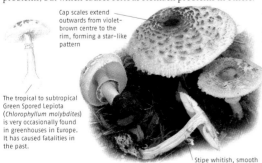

The tropical to subtropical Green Spored Lepiota (*Chlorophyllum molybdites*) is very occasionally found in greenhouses in Europe. It has caused fatalities in the past.

No groove on ring

Stipe base bulbous, stepped

Stipe whitish, smooth

Freckled Dapperling

Lepiota aspera (mushrooms with gills)
Cap 4–8(15) cm   July–October

☠

Habitat *On verges, compost, bark mulch and piles of leaves, also on jewelweed or nettles, nitrate indicator.*

> Gills unattached, always white
> Spores white
> Common throughout Europe

This species can often grow to be very large on well-fertilised ground which means that it is liable to be mistaken for edible Parasols (p. 130). However, parasols have a more solid ring which is not integrated with the stipe and which can be pushed along it, while the thin, hanging ring on the Freckled Dapperling is integrated with the stipe. Contrary to the advice in many of the older mushroom guides, this mushroom should not be eaten as it causes serious poisoning of the stomach and digestive tract.

Key features for identifying this species are the very crowded gills covered by a skin-like membrane when the mushroom is young.

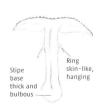

Ring skin-like, hanging

Stipe base thick and bulbous

132

Cap brown, becoming lighter towards the rim

Cap scales pyramidal, prominent

Did you know?
Lepiota perplexa *only has a slight fibrous zone instead of a ring. It is also poisonous.*

White Dapperling (❌)
Leucoagaricus leucothites (mushrooms with gills)
Cap 4–10 cm   June–October

There has been controversy over the edibility of the White Dapperling since a case of poisoning was recorded in Switzerland. Whether or not this was due to individual intolerance is uncertain since most people can eat it without any ill effects. However, it is no longer advisable to pick this mushroom. Beginners often confuse this mushroom with the Field Mushroom (p. 138) although the White Dapperling's gills remain more or less white like the lepiotas and amanitas.

It is very rare to find the smaller *Leucocoprinus cepistipes*. It grows on bark mulch and compost heaps, but is most common in greenhouses.

Habitat Grassy verges, embankments, gardens, newly arranged flower beds and on bark mulch.

> Gills unattached, often turning slightly pink when older
> Spores white
> Becoming increasingly common throughout Europe
> Similar species albino Deathcap

Ring skin-like, hanging

Gills un-attached, usually turning pale pink

Cap smooth, whitish or with slight colouring

133

Stipe white, smooth, ringed

Caution!
Confusion with the Deathcap could have fatal consequences. The Deathcap can be identified by its volva and stipe base which means removing the entire mushroom from the ground with the whole stipe. Just cutting the mushroom off at the base of the stipe is not enough to provide positive identification.

Plantpot Dapperling

Leucocoprinus birnbaumii (mushrooms with gills)
Cap 2–4 cm   Perennial

Habitat *Occurs sporadically in greenhouses and plant pots, never in open country.*

> Gills unattached, pale yellowish
> Spores white
> Common throughout the world

The Plantpot Dapperling is the most common of the tropical species which occur sporadically in Europe. It is spread via potting soil and occurs after houseplants have been re-potted. The mushroom does not damage plants and is also harmless to humans.

Cap yellow, slightly darker with flaky scales

Stipe pale yellow, ochre at base

Ring skin-like, yellowish

Flesh pale yellowish

The deadly poisonous *Lepiota elaiophylla* also only grows in flowerpots. While it looks similar to the Plantpot Dapperling, it is more solid and has no ring.

Bearded Dapperling

Cystolepiota seminuda (mushrooms with gills)
Cap 1–3 cm   August-November

Habitat *In beech or other deciduous forests, prefers moderately nutrient-rich soils.*

> Gills unattached, white
> Spores white
> Common throughout Europe

This species gets its name from the 'bearded' appearance of its cap rim. All *Cystolepiota* species (except the Lilac Dapperling) have an unpleasant metallic odour similar to that of puffballs (p. 284).

Cap rim bearded

Cap milky white, flaky

Stipe whitish with a fine, powdery coating

The Lilac Dapperling (*C. bucknalli*) is the same colour all over and has a very unpleasant odour of coal gas.

Gills crowded

Dewdrop Dapperling

Chamaemyces fracidus (mushrooms with gills)

Cap 3–6 cm   August–November

The Dewdrop Dapperling is the only one of the dapperlings to have gills which are attached to the stipe. It is therefore often mistaken for other species of mushrooms. However, the stocking-like stipe surface and the presence of droplets should make it fairly easy to identify.

Habitat *Under pines, very occasionally under spruces, on alkaline soils, prefers warmer conditions.*

> *Odour of cucumber skin*
> *Spores white*
> *Patchy distribution throughout Europe*

Cap ivory-coloured, greasy

Stipe surface like snakeskin

Young fruiting bodies have amber-coloured droplets on them if the weather is not too dry.

Gills almost unattached

Flesh whitish

135

Limacella guttata

No common name (mushrooms with gills)

Cap 5–12 cm   August–October

There are very few species of *Limacella* and they are all very rare. Only *Limacella guttata* is slightly more common and, as such, it is occasionally picked. It tastes very similar to St. George's Mushroom (p. 67). From a microscopic point of view, these mushrooms are more closely related to the amanitas than the lepiotas.

Habitat *On chalky soils in deciduous or coniferous forests, especially in montane regions.*

> *Strong odour of cucumber skin*
> *Cap moist, greasy*
> *Rare to patchy distribution in Europe although fairly common in some regions*

The slightly smaller *Limacella subfumacea* occurs in the Mediterranean region under Maritime Pines.

Cap creamy-white with a pinkish tinge

Stipe white with a hanging ring

Ring usually has olive-green flecks towards top

Pearly Powdercap

Cystoderma carcharias (mushrooms with gills)
Cap 2–5 cm   July–October

Habitat *In coniferous forests and mossy, hillside grassland, pine*

> **Strong, dust-like odour**
> **Flesh light, creamy-white**
> **Found throughout Europe**

For a long time, the Pearly Powdercap was thought to be a relative of the lepiotas. However, they have recessed, attached gills which are broad at the base, meaning that they are actually *Tricholomatacae*. They are described in this section of the book because of their similarity to lepiotas.

Cap creamy-pink, light powder coating on surface

As with all powdercaps, the cap surface appears to be covered in granules or a fine powder.

Gills white

Stipe has a flaky coating

Stipe ring upward-facing

Earthy Powdercap

Cystoderma amianthinum (mushrooms with gills)
Cap 2–4 cm   August–November

Habitat *In nutrient-poor coniferous forests, often together with lichens such as Reindeer Lichen.*

> **Odour slightly fruity or slightly earthy**
> **Spores white**
> **Found throughout Europe**

This species can vary considerably. It can be an intense, rust orange colour, orange-yellow or pale yellow. Rain can make the cap completely smooth, but it can also turn extremely wrinkly. The cap shape varies from conical to flat.

Very occasionally, the fruiting bodies of this species are attacked by a parasite known as the Powdercap Strangler (*Squamanita paradoxa*). Usually all that shows that this species has been present are the remains of its tiny stipe. It has only ever been found a few times in Europe.

Flesh whitish, orange-ochre on the stipe surface

Gills white, almost unattached

Cap surface has a fine, granular coating

Stipe surface flaky

Cystoderma granulosum
No common name (mushrooms with gills)
Cap 2–7 cm   July–October

Although this species was very common in all mountainous regions up until a few decades ago, it is in serious decline in lowland areas with intensive agriculture. Today, this species is found primarily in the montane regions of central Europe.

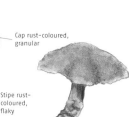

Habitat In coniferous forests and on well-used, hillside grassland, on acidic, generally nutrient-poor soils.

> *Mild, mushroomy odour*
> *Rare in southern Europe, patchy distribution on central Europe, more common in the north and east*

Cap rust-coloured, granular

Stipe rust-coloured, flaky

The claret-coloured, rare *Cystoderma superbum* is easily identified because of its colour.

Flesh pale, rust-brownish

Gills white, ascending

Golden Bootleg
Phaeolepiota aurea (mushrooms with gills)
Cap 15–25(30) cm   July–October

Despite the fact that this mushroom contains a relatively high concentration of prussic acid, it is often classed as edible. Nevertheless, it is not advisable to eat it. This is unfortunate, as it is a large and fruitful mushroom.

When young, the gills and cap are covered by a skin-like, granular membrane.

Habitat In ruderal locations such as embankments or gardens, often together with nettles, nitrate tolerant.

> *Slight odour of bitter almond*
> *Spores ochre-brown*
> *Rare throughout Europe, patchy distribution in the Alpine foothills*

Cap orange-ochre, granular

Stipe same colour as cap, fibrous

Ring upwards-facing, skin-like

Flesh pale ochre

Field Mushroom

Agaricus campestris (mushrooms with gills)
Cap 4–10 cm   June–October

Habitat *On moderately fertilised grassland and meadows, sensitive to slurry and artificial fertilisers.*

> *Odour mushroomy*
> *Spores dark brown*
> *Found throughout Europe, numbers generally declining*
> *Similar species Yellow Stainer, amanitas*

No poisonous, similar species grow in the Field Mushroom's typical habitats on meadows and grasslands, far away from trees. However, caution must be exercised if it is found growing near woodland (less than 30 metres from the tree line) since it may then be confused with certain *Amanita* species. A careful examination of the gill colour and stipe characteristics must be carried out to avoid any unnecessary trips to hospital!

Did you know?

Field Mushrooms sometimes have flaky caps. However, this variety does not differ in any other way and tastes just as good.

Flesh white, unchanging or turning slightly red

Gills vibrantly pink when young

138

If undisturbed, this species forms large fairy rings. This makes it possible to see where they grow, even if no fruiting bodies are visible.

Cap white

Stipe white, ringed

Horse Mushroom
Agaricus arvensis (mushrooms with gills)
Cap 8–15 cm   June–October

The Horse Mushroom is highly sought-after because it is so fruitful. However, the likelihood of finding one in woodland is greater than for the Field Mushroom, increasing the risk of confusion with the Yellow Stainer or even amanitas (p. 116).

Habitat On well-used pastures and grassland, sometimes in parks and even in spruce forests.

> Odour of aniseed
> Bruised areas turn yellowish
> Spores dark brown
> Found throughout Europe
> Similar species Yellow Stainer

Caution!
The Yellow Stainer (p 141) can easily be distinguished by the fact that its stipe flesh turns chrome-yellow. The inside of the Horse Mushroom's flesh does not turn yellow, only bruised, outer areas.

Flesh white

Gills pale grey-pink when young

The star-shaped, ripped underside of the ring is a key feature for identification.

139

Stipe white with a hanging ring

Cap white, often slightly flaky

Wood Mushroom
Agaricus silvicola (mushrooms with gills)
Cap 4–10 cm   June–October

Habitat In coniferous forests, also in deciduous forests, prefers relatively dry soils, otherwise no particular soil preference.

> Odour of bitter almond
> Bruised areas turn yellow
> Found throughout Europe
> Similar species amanitas

This mushroom also tastes very good. Although its flesh is relatively thin, it is very common and is often found growing in large numbers. However, all mushrooms that turn slightly yellow absorb a certain concentration of heavy metals (particularly caesium) from the ground. They should therefore only be eaten occasionally.

Specimens with off-centre, truncated basal bulbs are sometimes thought of as a separate species.

Gills pale grey-pink when young

Stipe base often very bulbous

Caution!
Since the Wood Mushroom can often become very yellow, it may be confused with the Deathcap (p. 116). In such cases, a careful examination of all distinguishing features must be carried out.

Stipe white with a hanging ring

Cap white, bell-shaped when young

Yellow Stainer

Agaricus xanthoderma (mushrooms with gills)

Cap 6–15 cm June–October

☠

The Yellow Stainer is the only member of the *Agaricus* family that is poisonous. Depending on the person, they can cause mild to serious stomach problems. The mushroom smells of carbolic (or sticking-plasters) and this becomes more intense when it is cooked.

Habitat *In ruderal locations in deciduous forests, gardens, parks and cemeteries on nutrient-rich soils.*

> *Odour of carbolic*
> *Bruised areas turn chrome-yellow*
> *Spores dark brown*
> *Common throughout Europe, becoming increasingly common*

Did you know?

There are a few varieties of Yellow Stainer, all of which are poisonous, such as the Flat-Top Agaricus (A. praeclaresquamosus) with its flaky cap. This group is easily identified by the fact that the flesh in the stipe base turns yellow.

Gills pale grey-pink when young

Stipe whitish with a ring

Inside of stipe base turns chrome yellow

Cap white, slightly angular

141

Spring Agaricus
Agaricus bitorquis (mushrooms with gills)
Cap 3–8 cm   June–October

Habitat *On roads and verges, always on highly compacted soils.*

> **Spores chocolatey brown**
> **Odour pleasantly mushroom-like**
> **Common throughout Europe**

Although mushrooms are relatively fragile structures, consisting mainly of water, their strength is quite unbelievable. The Spring Agaricus can easily break through tarmac when it grows and some roads and paths have to be repaired because of it.

Cap white, no discoloration

Double ring

Flesh white, turning slightly red

Gills pink when young

Agaricus bernardii has rough scales and grows along salted roads. It tastes unpleasant.

Rosy Wood Mushroom
Agaricus semotus (mushrooms with gills)
Cap 2–4 cm   July–October

Habitat *All forest types, slightly more common in coniferous forests, no soil preferences.*

> **Mild marzipan-like odour**
> **Spores chocolatey brown**
> **Found throughout Europe**

Very few people know that certain *Agaricus* species never grow larger than 4 to 5 cm, despite the fact that this is relatively commonplace. Most mushroom collectors ignore them although they are all edible.

The largest species among the 'dwarf' Agarics is the Lilac Mushroom (*A. porphyrhizon*). It is slightly more common in some regions.

Claret-coloured fibres in centre of cap

Stipe white, slightly pink towards the top

Flesh white, yellowish in the stipe

Gills pink when young

The Prince

Agaricus augustus (mushrooms with gills)

Cap 10–25 cm   July–October

It is easy to identify this good-tasting mushroom because of its size. The odour of marzipan and the flaky cap are further, clear characteristics. Although it usually only occurs individually, only a few of them are needed for a meal.

Agaricus macrocarpus has a white cap and has similarly large fruiting bodies. It is usually found on grassland.

Habitat *Primarily in coniferous forests, less common in deciduous forests or parks, prefers alkaline soils.*

> *Odour of bitter almond*
> *Spores chocolatey brown*
> *Common throughout Europe*
> *Similar species Freckled Dapperling*

Caution!

The Freckled Dapperling (p. 132) is faintly similar, although its gills remain white and it has quite an unpleasant odour.

Gills grey–pink when young

Flesh white, turning slightly yellow

143

Cap has brown scales on a cream-coloured base

Double ring

Blushing Wood Mushroom
Agaricus silvaticus (mushrooms with gills)
Cap 4–8 cm   August–October

Habitat *In coniferous forests on various soil types, sometimes also among fallen leaves in deciduous forests.*

> Spores chocolatey brown
> Odour dull, earthy
> Common throughout Europe
> Similar species Clustered Mushroom

The discolouration of the Blushing Wood Mushroom's flesh is obvious and happens quickly. Within a minute of being cut, the flesh turns from yellow-orange to orange-red and then a deep, blood red colour. This discoloration and the fact that its gills turn brown, mean that this mushroom should not be confused with any poisonous mushrooms. Blushing Wood Mushrooms are very tasty, but also very fragile.

The rare *Agaricus benesii* has white scales and looks almost like the rare albino form of Blushing Wood Mushroom.

Flesh rapidly turning blood red

Gills grey-pink when young

144

Cap brown with fibrous scales

Stipe white

Caution!
The Clustered Mushroom (A. vaporarius) does not turn as deeply red. Although it is not quite poisonous, it tastes unpleasant and can cause slight stomach upsets.

Shaggy Inkcap
Coprinus comatus (mushrooms with gills)
Cap 4–10 cm high   July–October

The ink from the Shaggy Inkcap mixed with a few drops of gum arabic produces an ink that can be used for writing and was actually used historically. Shaggy Inkcap spores can still be detected on some scrolls from centuries ago.

Habitat On heavily fertilised areas such as verges and the fringes of pastures, also on decomposing plant material on forest boundaries.

> *Spores blackish*
> *Flesh very fragile*
> *Common throughout Europe*
> *Similar species Common Inkcap*

Caution!
The Common Inkcap (p. 146) is poisonous if consumed with alcohol. Its stipe is shorter and its cap is smooth, grey-brown and less cylindrical.

Gills white when young, pink then black discoloration

Stipe white, hollow, ringed

145

Decomposing shaggy inkcaps are used to make soup in some countries. However, eating decomposing specimens may lead to food poisoning!

Cap cylindrical

Cap scales fringy, relatively prominent

Common Inkcap ⚔

Coprinus atramentarius (mushrooms with gills)
Cap 3–7 cm   May–October

Habitat *Grasslands, gardens, lowland forests, verges, no soil preference.*

> *Spores black*
> *Gills deliquescent*
> *Common throughout Europe*

Severe allergic reactions may occur if alcohol is drunk together with a meal containing Common Inkcaps. Symptoms may include redness, increased heart rate and circulation problems. These symptoms can also occur if alcohol is consumed two or three days after eating the mushrooms.

Stipe smooth, slightly broader at base, an ill-defined ring may be present

Flesh white

Gills white when young, black discoloration (not pink)

Stipe base thick, tuberous

Did you know?

The closely related Coprinus insignis *grows beneath living trees. It can easily be distinguished under a microscope by its warty spores.*

Cap grey, bell-shaped

Stipe white

Magpie Inkcap

Coprinus picaceus (mushrooms with gills)

Cap 5–12 cm high   July–October

This pretty-looking mushroom is the largest of the *Coprinus* species and is even larger than the Shaggy Inkcap (p. 145). The flaky, whitish velum remnants on the black background of the cap give the mushroom a dappled black-and-white appearance.

Cap black-grey with flaky, white velum remnants

Stipe white, slightly flaky

The smaller, similar *Coprinus stanglianus* grows on dry grassland. It was first discovered in 1988.

Cap covered by white velum when young

Habitat *In deciduous forests in alkaline, clay soils, primarily among fallen beech leaves.*

> Spores black
> Gills deliquescent
> Strong odour, often of mothballs
> Patchy distribution in southern and central Europe, very rare in northern Europe

Glistening Inkcap

Coprinus miccaceus (mushrooms with gills)

Cap 2–5 cm   July–October

Many mushroom guides advise against eating this mushroom in conjunction with alcohol, as is the case for the Common Inkcap (p. 146). Although there is no evidence that this causes problems, it is, nevertheless, sensible to follow this advice.

Coprinus ellsii grows individually on small pieces of wood lying on the ground.

Cap brownish-grey with sand-like velum granules

Stipe white, smooth

Cap acorn-shaped

Flesh brownish-yellow

Habitat *In all types of nutrient-rich deciduous forest, in parks and gardens, beneath trees or on buried wood.*

> Spores black
> Gills prone to withering
> Common throughout Europe

Firerug Inkcap

Coprinus domesticus (mushrooms with gills)
Cap 2–5 cm   April–September

Habitat In nutrient-rich deciduous forests, primarily in lowland forests, always on deciduous wood.

> Spores black
> Gills prone to withering
> Common throughout Europe

The Firerug Inkcap got its name from the 'fiery' appearance of its cap. It often occurs on wood used for the construction of buildings, and, very occasionally, so does the Glistening Inkcap (p. 147).

Cap ochre to yellow-brown with white scales

Cap rim slightly grooved

The Firerug Inkcap grows on a felt-like base called ozonium which occurs almost all year-round.

Velum remnants web/cotton wool-like, white

Stipe white, bulging at the base

Hare's Foot Inkcap

Coprinus lagopus (mushrooms with gills)
Cap 2–4 cm   June–October

Habitat On areas influenced by human activity in forests, bark mulch, wood chippings and other small pieces of wood.

> Gills roll inwards when decaying
> Spores black
> Common throughout Europe

Young specimens of this species are reminiscent of hares' feet because of the soft, white, furry velum. Little is known about the edibility of this mushroom although it is not thought to be poisonous.

Cap grey, covered with prominent, shaggy, white fibres

The rare *Coprinus erythrocephalus* is easy to identify when young by its fiery, orange-red, powdery cap and stipe.

Gills grey-black

Cap bent upwards when old, translucent

Stipe white with fine scales

Fairy Inkcap

Coprinus disseminatus (mushrooms with gills)

Cap 0.5–1.5 cm   May–October

Because this mushroom often occurs in large numbers in gardens and play areas, it is quite common for children to eat them. However, no cases of poisoning have been reported so far.

Habitat No biotope preferences, occurs on deciduous tree stumps, thick trunks and dead roots.

> *Gills prone to withering*
> *Spores black-brown*
> *Common throughout Europe*

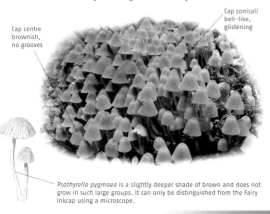

Cap centre brownish, no grooves

Cap conical/bell-like, glistening

Cap grey-beige, heavily grooved

Stipe grey-beige, smooth

Psathyrella pygmaea is a slightly deeper shade of brown and does not grow in such large groups. It can only be distinguished from the Fairy Inkcap using a microscope.

Coprinus auricomus

No common name (mushrooms with gills)

Cap 1–2 cm   May–November

Mushroom enthusiasts hoping to catch a glimpse of this and other *Coprinus* species have to be up early! The sensitive fruiting bodies decompose quickly and are sometimes unrecognisable by midday.

Habitat On verges, on forest paths, woodpiles and bark mulch.

> *Gills prone to withering*
> *Spores black-brown*
> *Common throughout Europe*

Cap brownish-grey when old, with wrinkly grooves

Stipe white to pale brown

The Pleated Inkcap (*C.plicatilis* agg.) looks very similar indeed, especially when it is mature.

Cap brownish-red when young, almost smooth

Gills grey-brown, very distant

Coprinus angulatus

✖

No common name (mushrooms with gills)

Cap 1–3 cm high   May–November

Habitat *On burnt areas in the early to late stages of regeneration.*

> *Gills deliquescent*
> *Spores black-brown*
> *Common throughout Europe*

There are hundreds of species of mushrooms that only grow or prefer to grow on burnt areas. *Coprinus angulatus* is the most common of these among the *Coprinus* species. It can be identified by its bare, brown cap.

Cap red-brown with wrinkly grooves

Stipe white

Cap cylindrical, no velum

Gills brownish-grey

Areas that have been affected by fire are often carpeted by the moss species *Funaria hygrometrica*.

Coprinus cinerus

✖

No common name (mushrooms with gills)

Cap 1–3 cm high   May–November

Habitat *On straw mixed with dung, old dung heaps and similar substrates with a high concentration of nitrates.*

> *Gills deliquescent*
> *Spores black-brown*
> *Common throughout Europe*

A large number of the approximately 100 European *Coprinus* species only grow on dung or droppings. It is not uncommon to find a number of different species growing on the same pile of dung at the same time.

Cap light grey, heavily grooved

The common *Coprinus stercoreus* grows directly on dung and its cap is between only 3 and 5 cm in diameter.

Cap whitish when young with a flaky velum

Stipe shaggy and flaky when young

Stipe white, smooth when old

Petticoat Mottlegill

Panaeolus papilionaceus (mushrooms with gills)
Cap 1–4 cm   June–November

The *Panaeolus* family are recognisable by their black gills with irregular flecks and their stipes, which have a frosted appearance from top to bottom. All but one member of this family grow on dung.

Habitat On horse droppings, cowpats and dung from many other herbivores.

> ***Gills irregularly brindled***
> ***Common throughout Europe***

Cap light grey, bell-shaped

Stipe finely frosted from top to bottom

The Egghead Mottlegill (*P. semiovatus*) can be identified by its sticky, smooth cap and its thin ring.

Cap rim draped

Stipe pale brownish to grey

Brown Mottlegill

Panaeolus foenisecii (mushrooms with gills)
Cap 1–3 cm   June–November

The Brown Mottlegill always grows on grassland which has just been mown. Specimens from certain areas have allegedly been known to contain small quantities of the psychedelic substance psilocybin although the substance has not been found in specimens from other areas. In any case, this mushroom causes food poisoning if eaten raw.

Habitat On horse droppings, cowpats and dung from many other herbivores.

> ***Gills irregularly brindled***
> ***Common throughout Europe***

Stipe pale brownish, slightly frosted

Cap ochre to red-brown, hygrophanous

The Banded Mottlegill (*P. cinctulus*) contains psychedelic substances and is slightly more common in some regions.

Gills dark brown, brindled

Flesh brownish

Pale Brittlestem
Psathyrella candolleana (mushrooms with gills)
Cap 2–6 cm   June–November

Habitat *Primarily on verges and on the fringes of grassland, no particular soil preferences.*

> **Stipe very fragile**
> **Spores black-brown**
> **Common throughout Europe**

Opinions on the edibility of the Pale Brittlestem differ. Although it is edible, it is very fragile and has little taste. However, young specimens can be used for soups and light sauces. Older specimens are unappetising due to their dark brown spores.

The violet-grey, very crowded gills are characteristic of the species.

Did you know?
The similar Psathyrella leucotephra *has a fibrous ring and grows in clumps. This species is relatively uncommon and grows in lowland forests or parks and prefers nitrate-rich substrates. It is not known whether it is edible.*

Flesh watery yellow

Stipe hollow

152

Cap brownish-grey, darkens when wet

Velum remnants web-like, white

Spring Brittlestem

Psathyrella spadiceogrisea (mushrooms with gills)

Cap 2–6 cm   (April)May–June

Although it is very occasionally found in autumn, this is usually due to confusion with other species. There are about a dozen other, very similar species which makes Spring Brittlestems the hardest *Psathyrella* species to identify, even for experts. However, none of these similar species are known to be poisonous.

The mushroom becomes very pale when dried, making it look like a completely different species.

Habitat *In open areas in deciduous forests, on verges and forest boundaries, usually avoids acidic soils.*

> **Stipe very fragile**
> **Spores dark brown**
> **Common throughout Europe**

Cap brown, white velum remnants on the rim

Flesh pale brownish

Gills earthy brown, narrow at base

153

Stipe white, slightly flaky when young

Did you know?

The easiest species of all to identify is the vernalis variety because of its lighter cap colour, its stipe that becomes yellow in the middle and early time at which it occurs (April).

Conical Brittlestem

🍴

Psathyrella conopilea (mushrooms with gills)
Cap 2–6 cm   (April) May–June

Habitat *On verges and open areas in deciduous forests, often among fallen leaves or in nutrient-rich areas.*

> Fine hairs visible on cap under microscope
> Spores dark brown
> Common throughout Europe

The Conical Brittlestem is the largest member of the *Psathyrella* family due to its long stipe, which can be up to 15cm long. It always grows in large groups and is rarely found growing individually. Although it is edible, it tastes insipid.

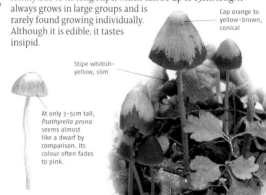

Cap orange to yellow-brown, conical

Stipe whitish-yellow, slim

At only 3–5cm tall, *Psathyrella prona* seems like a dwarf by comparison. Its colour often fades to pink.

Flesh pale brownish

Gills brown, crowded

Dune Brittlestem

✗

Psathyrella ammophila (mushrooms with gills)
Cap 2–5 cm   June–December

Habitat *On sand dunes, growing out of the underground parts of beach grass.*

> Spores dark brown
> Common in Europe's coastal regions

Mushrooms are everywhere, even at the beach! Surprisingly, some species grow on sand dunes, with the Dune Brittlestem being the most common of these. It is extremely rare to find one growing inland on sand.

The Clustered Brittlestem (*P. multipedata*) grows in thick clumps with 100 or more fruiting bodies sharing the same stipe base.

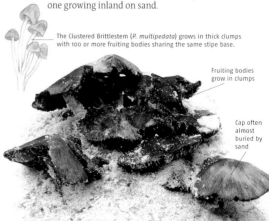

Fruiting bodies grow in clumps

Cap often almost buried by sand

Cap dark to grey-brown

Stipe whitish, tapered

Common Stump Brittlestem

Psathyrella piluliformis (mushrooms with gills)
Cap 2–5 cm   June–November

Although only very distantly related to the Sheathed Woodtuft, Common Stump Brittlestem's cap also changes colour when dried. Confusing the two would not, however, end in tragedy as they are both edible. The Common Stump Brittlestem does not have a particularly intense taste so it is advisable to avoid combining it with strong-flavoured foods.

When young, *Psahyrella sacchariolens* looks like it has been dusted with flakes of chocolate. Its obvious, sweetish odour is characteristic.

Habitat On rotting, thick pieces of deciduous wood or tree stumps in all types of forest.

> **Spores dark brown**
> **Grows in clumps**
> **Common throughout Europe**

Flesh creamy-white

Stipe hollow

Did you know?

Of around 60 Psathyrella *species, only one (*P. hirta*) grows on cowpats. As is the case for all* Psathyrella *mushrooms with fibrous flakes, they are only visible when the mushroom is young, after which they disappear rapidly.*

Cap orange to date-coloured, smooth

Gills earthy brown

Yellowfoot Brittlestem ⚔

Psathyrella cotonea (mushrooms with gills)
Cap 3–8 cm   June–November

Habitat *In beech forests on rotting tree stumps or buried wood, less common in other types of forest.*

> **Spores dark brown**
> **Grows in thick clumps**
> **Rare to patchy distribution throughout Europe**

This species belongs to a group of psathyrellas in which the velum is attached to the cap instead of lying loosely on top of it as with most psathyrellas. It is unknown whether it is edible or not.

The cap and entire stipe of the Medusa Brittlestem (*P. caput-medusae*) are covered with prominent scales.

Cap clay-coloured with rough, dark scales

Stipe white, slightly fibrous

Gills earthy brown

Stipe base and mycellium sulphur yellow

Weeping Widow ⛏

Lacrymaria lacrymabunda (mushrooms with gills)
Cap 3–8 cm   May–November

Habitat *On verges and fringes of grassland, on open forest boundaries, prefers nutrient-rich soils.*

> **Spores dark, violet-brown**
> **Grows in large groups**
> **Common throughout Europe**

When identifying this mushroom, it is important to check for the name-giving, watery droplets present on the gill blades. This species prefers to grow on verges and on the fringes of grassland. Although young specimens can be eaten, they do not taste particularly good.

Cap ochre to dark brown with fibrous scales

A bright rust orange variant also exists (var. *pyrotricha*)

White 'lashes' on gill blades

Clear, watery droplets

Stipe paler, fibrous

Conocybe tenera
No common name (mushrooms with gills)
Cap 1–3 cm   May–November

There are many members of the
Conocybe genus, most of which
can only be positively identified
with the aid of a microscope.
None of these species are
known to be edible and a few of
them are known to be poisonous.
It is therefore not advisable to eat
any of them.

Cap rust-coloured,
very smooth

Stipe rust brown,
finely frosted

With its gold-orange cap,
Conocybe aurea is one
of the more conspicuous
members of this family.

Habitat *Along
verges and fringes
of meadows, on
grassland, prefers
nutrient-rich areas.*

> *Spores rust brown*
> *Stipe very slim, fragile*
> *Common throughout
Europe*

Cap bell-shaped

Gills rust
brown

Conocybe subovalis
No common name (mushrooms with gills)
Cap 1–3 cm   May–November

A few conocybes have a thick, bulbous stipe base and this is
particularly apparent on this species. This and the light, olive
colour of its cap make this species easy to recognise. It is often
found growing in flower beds or flowerpots.

Habitat *Along verges
and on the fringes of
meadows, on grass-
land, in flower beds
and greenhouses.*

> *Spores rust-brown*
> *Fruiting body relatively
solid compared to other
conocybes*
> *Common throughout
Europe*

Cap olive-brown,
smooth

Stipe a
lighter shade
than cap,
finely frosted

Conocybe lactea occurs in
similar locations and its
cap is surprisingly high
off the ground

Flesh
creamy-
white

Stipe base
bulbous

Fool's Conecap

Pholiotina filaris (mushrooms with gills)
Cap 1–2 cm   May–October

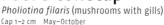

Habitat *On verges, areas formerly used for woodpiles, in gardens, often in freshly disturbed areas.*

> Spores rust brown
> Flesh pale ochre, brownish in the stipe base
> Patchy distribution throughout Europe

There have been reports from America of fatal poisoning due to this mushroom being mistaken for the Liberty Cap (p. 165). The American variant contains large concentrations of amatoxins, although this has not yet been detected in European specimens. Nevertheless, extreme caution is advised when handling this mushroom.

Cap honey brown, becoming slightly wrinkled

Gills rust brown

Stipe brownish, ringed

Pholiotina subnuda is similar and it is unknown whether or not it is also poisonous.

Ring white, upwards facing

Pholiotina aporos

No common name (mushrooms with gills)
Cap 1–2 cm   May–October

Habitat *On verges, on areas formerly used for woodpiles, in gardens and also in defoliated areas in deciduous forests.*

> Spores rust brown
> Gills ochre to rust brown
> Common throughout Europe

This species is characterised by the early time of year at which it occurs. However, it can only be distinguished from its many variants with the aid of a microscope. It is not known whether it is edible.

Cap red-brown with a few white velum remnants

Stipe brownish-yellow with a ring

Cap rim slightly grooved

Ring grooved at top

The extremely similar *Pholiotina arrhenii* only occurs in autumn.

Yellow Fieldcap

Bolbitius vitellinus (mushrooms with gills)
Cap 2–5 cm   May–October

Bolbitius species are usually fragile, short-lived mushrooms which are very similar in appearance to *Coprinus* species (p. 148/149). However, they do not become deliquescent and their spores are a much lighter shade of brown.

Grooves extend out from cap centre

Cap yellow, fades rapidly

The shape and size of this species can vary greatly. It is sometimes very solid and its cap can also be wrinkly.

Habitat *On grassy verges, on wood chippings, on meadows and in gardens, in nutrient-rich areas.*

> **Spores rust ochre**
> **Cap moist, greasy**
> **Common throughout Europe**

Gills ochre

Stipe white, slightly flaky

159

Netted Fieldcap

Bolbitius reticulatus (mushrooms with gills)
Cap 1–3 cm   June–October

All of the European *Bolbitius* species have a slightly venous to wrinkly cap surface. This becomes even more apparent when the mushrooms are dried, although a magnifying glass may occasionally be required.

Cap grey, greasy, grooved

Stipe white, slightly flaky

Some *Pluteus* species are similar, such as the Wrinkled Shield (p. 115).

Habitat *In all types of deciduous forest, always on rotting deciduous wood, particularly on thick, fallen tree trunks.*

> **Spores rust ochre**
> **Cap moist, greasy**
> **Patchy distribution throughout Europe, often overlooked**

Wrinkles/veins extend out from cap centre

Cap often slightly violet

Spring Fieldcap (❨ 🍴 ❩)

Agrocybe praecox (mushrooms with gills)
Cap 3–8(10) cm   May–July (October)

Habitat On verges, in ruderal locations and piles of wood chips, less common in open deciduous forests.

> Spores earthy brown
> Odour rancid, floury
> Taste slightly bitter
> Common throughout Europe

This species can usually be found between spring and the beginning of summer. Although it is edible, it is not very popular because of its slightly bitter, dull taste.

Did you know?

The Bearded Fieldcap (A. dura,– left) can be distinguished from the Spring Fieldcap by the very light colour of its cap and the Common Fieldcap (A. pediades, right) by its small fruiting body with no ring. Both occur on meadows and dry grassland.

Gills earthy brown

Stipe base has rooting threads

Cap ochre to olive-brown, smooth

Stipe creamy-white with a hanging ring

Dark Fieldcap

Agrocybe erebia (mushrooms with gills)
Cap 3–8 cm   July–October

This species is characterised by the very dark colour of its cap. Although there have not been any reports of poisoning, its bitter taste precludes it from being eaten.

Habitat *On verges and embankments, less common in open deciduous forests, prefers alkaline soils.*

> ***Spores earthy brown***
> ***Taste slightly bitter***
> ***Patchy distribution throughout Europe, although common in some regions***

Cap chocolate to leather-coloured, glistens when moist

Agrocybe arvalis grows out of a small sclerota which can be uncovered by digging carefully.

Stipe lighter brown, ringed

Gills earthy brown

Ring hanging

Poplar Fieldcap

Agrocybe cylindracea (mushrooms with gills)
Cap 4–10 cm   April–October

The Poplar Fieldcap was known by the Romans as a good-tasting mushroom and it is still often picked today in southern Europe. Its culture is extremely simple and it is occasionally cultivated.

Habitat *In lowland forests and damp, deciduous coppices, prefers warm conditions, only ever grows on poplar wood.*

> ***Spores earthy brown***
> ***Taste mild***
> ***Common in southern Europe, rare north of the Alps***

The much larger Poplar Pholiota (p. 172) also grows on poplar wood. It cannot be eaten because it tastes so bitter.

Cap cream to leather-coloured, slightly wrinkly.

Stipe whitish, ringed

Flesh creamy-brown

Gills earth brown, pale for quite some time

Verdigris Agaric

Psilocybe aeruginosa (mushrooms with gills)

Cap 3–7 cm   August–December

Habitat *On verges and on forest boundaries, in nutrient-rich, open areas in deciduous or coniferous forests.*

> *Spores violet-brown*
> *Odour slightly radish-like*
> *Common throughout Europe*

Flesh pale greenish, blue-green on stipe surface

Gills violet-brown

Mushroom experts are often confronted with looks of disbelief when they say that this 'poisonous-looking' species can be eaten. Nevertheless, the Verdigris Agaric can be eaten, despite its rather bright colouring. Conversely, many 'edible-looking' mushrooms are actually poisonous.

Did you know?

The Blue Roundhead (P. caerulea) can be distinguished by its less prominent velum or the slightly different colour of its gills.

The blue-green pigmentation seems to be sensitive to light since it fades in both species when they come into contact with direct sunlight.

Velum white with prominent scales

Cap intensely blue-green

Garland Roundhead

Stropharia coronilla (mushrooms with gills)

Cap 2–4 cm   July–November

Some mushroom specialists say that the Garland Roundhead is edible and others believe it to be poisonous. I suffered no ill effects after trying it myself, although it is recommended to avoid picking it. It can easily be confused with the Rosy Wood Mushroom (p. 142).

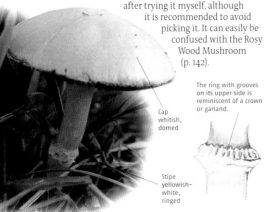

Habitat On well-used grasslands, on harvested fields, occasionally in gardens.

> *Spores violet-brown*
> *Mild odour of herbs*
> *Common throughout Europe*

The ring with grooves on its upper side is reminiscent of a crown or garland.

Cap whitish, domed

Stipe yellowish-white, ringed

Gills chocolatey brown

Flesh creamy-brown

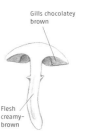

Scaly-Stalked Psilocybe

Psilocybe squamosa (mushrooms with gills)

Cap 2–4 cm   July–November

This species is thought to be poisonous or at least slightly poisonous. Although this has not been proven, it is recommended to avoid eating this mushroom altogether.

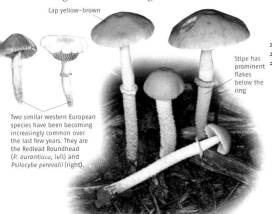

Cap yellow-brown

Habitat On verges and forest boundaries, in open areas in deciduous forests, on bark chippings and woodpiles.

> *Spores chocolatey brown*
> *Mild, radish-like odour*
> *Common throughout Europe*

Stipe has prominent flakes below the ring

Two similar western European species have been becoming increasingly common over the last few years. They are the Redlead Roundhead (*P. aurantiaca*, left) and *Psilocybe perevalii* (right).

Flaky velum remnants on cap rim

Ring white, grooved on the upper side

Burgundy Mushroom

Psilocybe rugoso-annulata (mushrooms with gills)
Cap 8–20 cm   June–November

🍴

Habitat *In cereal fields, on bark chippings and, increasingly, also on verges.*

> *Spores violet-brown*
> *Odour and taste slightly earthy*
> *Relatively common in Europe, becoming more common*
> *Similar species Conifer Roundhead*

This species was cultivated successfully for the first time in what used to be East Germany. Opinion on its taste is divided since many people do not like its slightly earthy aftertaste.

Sometimes mycellia occur which only bear yellow fruiting bodies.

Flesh whitish, firm

Gills grey-violet

Caution!
The poisonous Conifer Roundhead (P. hornemannii) is primarily found in northern Europe, identifiable by its flaky stipe and the fact that it grows in coniferous forests.

Cap red-brown, smooth

Stipe white to leathery yellow with a skin-like ring

Liberty Cap

Psilocybe semilanceata (mushrooms with gills)

Cap 1–2 cm   June–November

All bluing psilocybes are poisonous in that they have hallucinogenic effects. However, the mushroom is often picked for this very reason. Doing so without very specific knowledge can have fatal consequences as there are many poisonous, similar species.

Habitat On well-used grassland, sometimes along grassy verges, never grows directly on dung.

> *Spores violet-brown*
> *Odour and taste slightly earthy*
> *Patchy distribution in Europe, common in some regions*

Caution!

Even if the Liberty Cap causes no lasting damage, the consequences of confusing it with one of the many similar, poisonous species could be fatal since some of them contain chemicals which attack the liver.

Cap pointed

Stipe usually turns blue when bruised

165

Cap brownish, grooved, sticky when moist

Stipe creamy to leathery-yellow, smooth

The Indigo Psilocybe (*P. azurescens*), discovered in the USA in 1995, contains the highest concentration of psilocybin. It was discovered in Europe for the first time in 2000.

Conifer Tuft

Hypholoma capnoides (mushrooms with gills)
Cap 2–4 cm   (August) October–March

Habitat In dry mixed coniferous forests, always on rotting coniferous tree stumps.

> Spores violet-black
> Taste mild, slightly tart
> Common throughout Europe
> Similar species Sulphur Tuft

The Conifer Tuft is one of the few edible mushrooms which grow in large numbers during the winter months. With the right weather conditions, it has also been known to grow in August and into May. It tastes best when steamed or in soup.

The difference in gill colour between the Conifer Tuft (right) and the Sulphur Tuft (left) is more obvious on younger specimens.

Gills smoky grey when young

Stipe pale yellow-brown

166

Cap yellow-brown, hygrophanous

Gills covered with a thin veil when young

Caution!
The Sulphur Tuft (p. 167) tastes bitter and is also poisonous.

Sulphur Tuft

Hypholoma fasciculare (mushrooms with gills)
Cap 2–6 cm   April–December

Many people have difficulty distinguishing the Sulphur Tuft from the Conifer Tuft. Tasting a small sample (do not swallow it!) will make it easier. If it tastes mild then it is a Conifer Tuft and if it tastes bitter then it is a Sulphur Tuft. This comparison should only be carried out for the two species described here. It is not recommended as a general method for identifying mushrooms.

Habitat In all types of forest, on rotting deciduous or coniferous wood, on tree stumps, roots or on buried wood.

> Spores violet-black
> Taste bitter
> Very common in Europe

Did you know?
There is a very small, almost completely yellow-green variant (H. f. viridis) of the Sulphur Tuft. It is just as poisonous and bitter as the common Sulphur Tuft, but is harder to mistake for an edible species because of its size and colour.

Gills green-yellow when young

Stipe greenish yellow-brown

Cap yellow to orange-brown, hygrophanous

167

Brick Tuft
Hypholoma lateritium (mushrooms with gills)
Cap 3–8 cm   August–December

Habitat In all types of forest, always on thick, rotting pieces of deciduous wood, less common on buried wood.

> **Spores violet-black**
> **Taste slightly bitter**
> **Common throughout Europe**

The Brick Tuft only has a slight bitter taste and is eaten by some people because it is supposed to aid in the treatment of rheumatism. This is, however, the subject of controversy and its use as a treatment is frowned upon in orthodox medicine. While its tartness will appeal to some people, most people do not like it.

Did you know?
There are a number of wood-dwelling species with striking orange to brick-red caps, such as the Conifer Scalycap (Pholiota astragalina, left) or the Redlead Roundhead (Psilocybe aurantiaca, right).

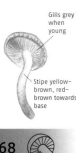

Gills grey when young

Stipe yellow-brown, red-brown towards base

168

Grows in thick clumps

Cap brick red with velum scales

Sphagnum Brownie

Hypholoma elongatum (mushrooms with gills)
Cap 1–3 cm   July–October

Four different *Hypholoma* species grow in bogs and the only way to identify any of them positively is by using a microscope. The Sphagnum Brownie is easily the most common among them.

Cap yellow-brown, grooved at rim

The Peat Brownie (*Pholiota udum*) also grows on bogs and peat with no moss covering.

Stipe has very small, white flakes

Habitat In peat bogs and boggy areas in coniferous forests, always in or around sphagnum moss.

> ***Spores violet-black***
> ***Taste slightly bitter***
> ***Common throughout Europe***

Gills beige-grey

Stipe light brown-yellow, usually very long

Snakeskin Brownie

Hypholoma marginatum (mushrooms with gills)
Cap 1–3 cm   July–October

This mushroom gets its name from the snakeskin-like appearance of its stipe surface. In order to get a clear view of this, turn the mushroom on its side and look along the stipe from the cap rim downwards.

Cap yellow-brown, smooth

The Rooting Brownie (*H. radicosum*) grows in similar biotopes and can be identified by its very long stipe root.

Cap rim white

Habitat In damp coniferous forests, on rotting wood or on the ground, primarily in hilly regions.

> ***Spores violet-black***
> ***Taste slightly bitter***
> ***Common in some parts of Europe***

Gills violet-grey

Stipe has a white, snakeskin-like pattern on it

Shaggy Scalycap

Pholiota squarrosa (mushrooms with gills)
Cap 3–8 cm   July–October

Habitat *In all types of forest, in parks, orchards, at the base of living trees.*

> Spores earthy brown
> Taste bitter
> Grows in clumps
> Common in Europe

This mushroom usually grows in clumps at the bases of living trees (deciduous and coniferous). Its spores enter the tree via wounds and can cause white rot. It is the only shaggy *Pholiota* species with a dry cap and stipe. Similar species either have a slimy cap or no prominent scales. It is sometimes eaten despite its bitter taste.

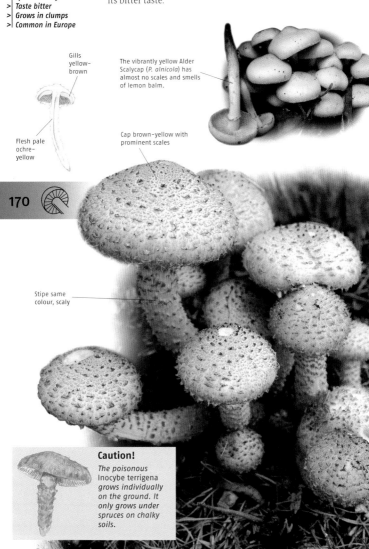

Gills yellow–brown

The vibrantly yellow Alder Scalycap (*P. alnicola*) has almost no scales and smells of lemon balm.

Flesh pale ochre–yellow

Cap brown-yellow with prominent scales

Stipe same colour, scaly

Caution!
The poisonous Inocybe terrigena grows individually on the ground. It only grows under spruces on chalky soils.

Flaming Scalycap

Pholiota flammans (mushrooms with gills)

Cap 2–6 cm July–October

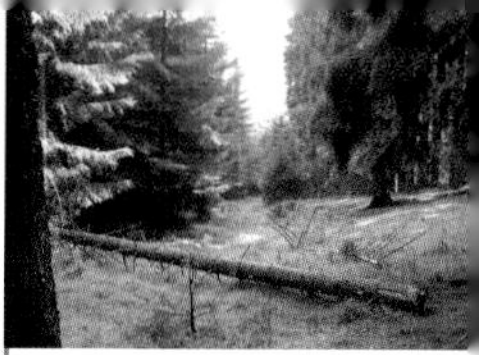

Habitat *In coniferous forests or mixed forests, always on rotting coniferous wood.*

With its vibrant, orange-yellow cap, it is easy to see how the Flaming Scalycap got its name. As with almost all *Pholiota* species, it tastes too bitter to be eaten.

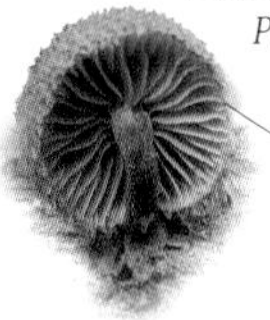
Phaeomarasmius erinaceus has spiky scales.

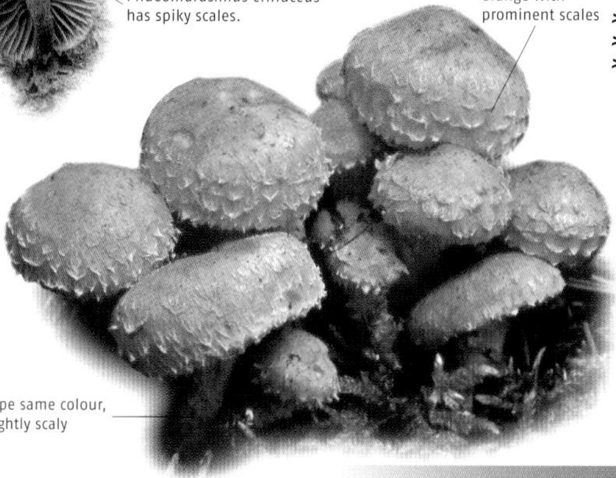
Cap yellow-orange with prominent scales
Stipe same colour, slightly scaly

> ***Spores earthy brown***
> ***Taste bitter***
> ***Common in Europe***

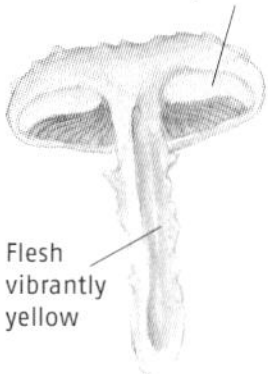
Gills luminous orange-yellow
Flesh vibrantly yellow

Golden Scalycap

Pholiota cerifera (mushrooms with gills)

Cap 3–7 cm July–October

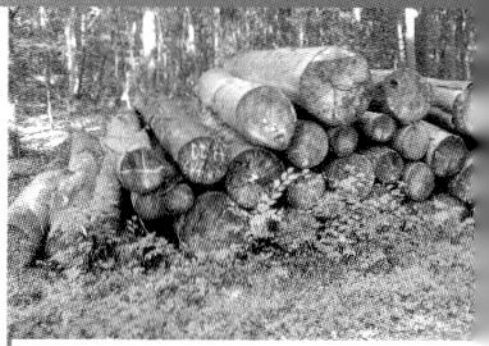

Habitat *In deciduous forests on living beech trees and other deciduous trees, on fallen trees, less common on coniferous trees.*

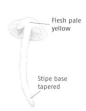

This species can grow many metres high up on apparently healthy trees. It often grows in branch holes and other wounds on trees. However, it is only slightly parasitic and it only causes superficial damage to trees.

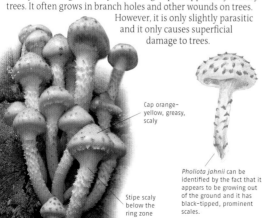

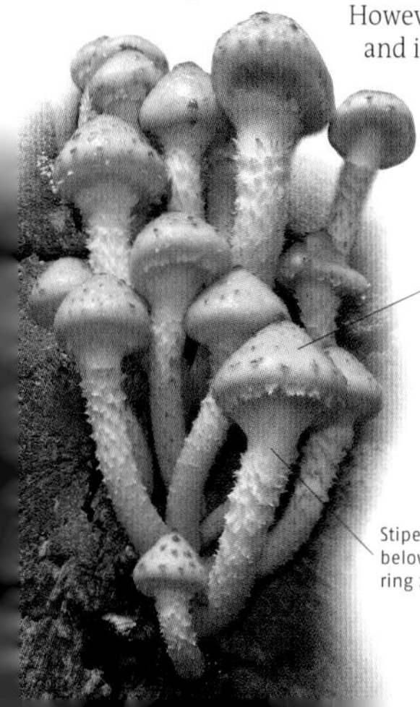
Cap orange-yellow, greasy, scaly
Stipe scaly below the ring zone

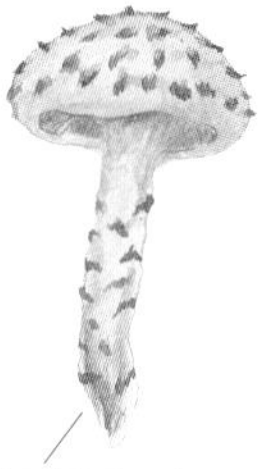

Pholiota jahnii can be identified by the fact that it appears to be growing out of the ground and it has black-tipped, prominent scales.

> ***Spores earthy brown***
> ***Taste bitter***
> ***Common in Europe***

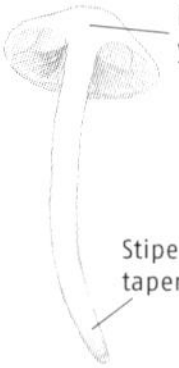
Flesh pale yellow
Stipe base tapered

Poplar Pholiota
✂

Pholiota destruens (mushrooms with gills)
Cap 6–15 cm   July–November

Habitat In lowland forests, in rows of trees on riverbanks, always on upright or fallen poplar trees.

> Spores earthy brown
> Taste bitter
> Common near major rivers in Europe, otherwise uncommon

The Poplar Philiota has robust, long-lasting fruiting bodies with firm flesh. As such, it is often still possible to see their blackened remains on poplar trees in spring.

Cap ochre to brown with thick, shaggy scales

Flesh white, firm

Gills pale earthy-brown

As its name suggests, this species only grows on poplar trees.

Stipe has shaggy scales beneath the ring zone

Pholiota lenta
✂

No common name (mushrooms with gills)
Cap 4–8 (10) cm   September–November

Habitat In nutrient-rich deciduous forests, particularly among tree debris and branches, always on or near wood.

> Spores earthy brown
> Taste slightly bitter
> Common throughout Europe

This species mainly occurs between late summer and late autumn. However, if the conditions are right, it can also grow in spring like the Wood Blewit (p. 65). It grows in clumps, although not usually in such concentration as shown in the photograph.

Flesh cream-coloured

Gills ochre-brown

Cap pale to pinkish-brown, slimy

Cap scales white, removable

The Sticky Scalycap (*P. gummosa*) can be identified by its olive fruiting body and its rust-coloured stipe base.

Sheathed Woodtuft
Pholiota mutabilis (mushrooms with gills)
Cap 2–5 cm   May–October

The Sheathed Woodtuft is a highly sought-after edible mushroom because of its taste and the fact that it grows in thick clumps. It is particularly suited for adding to soups although the stipes are so fragile that only the caps are picked. However, if you need a mushroom expert to identify what you think is a Sheathed Woodtuft, you must show them the complete mushroom, otherwise positive identification may not be possible.

Only the stipe characteristics can be used to positively identify the Funeral Bell (left, silvery, with longitudinal fibres and a fibrous ring zone) or the Sheathed Woodtuft (right, with brown scales and a skin-like ring). Other characteristics such as taste, cap grooves and shape are very unreliable by comparison.

Habitat *On dead, rotting deciduous wood, less common on coniferous wood, usually occurs on tree stumps.*

> **Taste pleasantly nutty**
> **Spores earthy brown**
> **Common in Europe**
> **Similar species Funeral Bell**

Flesh brownish

Gills nut brown

Caution!
The deadly poisonous Funeral Bell (p. 173) can look highly similar after various stages of moisture uptake. Anyone wanting to pick Sheathed Woodtufts must know how to identify Funeral Bells.

173

Cap yellow to orange-brown, hygrophanous

Stipe tip cream-coloured

Stipe has a skin-like ring zone with brown scales beneath it

Winter Twiglet

Tubaria hiemalis (mushrooms with gills)

Cap 2–5 cm   September–February

Habitat *No biotope preference, on bark mulch, wood chippings and similar material.*

> **Spores dirty/rust brown**
> **Velum white, scarce**
> **Common throughout Europe**

Gills orange–brown, triangular

Flesh brownish–orange

The *Tubaria* family consists mainly of relatively small, inconspicuous, rust-brown species. One characteristic they all have in common is that the base of their gills is completely attached to the stipe. The cross-section of the gills therefore appears almost triangular.

The Scurfy Twiglet (*T. furfuracea*) grows in summer and autumn and has more apparent velum remnants on its cap rim.

Cap orange to rust brown, rapidly becoming bare

Stipe pale orange-brown

Hawthorn Twiglet

Tubaria dispersa (mushrooms with gills)

Cap 1–3 cm   July–October

Habitat *Beneath whitethorn (*Crataegus* spp.), primarily on alkaline, clay soils.*

> **Spores dirty/rust brown**
> **Taste slightly bitter**
> **Patchy distribution throughout Europe**

Gills vibrantly ochre-yellow

Always occurs near whitethorn

Once it has been recognised as a *Tubaria* species, the Hawthorn Twiglet is easy to identify because of its conspicuous, ochre-yellow gills. The location it grows in is also characteristic.

Cap ochre-yellow, bare

The Felted Twiglet (*T. conspersa*) grows on clay soil on verges and has prominent velum remnants on its cap and stipe.

Stipe has a covering of whitish fibres

Flammulaster carpophilus

No common name (mushrooms with gills)
Cap 1–2 cm   May–July

Good eyesight is required in order to spot this small species among fallen beech leaves, despite the fact that it often grows in large numbers. It is characterised by the granular surface of its cap and the locations in which it grows.

Gills beige, distant

The darker *Flammulaster granulosus* grows on defoliated clay soil and on embankments.

Whole stipe has fine scales

Habitat *Among fallen leaves in beech forests, on leaves, cupules and small branches, most common on alkaline soils.*

> *Spores ochre-brown*
> *Whole fruiting body one colour of beige*
> *Patchy distribution throughout Europe*

Cap beige, covered with tiny granules

Peeling Oysterling

Crepidotus mollis (mushrooms with gills)
Cap 2–5 cm   May–October

The Peeling Oysterling belongs to a group of mushrooms which have very short or no stipes and grow laterally or on peaked substrates. Experts call this kind of growth 'crepidotoid,' which corresponds to the scientific name for this family of mushrooms. However, this type of growth is occasionally also seen in other species.

Short stipe laterally affixed

Cap yellow-brown, fading to whitish

Habitat *In relatively nutrient-rich deciduous forests, on fallen trees or on deciduous tree stumps.*

> *Spores earthy brown*
> *No stipe on fruiting body*
> *Common throughout Europe*

None of the other species in this family has a jelly-like layer in their caps. The most common among them is *Crepidotus cesati*.

Cap skin jelly-like, flexible

Split Fibrecap

Inocybe rimosa (mushrooms with gills)
Cap 2–6 cm   June–October

☠

Habitat *In deciduous and coniferous forests, on alkaline soils, along verges, often also on acidic soils.*

> *Spores earthy brown*
> *Odour acidic*
> *Very common throughout Europe*

Between 150 and 200 *Inocybe* species in central Europe are poisonous, or are at least thought to be poisonous. The characteristics they have in common are their longitudinally fibrous caps which are often split open, their earth-coloured spores and other microscopic details. The Split Fibrecap is one of the most variable species as far as colour, cap shape and size are concerned.

Did you know?

The only Inocybe *species which does not contain any poisonous substances is* Inocybe adaequata. *However the danger of confusion with other* Inocybe *species is so great that it is recommended to avoid picking it altogether.*

Cap pointed, bell-shaped

Gills yellow-brown, slightly olive-coloured

176

Cap whitish, ochre, yellow to dark brown

Stipe whitish with a covering of fine fibres

The equally variable Frosty Fibrecap (*I. maculata*) can look very similar.

Bulbous Fibrecap ☠

Inocybe napipes (mushrooms with gills)
Cap 2–4 cm   July–October

In order to identify an inocybe positively, it is necessary to ensure that the stipe base does not break away when the mushroom is picked. This is because the presence or absence of a basal bulb is one of the most important factors in determining the species.

Habitat *In damp coniferous forests, on the fringes of bogs and in boggy areas, always under spruces, firs or pines.*

The Woolly Fibrecap (*I. lanuginosa*) grows in the same locations and looks almost like a cuddly toy when young.

Cap brown with a pointy hump

> **Spores earthy brown**
> **Odour acidic**
> **Common throughout Europe**

Stipe whitish, brownish when older

Stipe base bulbous

Gills earthy brown

Fleecy Fibrecap ☠

Inocybe flocculosa (mushrooms with gills)
Cap 2–4 cm   July–October

The wide range of opinions on *Inocybe* species is particularly apparent when it comes to the Fleecy Fibrecap. While some mycologists view it as one, variable species, others are of the opinion that it has up to eight different subspecies. Whatever the case may be, they are all poisonous and so the argument is of little interest to collectors of edible mushrooms.

Habitat *In deciduous and coniferous forests or under individual trees in parks and gardens, prefers chalky soils.*

Cap becomes slightly scaly towards the rim

Stipe brownish-grey, fibrous

> **Spores earthy brown**
> **Odour acidic**
> **Common throughout Europe**

Gills earthy brown

Stipe cylindrical

Inocybe fuscidula is also very common and occurs almost exclusively in coniferous forests.

Deadly Fibrecap
Inocybe erubescens (mushrooms with gills)
Cap 3–8 cm   April–June

Habitat In deciduous forests, parks and under individual, older beeches or oaks, always on chalky soil.

> Spores earthy brown
> Flesh reddens slowly
> Odour acidic
> Uncommon to patchy distribution throughout Europe, common in some regions

The Deadly Fibrecap often causes serious poisoning because it occurs near St. George's mushrooms (p. 67) and looks very similar when young. The poison is called muscarine and it is the only fungal poison for which there is an antidote. This is called atropine, the poisonous substance contained in the Deadly Nightshade plant. It has an immediate effect and patients are usually discharged without further ado. However, if muscarine poisoning is not treated, it can lead to circulatory collapse and cardiac arrest.

Inocybe godeyi is a brick red colour throughout its life and has a white, rimmed basal bulb.

Gills earthy brown

Stipe, at most, only slightly thickened

178

Did you know?
It is harder to mistake older specimens for St. George's Mushrooms because of their reddish colour and brown gills. St. George's Mushroom never has any redness to it, its gills stay creamy–white and it has a strong, floury odour.

Cap whitish at first, slowly turning reddish

Stipe white, fibrous

Greenflush Fibrecap

Inocybe corydalina (mushrooms with gills)
Cap 3–8 cm   July–October

Odour plays an important role in identifying inocybes. Most of them have an acidic odour, but there is a variety of other odours, including fish, wine cask, bitter almond, geranium leaves, pear blossom and larkspur. This species smells of sweet flowers.

Inocybe haemacta, which grows under hazel trees, can be identified by its odour of stables.

Cap grey-white, with darker scales

Peak grey-green

Habitat In deciduous forests on alkaline, clay soils, primarily under beeches and oaks.

> *Spores earthy brown*
> *Odour sweetish, blossom-like*
> *Patchy distribution in Europe, largely absent in northern Europe*

Gills grey-brown

Flesh sometimes reddening slightly

Inocybe cervinus

No common name (mushrooms with gills)
Cap 2–6 cm   June–October

This is sometimes the most common inocybe present in montane coniferous forests. It is quite easy to identify because of its cloudy, brown-red colour and the characteristic odour of old wine casks.

The Greenroot Fibrecap (*I. calamistrata*) also grows in montane coniferous forests. It is easy to identify by its blue-green stipe base.

Cap red-brown with rough scales

Habitat In moderately damp coniferous forests, usually on acidic, sandy soils, occasionally also under deciduous trees.

> *Spores earthy brown*
> *Odour mildewy, like old wine casks*
> *Common in Europe*

Flesh discolours slightly to brown-red

Stipe brownish-red, fibrous

Stipe slim, cylindrical

Inocybe dulcamara
No common name (mushrooms with gills)
Cap 2–6 cm   June–October

Habitat Along paths, on dumps and in gravel pits, primarily on dug ground, under deciduous trees or pines.

> Spores earthy brown
> Odour mildly acidic
> Common in Europe

This inocybe belongs to a group of species which have felted cap surfaces that do not split open and whose gills are an unusual olive colour. It does not have a bittersweet taste as the scientific name 'dulcamara' might suggest. The reason behind its name is unknown.

The only yellow-brown inocybe with a squarrose stipe is *Inocybe terrigena* which only grows on chalky soils.

Cap olive-yellow to brown-olive, felted

Stipe paler, fibrous

Gills olive when young

Stipe cylindrical

Collared Fibrecap
Inocybe cincinnata (mushrooms with gills)
Cap 2–4 cm   July–October

Habitat In coniferous forests on relatively alkaline soils or chalky areas, very occasionally found under deciduous trees.

> Spores earthy brown
> Odour acidic
> Common in Europe

The violet colours on the stipe tip are very important for identifying this species. If the mushroom's size and scaly cap are also taken into consideration, it will usually be possible to identify it clearly without the aid of a microscope. Like all inocybes, the Collared Fibrecap is poisonous.

Inocybe pusio grows under deciduous trees. It is the only species to have a longitudinally fibrous cap as well as a purple stipe.

Cap brown with prominent scales

Stipe tip pink-violet

Flesh whitish, violet on the stipe tip

Stipe cylindrical

White Fibrecap

Inocybe geophylla (mushrooms with gills)
Cap 1–3 cm   July–October

The White Fibrecap looks almost like a *Mycena* species (p. 97). Its silky cap, which becomes greasy in wet weather is also atypical for Inocybes. Viewed under a microscope, however, it becomes clear that it is, indeed, an inocybe.

Inocybe sindonia is almost as lightly-coloured but the hump on its cap is slightly scaly.

Habitat In deciduous and coniferous forests, on verges, on the banks of streams, no soil preferences.

> Spores earthy brown
> Odour acidic
> Very common throughout Europe

Did you know?

There are many varieties which are different shades of violet, some of which can turn ochre-yellow.

Gills strikingly clay brown

Stipe cylindrical

Cap white, with a silk-like sheen

181

Stipe whitish

Veiled Poisonpie

Hebeloma mesophaeum (mushrooms with gills)
Cap 2–5 cm   August–October

Habitat *No biotope preference, under deciduous or coniferous trees, particularly under young spruces.*

> *Odour radish-like*
> *Spores earthy brown*
> *Common in Europe*

It is often difficult to distinguish between the many different members of the *Hebeloma* genus. They are all cream-coloured with ochre to dark brown flesh and most have a radish-like odour. None of them are edible and some are known to be poisonous.

Did you know?

Mountaineers may come across Hebeloma bruchetii, which is also veiled. It only grows at heights greater than 1,800 m above sea level in symbiosis with creeping, alpine forests.

Gills earthy brown, attached, ascending

Stipe base darker

Cap dark brown, light fibrous covering on rim

A web-like veil is present between the cap rim and stipe of younger fruiting bodies. This is a key characteristic within the *Hebeloma* genus.

Stipe ochre-brown, darker towards base

Poisonpie

Hebeloma crustuliniforme (mushrooms with gills)
Cap 3–8 cm   August–October

If the weather is relatively wet, the gills of the Poisonpie can be seen 'weeping' in a similar way to those of the Weeping Widow (p. 156). This characteristic is common to a whole group of very closely related hebelomas and never occurs in any of the other species.

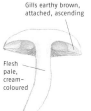

The thinner *Hebeloma velutipes* normally grows under willows, but also grows under other deciduous trees. The scales on its stipe tip are much finer.

Stipe beige with rough scales at the tip

Cap clay brown, smooth

Habitat *In parks, avenues, on dumps, less common in open forests, under decidu- ous trees, particularly in pioneer vegetation.*

> Odour radish-like
> Spores earthy brown
> Common in Europe

Gills earthy brown, attached, ascending

Flesh pale, cream- coloured

Hebeloma incarnatulum

No common name (mushrooms with gills)
Cap 3–8 cm   July–October

This mushroom cannot be identified by its long stipe alone. Positive identification is only possible if the mushroom's surroundings are taken into account. When it grows in moss beds on bogs, its stipe is long in order to keep the cap above the bog-dwelling plants. When it grows on defoliated areas, the mushroom's stipe is usually short.

Hebeloma helodes grows in similar, damp locations but always under deciduous trees. The centre of its cap is much darker and it is smaller.

Cap flesh-coloured, lighter at rim

Stipe beige, scaly at tip

Habitat *In damp coniferous forests and in bogs, on acidic, nutrient-poor soils, particularly under spruces.*

> Odour radish-like
> Spores earthy brown
> Patchy distribution in Europe, more common in the north

Flesh pale, cream-coloured

Stipe base thick, bulbous

Bitter Poisonpie

Hebeloma sinapizans (mushrooms with gills)
Cap 6–15 cm   August–October

Habitat *In deciduous forests and parks, also in gardens, on neutral to acidic soils, particularly under beeches.*

> *Odour radish-like*
> *Spores earthy brown*
> *Common in Europe*

It would be nice if this large, fleshy mushroom, which often grows in large numbers, were edible. Unfortunately it is not and causes severe food poisoning as well having a bitter taste.

This species usually grows in long rows or large rings.

Gills earthy brown

Stipe becomes hollow, downwards-pointing cone like structure inside tip

Cap completely flesh to red-brown

Stipe whitish with rough scales

184

Did you know?
Hebeloma laterinum *is often found on chalky soils under coniferous trees. It has a lighter-coloured cap with a grooved rim and a pleasant, flowery odour.*

Sweet Poisonpie

Hebeloma sacchariolens (mushrooms with gills)
Cap 3–8 cm   July–October

Both the English and scientific names provide clues about the unique odour of this mushroom. It has a particularly sweet odour, reminiscent of caramelised sugar. However, this does not indicate that it is edible!

Cap pinkish-brown, slightly darker in the centre

Gills broad, relatively distant

Brown to black discoloration occurs from the stipe base upwards on older fruiting bodies.

Habitat In deciduous forests, on neutral to alkaline, clay soils, often on areas with relatively poor drainage.

> *Odour sweetish*
> *Spores earthy brown*
> *Patchy distribution in Europe*

Flesh pale brownish

Stipe tapered

Rooting Poisonpie

Hebeloma radicosum (mushrooms with gills)
Cap 3–8 cm   July–October

The Rooting Poisonpie is fairly unique among the hebelomas in that it has a scaly cap and a skin-like ring. The method by which it receives nutrients is also unique. It uses its long root to reach the nitrate-rich droppings in under-ground mouse nests.

Cap beige, rim is scaly

Ring skin-like, solid

Habitat In deciduous and coniferous forests, on acidic, alkaline or neutral soils.

> *Odour marzipan-like*
> *Spores earthy brown*
> *Found throughout Europe*

Flesh pale brownish

Stipe rooting

Naucoria melinoides

No common name (mushrooms with gills)

Cap 2–5 cm   July–October

Habitat *In outcrops of alder trees, boggy areas or other damp areas in deciduous forests, always under alder trees.*

> Flesh slightly bitter
> Spores earthy brown
> Found throughout Europe

Many *Naucoria* species often grow in 'communities' under alder trees. It is not uncommon to find three, four or more different species growing in a group. However, none of them are edible since they taste bitter and at least a few of them are thought to be poisonous.

Cap yellow-brown, pale ochre-yellow when dry

Stipe yellow-brown with a paler fibres

Gills ochre-brown, attached, ascending

Flesh moist, brownish-yellow

One of the few *Naucoria* species that grows under willows instead of alders is *Naucorai salicis*.

Spectacular Rustgill

Gymnopilus junonius (mushrooms with gills)

Cap 6–15 cm   July–October

Habitat *In all forest types, prefers relatively warm conditions, grows on dead deciduous wood.*

> Taste bitter
> Spores light rust brown
> Patchy distribution in Europe, rare in some regions, more common in the south

The Spectacular Rustgill is unique among the *Gymnopilus* species in that it has a skin-like ring on its stipe and unusually large fruiting bodies. It can be distinguished from the Poplar Fieldcap (p. 161) by the fact that it is typically an orange-yellow colour.

Cap rust orange, domed

This species can easily be confused with the Golden Bootleg (p. 137) if its skin-like ring is not taken into account along with the fact that it grows on wood

Flesh yellowish-orange

Stipe ascending

Common Rustgill

Gymnopilus penetrans (mushrooms with gills)

Cap 2–7 cm   July–October

☠

The *Gymnopilus* species are a small group of brown-spored mushrooms with strikingly yellow gills. They are all bitter and some are even slightly poisonous. They are, therefore, of little interest to collectors of edible mushrooms. However, they are sometimes very common and are often confused with the Sheathed Woodtuft (p. 173) or the Conifer Tuft (p.166).

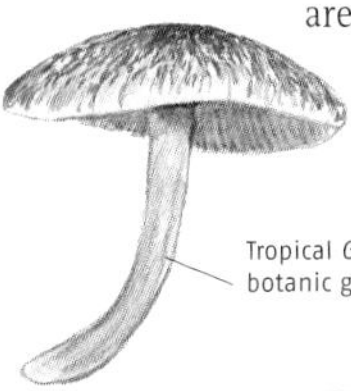

Tropical *Gymnopilus* species are sometimes found in botanic gardens, such as *Gymnoplius pupuratus*.

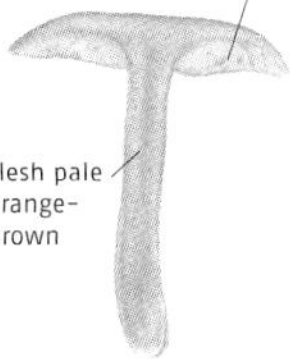

Habitat In all forest types, on dead coniferous wood and tree stumps, less common on deciduous wood.

> Taste bitter
> Spores light rust brown
> Common in Europe

Gills orange-yellow, attached, broad at base

Flesh pale orange-brown

187

Cap orange to rust brown

Stipe has white fibres

Did you know?

When older, the Common Rustgill can be identified by the rust-coloured flecks on its gills. When young, however, these flecks are orange-yellow.

Cinnamon Webcap

Cortinarius cinnamomeus (mushrooms with gills)
Cap 4–8 cm   August–October

Habitat *In coniferous forests, on embankments and verges, on acidic, sandy, nutrient-poor soils.*

> Spores rust brown
> Flesh yellowish
> Common in Europe

The Cinnamon Webcap is often used to dye wool in Scandinavia as it contains highly soluble pigments. This can also be observed at home by pressing a fruiting body against a paper tissue soaked in spirit. Depending on the species, the colours produced may include yellow, orange or red and sometimes the gills, flesh and velum produce different colours.

Cortinarius croceus grows in similar locations but can be distinguished by its gills which are golden when young.

Gills bright orange when young

Did you know?

The liquid from Cinnamon Webcaps boiled in brine can be used to dye wool different shades of red or yellow. Other species of mushroom exist which also contain pigments, such as the Velvet Rollrim and the Scaly Tooth.

Stipe wood-coloured to yellowish

Cap orange to red-brown

Bloodred Webcap

Cortinarius sanguineus (mushrooms with gills)
Cap 2–6 cm   August–October

It is usually only possible to identify *Cortinarius* species positively when the fruiting bodies are young. This is because the characteristic gill colour is covered by the rust-brown spores on older mushrooms. The Bloodred Webcap can be identified clearly because it is completely red. Some *Cortinarius* species, including this one, are highly poisonous!

Habitat In damp coniferous forests, usually on acidic, sandy, nutrient-poor soils.

> *Spores rust brown*
> *Flesh pale cherry red*
> *Common in Europe*

Stipe same colour

The larger Surprise Webcap (*C. semisanguineus*) has a yellow-brown cap and yellowish stipe and usually grows in relatively dry locations.

Gills blood red when young

Cap blood to brownish-red

Violet Webcap

Cortinarius violaceus (mushrooms with gills)
Cap 10–15 cm   August–October

The Violet Webcap is one of the few *Cortinarius* species which is easy to identify. The combination of its colour and cap surface is unmistakable. Although it is edible, it does not have a particularly exciting taste and is best eaten along with other edible mushrooms.

Habitat In dewy to damp coniferous forests, usually on acidic, nutrient-poor soils, rare in deciduous forests.

> *Spores rust brown*
> *Odour similar to cedar wood*
> *Relatively common in Europe*

The felted cap surface is a key characteristic.

Cap violet, felted

Stipe same colour

Flesh dark violet

Stipe base thick

Fool's Webcap
Cortinarius orellanus (mushrooms with gills)
Cap 4–8 cm   July–October

☠

Habitat *In warm, dry, mixed oak and pine forests, usually on slightly acidic, nutrient-poor soils.*

> Spores rust brown
> Odour slightly mushroomy
> Rare in Europe, becoming more common in some regions

Up until around 50 years ago, it was not known that any of the *Cortinarius* species were poisonous, let alone the fact that some are deadly poisonous. It was not until a few mass poisonings occurred in Poland at the end of the 1950s that more detailed analyses of these species were carried out. One of the poisons discovered in the Fool's Webcap was named orellanline which corresponds to the mushroom's scientific name. This poison attacks the kidneys.

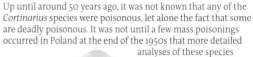

Cortinarius venetus is a similar shape, but it is completely yellow-green. Although it does not contain orellanine, it is still poisonous.

Flesh light orange-ochre

Gills vibrantly rust orange

Cap rust orange, slightly rough

Stipe brownish-yellow, smooth

Caution!
At a glance, very young specimens can be mistaken for small Chanterelles. It is therefore necessary to check each mushroom individually when you pick them.

Deadly Webcap

Cortinarius speciosissimus (mushrooms with gills)
Cap 4–8 cm   July–October

The Deadly Webcap is aptly named. Although there are no similar edible mushrooms, it is not uncommon to find this species growing around Trumpet Chanterelles (p. 243) which often grow in large numbers. Mushroom pickers must not allow the excitement of finding a group of Trumpet Chanterelles to cloud their judgement. Care must be taken to avoid mixing Deadly Webcaps with the edible mushrooms otherwise the consequences can be severe.

Habitat In Spruce and bog forests, on acidic, nutrient-poor soils.

> **Spores rust brown**
> **Odour slightly mushroomy**
> **Patchy distribution throughout Europe, less common in the south**

Caution!
Ignorance almost killed three youths in 2003. Although they were looking for hallucinogenic Liberty Caps (p. 165) they accidentally ate some Deadly Webcaps because of the similar cap shape. Kidney transplants saved all three at the last minute.

Gills rust brown

Flesh brownish-yellow

191

Cap rust orange, slightly rough, with a hump in the centre

Related species, such as the Sunset Webcap (*C. limonius*), are also all very poisonous.

Stipe same colour with a yellow, snakeskin-like pattern

Belted Slimy Cort
Cortinarius collinitus (mushrooms with gills)
Cap 5–12 cm July–Ocober

Habitat *In coniferous forests on acidic, nutrient-poor soils, always under spruces.*

> Spores rust brown
> Odour weak, not honey-like
> Common to patchy distribution in Europe, exceptionally common in some regions
> Similar species other Cortinarius *species with slimy stipes*

Gills brownish

Flesh pale, turning ochre-yellow from the stipe base upwards

A good rule of thumb is that *Cortinarius* species with slimy stipes and mild-tasting flesh are edible. The species with bitter-tasting flesh can easily be identified by tasting a sample. However, the fact that the slime layer on the stipe may dry out may make identification more difficult. If positive identification is impossible then mushrooms should not be picked or they should be taken to a mushroom expert.

Caution!
There are many similar, poisonous species of Cortinarius *which have slimy caps instead of slimy stipes such as the rare* Cortinarius camptoros.

192

Cap red to orange-brown, slimy

The Purple Stocking Webcap (*C. stillatitius*) tends to grow individually. It has an olive-brown cap and its stipe base gives off a honey-like odour.

Stipe same colour covered with a layer of violet slime

Yellow Webcap

Cortinarius delibutus (mushrooms with gills)

Cap 5–10 cm   July–October

This species is easy to identify by its violet-blue gills and the ochre-yellow slime on its stipe. However, even experts find it difficult to identify once the violet-blue colour has faded and dry weather makes the sliminess much less apparent.

Habitat *In various types of beech and coniferous forest, prefers acidic, nutrient-poor soils.*

> *Spores rust brown*
> *Odour mild, unspecific*
> *Common in Europe*

Cap yellow-brown, slimy

The far less common *Cortninarius salor* is one colour and can often be found under silver firs.

Stipe slightly bluish with an ochre-yellow slime layer

Flesh pale ochre-yellow

Gills remain violet for a long time

193

Cortinarius vibratilis

No common name (mushrooms with gills)

Cap 2–6 cm   July–October

Even touching the flesh of this mushroom with the tip of the tongue is enough to find out just how bitter it tastes. It is part of a group of *Cortinarius* species whose stipes are only slimy when it is rainy, which makes them quite hard to identify when the weather is dry.

Habitat *In damp coniferous forests, prefers acidic, nutrient-poor soils.*

> *Spores rusty brown*
> *Odour mild, unspecific*
> *Patchy distribution in Europe*

The only bitter-tasting *Cortinarius* with a violet-blue cap is *C. croceocaeruleus*. It grows in alkaline soils in Beech forests.

Cap orange-ochre, slimy

Stipe same colour, paler, often almost white

Flesh orange-ochre

Stipe base tapered

Goliath Webcap

Cortinarius praestans (mushrooms with gills)
Cap 15–25 cm   July–October

Habitat In deciduous forests under beeches, oaks or lime trees, on alkaline soils.

> **Spores** rusty brown
> **Odour** fresh, aromatic, cheese-like when dry
> **Patchy distribution** in southern Europe, rare north of the Alps
> **Similar species** *Cortinarius variecolor*

The Goliath Webcap is one of the few *Cortinarius* species that is a prized edible mushroom and is even sold at markets in southern Europe. Its popularity has less to do with its taste (which is quite average) than its size, as mature fruiting bodies can often weigh up to and in excess of 1.5 kilos. This mushroom has become quite rare in central Europe and should, therefore, not be picked in this region.

The common name for this mushroom relates to the extraordinary size to which the fruiting bodies can grow.

Flesh bluish in the upper part of the stipe

Gills blue–violet when young

Caution!

There are many brown and violet Cortinarius species, a few of which are thought to be poisonous. The most common of these is Cortinarius variecolor (p. 195).

Stipe white with violet tinges

Cap chocolate brown, slimy

Cortinarius variecolor

No common name (mushrooms with gills)

Cap 8–15 cm   July–October

Although some people find this mushroom's odour unbearable, even to the point of causing headaches in enclosed spaces, others can barely detect any odour. The 'dusty' odour is similar to that found in old, unused stables or barns.

Habitat In coniferous forests, particularly in hilly areas, prefers alkaline soils.

> **Odour strong, dusty**
> **Spore rusty brown**
> **Patchy distribution in Europe, common in Alpine regions**

Cap brown, remaining violet at the rim for some time

Flesh violet, fading rapidly

The otherwise similar Bruising Webcap (*C. purpurascens*) can be identified by the purple flecks which appear on its flesh of when it is touched.

Stipe thick, club-like

Stipe whitish with some hints of violet velum remnants

Mealy Bigfoot Webcap

Cortinarius caerulescens (mushrooms with gills)

Cap 6–12 cm   August–October

The blue-violet colour of many *Cortinarius* species fades rapidly. The blue colour of the Mealy Bigfoot Webcap quickly fades to ochre-yellow. Since it is often impossible to tell whether old specimens were once blue-violet, they must remain unpicked.

Habitat In beech forests, only on alkaline soils.

> **Odour slightly earthy, becoming stronger with age**
> **Spores rusty brown**
> **Patchy distribution in Europe, very rare towards the north**

One of the many similar, blue species is the Bitter Bigfoot Wecap (*C. sodagnitus*). It can be identified by the fact that it turns bright red when it comes into contact with lime potash.

Cap blue–violet with whitish to ochre-yellow velum remnants

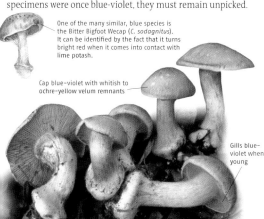

Flesh with bluish mottling, ochre-yellow in stipe base

Gills blue-violet when young

Stipe has a rimmed basal bulb

Splendid Webcap
Cortinarius splendens (mushrooms with gills)
Cap 6–12 cm   August–October

Habitat *In coniferous forests under spruces and firs and in deciduous forests under beeches and oaks, only on alkaline soils.*

> *Odour slightly aromatic to earthy, not floury*
> *Spores rusty brown*
> *Rare to patchy distribution in Europe, very rare in the north*

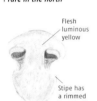

Flesh luminous yellow

Stipe has a rimmed basal bulb

It was not known that this mushroom is deadly poisonous until it poisoned 17 people in Lyon at the end of the 1970s. It had been confused with the Golden Tricholoma (p. 74) which also only seems to cause poisoning after it has been consumed a number of times. It has not yet been possible to determine which poison this mushroom contains but the substances it does contain are very similar to those in the Golden Tricholoma. Despite this uncertainty, this mushroom must be categorised as deadly poisonous.

Caution!
Despite the fact that the Golden Tricholoma is now classed as poisonous, many people still pick it. However, it is absolutely necessary to be able to distinguish it from the deadly poisonous Splendid Webcap.

There are many other species with yellow flesh and all of them are thought to be poisonous apart from *Cortinarius odorifer* (p. 197). The Olive Webcap (*C. atrovirens*) has the darkest coloured cap and also has a strong, peppery odour.

Gills vibrantly yellow when young

Centre of cap has olive-brown velum remnants

Cap sulphur yellow, slimy

Cortinarius multiformis (❨❅❩)
No common name (mushrooms with gills)
Cap 6–12 cm   August–October

The majority of *Cortinarius* species grow on alkaline soils. This species, however, grows on acidic soils in coniferous forests. It is also identifiable by its slightly bulbous stipe and its irregularly serrated gill blades. Although it is edible, it can easily be confused with many other species which are thought to be poisonous.

Habitat *In coniferous forests under firs, pines and spruces on relatively acidic soils.*

> **Odour usually slightly honey-like**
> **Spores rusty brown**
> **Patchy distribution throughout Europe**

Cap ochre-yellow with ingrown fibres

Stipe white with a silky, fibrous covering

Flesh pale, ochre-yellow in the stipe tip

Stipe thick, bulbous

The Birch Webcap (*C. triumphans*) can be identified by the obvious, yellow velum rings on its stipe. Its stipe is only slightly bulbous, its gills are violet when young and it only grows under birches.

Cortinarius odorifer ❅❅
No common name (mushrooms with gills)
Cap 6–12 cm   August–October

Although the strong, aniseed-like odour of this species is unique, there are at least a dozen other species which look very similar. Some are even deadly poisonous, such as the Splendid Webcap (p. 196).

Habitat *In coniferous forests under firs, pines and spruces on relatively acidic soils.*

> **Odour strong, aniseed-like**
> **Spores rusty brown**
> **Patchy distribution in Alpine regions, otherwise relatively rare**

Cap olive-grey, rapidly turning rust-coloured

Gills yellow when young

Flesh intensely lemon-coloured

Stipe has a rimmed basal bulb

Cortinarius elegantissimus grows under beeches and can be identified by, among other things, its earthy odour.

Contrary Webcap

Cortinarius varius (mushrooms with gills)

Cap 5–10 cm   August–October

Habitat In coniferous forests under firs, spruces and pines on chalky soils.

> Odour strong, aniseed-like
> Spores rusty brown
> Common in Alpine regions and some other regions, otherwise very rare
> Similar species other Cortinarius species

The Contrary Webcap is extremely common in some regions where it is often picked in large numbers for eating. While there is absolutely nothing wrong with this, it must be noted that of the 1,000 or so *Cortinarius* species in central Europe, there are many similar species which may or may not be poisonous.

The almost identical *Cortinarius variiformis* can be distinguished by the brownish velum remnants on its stipes and the fact that it grows under oaks. It is also thought to be edible.

Flesh white

Stipe thick, club-like

198

Caution!

Many Cortinarius *species look similar and only have minute differences. A few of them are known to be poisonous, including* Cortinarius glaucopus.

Cap orange-brown

Stipe pure white

Gills remain violet for some time

Cortinarius calochrous

No common name (mushrooms with gills)

Cap 4–8 cm   August–October

This mushroom represents a whole group of very similar species which all have the same colour of gills and a prominent rim on their basal bulbs. They are all thought to be poisonous.

Habitat In coniferous forests under spruces and firs and in deciduous forests under beeches and oaks, only on alkaline soils.

> **Odour mild, slightly aromatic**
> **Spores rusty brown**
> **Rare to patchy distribution in Europe**

Cap ochre to sulphur yellow, slimy

Cortinarius suaveolens can be distinguished by its strong odour of orange blossom.

Stipe whitish, violet towards top

Flesh pale yellow in cap, otherwise violet

Gills remain pinkish–violet for some time

 199

Bitter Webcap

Cortinarius infractus (mushrooms with gills)

Cap 5–10 cm   August–October

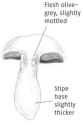

The Bitter Webcap is one of the most bitter-tasting mushrooms and even the feared Bitter Bolete is nothing by comparison. Merely touching the cap surface with the tip of the tongue will suffice as confirmation.

Habitat In coniferous forests under spruces and firs, less common in deciduous forests, on alkaline soils.

> **Flesh very bitter**
> **Spores rusty brown**
> **Patchy distribution in Europe**

Only *Cortinarius subtortus* has gills with a similar olive-grey colour. It only grows in boggy areas and has an odour of incense.

Cap dusky olive-grey, slimy

Gills typically olive-grey

Flesh olive-grey, slightly mottled

Stipe base slightly thicker

Gassy Webcap

Cortinarius traganus (mushrooms with gills)
Cap 5–10 cm   August–October

Habitat *In coniferous forests on acidic, nutrient-poor soils, especially among blueberries.*

> *Odour strong, sweet, like alcoholic spirits*
> *Spores rusty brown*
> *Patchy distribution in Europe*

The Gassy Webcap has a particularly broad stipe base. The diameter of the stipe base even exceeds that of the cap on some specimens.

Cap violet with silvery-white fibres

The Goatcheese Webcap (*C. camphoratus*) has an absolutely disgusting odour, reminiscent of billy goats. It can be distinguished by its violet flesh.

Gills rusty brown, even when young

Flesh brown-orange, mottled

Stipe base thick, club-like

200

Variable Webcap

Cortinarius anomalus (mushrooms with gills)
Cap 3–8 cm   August–October

Habitat *In coniferous forests on acidic, nutrient-poor soils, primarily under spruces.*

> *Stipe base cylindrical*
> *Spores rusty brown*
> *Common in Europe*

The colour of the velum remnants on the stipe is a key characteristic on all *Cortinarius* species. It is often very prominent, making it easy to spot. If it is not, as is usually the case, it may help to hold the fruiting body horizontally against the light and look down the stipe from the cap rim to the stipe base.

The Freckled Webcap (*C. spilomeus*) is slightly redder and can be distinguished by the fine, brown-red velum remnants on its stipe.

Cap beige-grey, shimmers slightly when dry

Cap blue-grey when wet, beige when dry

Stipe has ochre-yellow velum rings

Gills tender and violet when young

Gypsy Mushroom

Cortinarius caperatus (mushrooms with gills)

Cap 5–12 cm   August–October

The origins of this mushroom's common name are unknown. It used to be classed in a separate genus (*Rozites*) because of the skin-like velum ring on its stipe.

Only the Red Banded Webcap (*C. armillatus*) has such bright red velum rings. Although it is eaten by some, it cannot be recommended because of the substances it contains.

Habitat In coniferous forests, especially in heathery spruce forests, on dry, acidic, nutrient-poor soils, rarely under deciduous forests.

> Ring skin-like and solid
> Spores rusty brown
> Common in Europe but declining in many areas
> Similar species other *Cortinarius* species

Caution!

The Gypsy Mushroom may be confused with many *Cortinarius* species if the structure of the velum zone is not taken into account. Two such examples are C. patibilis *(left)* and the hygrophanous C. malachiu *(right)*.

Gills brownish

Flesh pale brownish

Cap ochre-brown with a light violet band in the centre

Stipe same colour with obvious, longitudinal fibres

Cortinarius acutus

No common name (mushrooms with gills)
Cap 1–3 cm   August–October

Habitat *In damp coniferous forests on acidic, nutrient-poor soils, primarily under spruces.*

> *Always grows in groups*
> *Spores rusty brown*
> *Common in Europe*

This is one of the smallest *Cortinarius* species although it is often found growing in large numbers in damp, mossy areas. Although it may appear similar to *Galerina* (p. 205) species at a glance, there are microscopic differences. There are hundreds of small, brown *Cortinarius* species.

Cap brown–orange, grooved, with a pointy hump

Flesh watery orange–brown

Stipe longer than cap diameter

Stipe same colour with white velum remnants

The slightly larger *Cortinarius albovariegatus* grows in very damp areas, usually in bogs. It occurs especially early in the year.

Earthy Webcap

Cortinarius hinnuleus (mushrooms with gills)
Cap 2–8 cm   August–October

Habitat *In deciduous forests, parks and gardens under various deciduous trees on relatively dry soils.*

> *Odour reminiscent of barn dust*
> *Spores rusty brown*
> *Common in Europe*

The Earthy Webcap has a prominent, white velum ring on its stipe when young, but unlike some species of *Cortinarius*, such as *C. acutus*, its cap is not hygrophanous.

Cap has a domed hump

Flesh pale brownish

Cortinarius brunneus is quite similar although it is a darker colour of brown. It grows in damp, acidic coniferous forests.

Cap orange–ochre, smooth

Gills distant

Wetted Cortinarius

Cortinarius evernius (mushrooms with gills)
Cap 2–6 cm   August–October

This mushroom gets its name from the fact that its cap is highly hygrophanous. It is thought to be poisonous and should not be picked.

Habitat *In damp coniferous forests on acidic soils under pines, firs and spruces.*

> **Odour mild, slightly earthy**
> **Spores rusty brown**
> **Patchy distribution in Europe, more common in some regions**

Cap red-brown, smooth, darker at the rim

Stipe violet with white fibres

The intensely violet *Cortinarius scutulatus* is closely related. Its velum is more prominent and has a radish-like odour.

Flesh becomes a darker and darker shade of violet towards the stipe base

Stipe base tapered

Pelargonium Webcap

Cortinarius flexipes (mushrooms with gills)
Cap 2–5 cm   August–October

Despite the wide range of colours displayed by the Pelargonium Webcap, from brown to violet-grey, its distinct odour of geraniums and the white velum rings around its stipe make it easy to identify.

Habitat *In coniferous forests on damp, acidic soils under spruces.*

> **Odour of geraniums**
> **Violet mycellium at stipe base**
> **Spores rusty brown**
> **Common in Europe**

Stipe covered with white flakes and velum rings

Cap has small, prominent scales

The Frosty Webcap (*C. hemitrichus*) only grows under birches.

Gills rusty brown with a hint of violet

Flesh violet in stipe tip

Funeral Bell
Galerina marginata (mushrooms with gills)
Cap 1–4 cm   (March) June–December

☠

Habitat *On dead, moderately rotten coniferous and deciduous wood, also on bark mulch or on buried wood.*

> **Odour usually slightly floury**
> **Spores rusty brown**
> **Common in Europe**

The Funeral Bell is deadly poisonous and contains the same poison as the Deathcap. It grows primarily in low-lying areas under coniferous and deciduous trees. Caution must be exercised as it has been found growing on the same piece of wood as the highly edible Sheathed Woodtuft (p. 173).

Galerina sideroides has a characteristic white covering on its stipe. It is also thought to be poisonous.

Flesh brownish

Gills rusty brown

Did you know?
The Funeral Bell often appears to be growing out of the ground. In such cases, it usually found in-dividually and so is less likely to be confused with the Sheathed Woodtuft (p. 173). However, it grows in thick clumps on bark mulch which greatly increases the danger of confusion.

204

Cap brown, hygrophanous, slightly grooved

Stipe white, ringed, with longitudinal fibres

Bog Bell
Galerina paludosa (mushrooms with gills)
Cap 1–3 cm   July–October

Cap honey brown, grooved

This species is one of very few mushrooms which are able to survive in the middle of bogs. It is common and can be found in just about every bog by those who are willing to brave the treacherous conditions underfoot. It can often be found growing in unison with the equally common Sphagnum Greyling (p. 84).

White, snakeskin-like pattern on stipe

Phaeogalera stagnina is much less common and also only ever grows in bogs.

Gills rusty brown

Stipe much longer than cap diameter

Habitat In bogs and damp coniferous forests, always in bogs covered with sphagnum (the mushroom is connected to this moss).

> *Cap covered by white velum when young*
> *Spores rusty brown*
> *Common in Europe*

Hairy Leg Bell
Galerina vittiformis (mushrooms with gills)
Cap 1–3 cm   July–October

Not much is known about the toxicity of this species and other small *Galerina* species. It is thought to be harmless and children who have eaten this mushroom have not suffered any ill effects. However, there are so many highly poisonous *Galerina* species that it is not advisable to eat any of them.

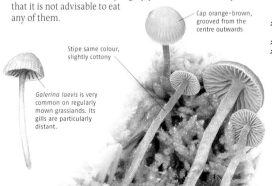

Cap orange-brown, grooved from the centre outwards

Stipe same colour, slightly cottony

Galerina laevis is very common on regularly mown grasslands. Its gills are particularly distant.

Cap surface glistens, grooved from the centre outwards

Habitat On mossy grassland in forests and in the open, no particular biotope preferences.

> *Cap and stipe slightly cottony*
> *Spores rusty brown*
> *Common in Europe*

False Saffron Milkcap

Lactarius deterrimus (mushrooms with gills)

Cap 5–10 cm   July–October

Habitat In forests, nurseries and on verges, always under spruces, usually on alkaline soils.

> Odour slightly tart, woody
> Spores light ochre
> Common throughout Europe
> Similar species Birch Milkcap

As a rule of thumb, all *Lactarius* species which exude an orange latex are edible. However, the quality varies somewhat. While the False Saffron Milkcap tastes slightly resinous, the Blood Milkcap (p. 207) tastes very good. *Lactarius* mushrooms can be fried quickly like a medium steak, pickled in vinegar or put into salads and soups. They are not, however, suitable for stewing or steaming. Eating *Lactarius* mushrooms dyes the urine red, but this is a perfectly normal and harmless side effect!

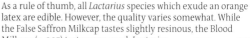

The latex from *Lactarius semisanguifluus* changes colour even more rapidly within 5–7 minutes. It only grows on chalky soils under pines.

Stipe cottony, becoming hollow

Latex orange, becomes blood red after 15 minutes

Caution Poisonous!

The Birch Milkcap (left, p. 208) causes food poisoning if pre-pared normally and the Larch Lactarius (right, L. porninsis) be-comes bitter. Although they both look very similar to the edible Lactarius species from above, they can be distinguished by the white latex they exude.

Stipe has no dimples

Cap orange, with more or less distinct zones, funnel-shaped

Saffron Milkcap

Lactarius deliciosus (mushrooms with gills)

Cap 5–10(12) cm   July–October

The latex of the Saffron Milkcap turns green within a day of exposure to the air, rather than turning dark red. It can easily be identified by the silvery sheen on its cap, reminiscent of a dried snail trail.

Habitat *In pine forests on relatively acidic, sandy soils but also on shell limestone on Juniper heaths.*

The Stone Milkcap (*L. salmonicolor*) is completely salmon pink and has no green discoloration. It only grows under Silver Firs and its latex turns dark red after 1–2 hours.

> *Fruiting bodies robust with thick flesh*
> *Spores pale ochre*
> *Common throughout Europe*

Stipe dimpled

Cap orange with water spots and silvery zones

Latex orange, initially unchanging, turns green within a day

Stipe robust, short, becoming hollow

Blood Milkcap

Lactarius sanguineus (mushrooms with gills)

Cap 6–15 cm   July–October

This mushroom is the best tasting of all the edible *Lactarius* species and is most common in southern Europe. Although it is the most commonly sold wild mushroom in Spain, it is usually quite rare in central and northern Europe and is even protected in some countries.

Habitat *On the boundaries of pine forests and on juniper heaths, prefers warmer conditions, only grows on shell limestone.*

Sometimes mildewy Blood Milkcaps are found which have a white layer where their gills are normally located. They are particularly firm and taste very good indeed.

> *Fruiting bodies robust with thick flesh*
> *Spores pale ochre*
> *Common in southern Europe, rare to patchy distribution north of the Alps*

Stipe pale violet

Cap orange, fading rapidly

Latex remains blood red throughout

Woolly Milkcap
Lactarius torminosus (mushrooms with gills)
Cap 5–10 cm   July–October

Habitat *In various types of forest, in avenues, gardens and parks, always under birches, usually on alkaline soils.*

> Latex white, unchanging
> Flesh white, hot-tasting
> Spores pale cream-coloured
> Common throughout Europe, particularly in the north and east

As with all hot-tasting *Lactarius* mushrooms, this species is inedible if prepared normally and can cause serious food poisoning in some individuals. However, it can be made edible by ensilaging or by lactic acid fermentation. Both methods are common in eastern Europe and Scandinavia.

The Bearded Milkcap (*L. pubescens*) looks like a paler version of the Woolly Milkcap. It often grows in parks and gardens and it is unusual to find it growing in forests.

Cap rim rolled up with a thick fringe

Did you know?
Where birches and pines are found growing together, poisonous Woolly Milkcaps (right) and edible Saffron Milkcaps (left) can also sometimes be found growing in unison. The colour of the latex is a key factor for identifying them positively.

Stipe pale salmon pink

Cap pink-orange, zoned, usually slightly recessed

Velvety Milkcap

Lactarius lignyotus (mushrooms with gills)
Cap 4–8 cm   July–October

The Velvety Milkcap and the Tawny Milkcap (p. 218) are the only two edible *Lactarius* mushrooms which exude a white latex. All of the others have a bitter or hot taste and some are even poisonous. Unusually, both of these species can be eaten raw and taste excellent with some salt in sandwiches.

Lactarius picinus has a smooth stipe tip and a velvety cap with no wrinkles. It also grows in coniferous forests in mountainous regions and tastes slightly bitter.

Caution!
There are other Lactarius *mushrooms which exude a latex which turns pink and all of them have a hot or bitter taste. Most of them have a lighter coloured stipe and grow in deciduous forests such as* L. pterosporus.

Habitat In semi-natural, damp forests in mountainous regions, always under spruces.

> Latex white, turning pink
> Flesh mild
> Spores cream-coloured
> Patchy distribution throughout Europe, more common in some regions

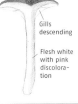

Gills descending

Flesh white with pink discoloration

209

Cap brown–black, slightly wrinkled

Stipe tip grooved

Stipe dark brown

Purple Staining Milkcap ✕

Lactarius uvidus (mushrooms with gills)
Cap 3–7 cm   July–October

Habitat *In semi-natural, damp forests in mountainous regions and on the fringes of bogs, always under birches or spruces.*

> **Latex white at first then violet**
> **Flesh mild at first, then becoming hot-tasting**
> **Spores pale cream-coloured**
> **Common in northern Europe otherwise uncommon to patchy distribution**

The white latex exuded by this mushroom turns an unusual violet after a few minutes and is often only noticed by collectors once they have unpacked their mushrooms at home.

Cap grey, very slimy when wet

Stipe whitish

Stipe becomes hollow

Flesh white with violet discoloration

Lactaria violascens is characterised by its dry, solid fruiting bodies and the fact that it occurs on chalky soils in deciduous forests. It is close to extinction in Europe.

Yellow Bearded Milkcap ☠

Lactarius repraesentaneus (mushrooms with gills)
Cap 6–15(20) cm   July–October

Habitat *In semi-natural, damp forests in mountainous regions and on the fringes of bogs, always under birches or spruces.*

> **Latex white, violet when dry**
> **Flesh tastes very hot**
> **Spores pale cream-coloured**
> **Common in northern Europe otherwise uncommon**

This handsome mushroom is picked in large quantities in northern and north-eastern Europe. Salt is added and the mushrooms are placed in casks or ensilaged. These hot-tasting mushrooms are a delicacy in Finland and are even more popular than boletes. However, if prepared normally, they are inedible and possibly even poisonous.

Lactarius citriolens grows in deciduous forests. It can be identified by its latex which turns yellow and its slight odour of lemon balm.

Cap ochre-yellow, greasy

Scales prominent, same colour as cap

Stipe dimpled

Flesh white with violet discoloration

Cap rim shaggy

Lactarius scrobiculatus

No common name (mushrooms with gills)
Cap 8–20 cm   July–October

This large and striking mushroom can occupy large areas of ground in mountain pine forests. Its Latin name means 'pock-marked' or 'pitted' and refers to the many dimples present on the stipe. Although many *Lactarius* mushrooms display this characteristic, it is particularly apparent on this species.

Lactarius intermedius is relatively rare and only grows under silver firs. It is paler, hardly has any zoning on its cap and the fringe on the cap rim is the same colour as its cap.

Habitat In relatively dry coniferous forests on chalky soils, primarily in higher locations, always under spruces.

> **Flesh tastes very hot**
> **Spores pale cream-coloured**
> **Patchy distribution in Europe, common in some regions**

Cap yellow-ochre, zoned

Latex white, rapidly discolouring to lemon yellow

Cap rim has a darker coloured fringe

Stipe grooved

Lactarius acerrimus

No common name (mushrooms with gills)
Cap 6–12 cm   July–September

Occasionally, fruiting bodies grow in a twisted, crooked fashion, for example, when they encounter obstacles. However, this is a key characteristic of this mushroom since it always has an irregular shape, even when there are no obstacles which might hinder its growth.

Habitat Primarily in parks, open deciduous forests and open woodland, usually under oaks.

> **Flesh tastes very hot**
> **Spores pale cream-coloured**
> **Patchy distribution in Europe**

Gills cross-linked

Lactarius insulsus is never crooked and has particularly regular zoning on its cap.

Cap orange-ochre, zoned

Flesh and latex whitish

Stipe short, crooked

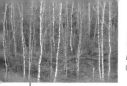

Lilacscale Milkcap

Lactarius spinosulus (mushrooms with gills)

Cap 2–5 cm   August–October

Habitat *In parks and open deciduous forests, particularly on acidic soils, only under birches.*

> Flesh hot-tasting
> Spores pale cream-coloured
> Rare to very patchy distribution in Europe

The prominent scales on this mushroom's cap are very unusual for *Lactarius* species and are only found on this species in Europe. Most *Lactarius* mushrooms have smooth or felted caps and it is less common for them to have shaggy scales.

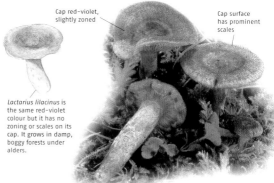

Cap red-violet, slightly zoned

Cap surface has prominent scales

Lactarius lilacinus is the same red-violet colour but it has no zoning or scales on its cap. It grows in damp, boggy forests under alders.

Gills descending slightly

Flesh and latex whitish

Fenugreek Milkcap

Lactarius helvus (mushrooms with gills)

Cap 5–12 cm   July–October

Habitat *In damp to boggy coniferous forests, less common on dry heath land, under pines and spruces.*

> Flesh mild
> Latex clear, watery
> Odour similar to lovage
> Spores whitish
> Common in northern Europe, rare to patchy distribution in the south

This noticeably aromatic mushroom causes serious food poisoning if it is eaten fresh. However, once it has been dried and ground to a powder, it makes a good seasoning. Caution is, however, advised since this is the only mild-tasting *Lactarius* mushroom which is poisonous.

The Curry Milkcap (*L. camphoratus*) also develops an aroma of seasoning once dried. When it is dry it has a relatively tart aroma and is less suitable for use as a seasoning.

Cap leather brown, felted

Flesh creamy-white

Gills light ochre, broad at base

Ugly Milkcap

☠

Lactarius turpis (mushrooms with gills)
Cap 4–10 cm   July–October

Although the Ugly Milkcap is edible if prepared in certain ways and is often picked in eastern Europe, it has recently been found to contain carcinogenic substances. As such, it is advisable to avoid picking it. It is also poisonous if steamed or cooked like other mushrooms.

Habitat *In all types of deciduous and coniferous forests, particularly on acidic, nutrient-poor soils under spruces or birches.*

Young specimens have striking chrome yellow felt on the cap rim. It turns an intense pink-violet colour on contact with lime potash.

Gills crowded

> *Flesh tastes very hot*
> *Spores pale cream-coloured*
> *Common in Europe*

Gills creamy-white

Stipe becomes hollow

Cap dark olive, smooth

Beech Milkcap

✗

Lactarius blennius (mushrooms with gills)
Cap 4–8 cm   July–October

The Beech Milkcap is one of the most common mushrooms found growing around beeches. This species has begun to develop root symbioses with lime trees in eastern Europe where beech forests are on the decline. Strangely enough, this has never been observed in central Europe.

Habitat *In various types of beech forest or under beeches in other types of forest, no particular preferences.*

The Pale Milkcap (p. 216) also only grows under beeches.

> *Flesh hot-tasting*
> *Spores cream-coloured*
> *Common in Europe*

Stipe pale grey, smooth

Cap greenish-grey with water spots

Gills creamy-white

Latex grey-green when dry

Lactarius circellatus

No common name (mushrooms with gills)

Cap 8–15 cm   July–October

Habitat In open deciduous forests, parks and gardens, only under hornbeams, prefers alkaline soils.

> Latex white, grey-green when dry
> Tastes hot
> Spores cream-coloured
> Patchy distribution in Europe, common in Alpine regions

All *Lactarius* mushrooms grow in root symbiosis with trees. Quite a few of them have no particular preference with regard to the species of their host tree. This is the only *Lactarius* mushroom which only grows together with hornbeams.

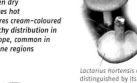

Lactarius hortensis can be distinguished by its more widely spaced gills, its only slightly zoned cap and the fact that it only grows under hazel trees. It is one of the most hot-tasting *Lactarius* mushrooms.

Cap zoned

Gills ochre, crowded

Flesh whitish

Gills broad at base

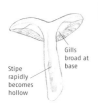

Northern Milkcap

Lactarius trivialis (mushrooms with gills)

Cap 6–12(15) cm   August–October

Habitat In damp coniferous forests and in bogs, usually under spruces.

> Latex white, grey-green when dry
> Tastes hot
> Spores cream-coloured
> Common in northern Europe, distribution otherwise patchy, rare in the south

This is the most popular edible mushroom in Finland. The mushrooms are chopped roughly and placed in water for 24 hours. They are mixed with salt and layered in casks before being left for 6-8 weeks. The mushrooms are then ready just in time for Christmas.

The pretty bluish colour of young specimens fades quickly and older specimens are usually completely ochre.

Cap blue-violet when young, greasy

Gills ochre, crowded

Gills broad at base

Stipe rapidly becomes hollow

Coconut Milkcap

Lactarius glyciosmus (mushrooms with gills)
Cap 2–5 cm   July–October

This mushroom looks very similar to many other species and does not seem to have any particularly unique characteristics. Its odour, however, is unique. No other mushroom has such a coconut-like odour. Despite this pleasant aroma, its hot taste makes it inedible.

Habitat *In all types of forest, on embankments, in parks and avenues, on dry, relatively acidic, nutrient-poor soils, only under birches.*

Cap pinkish-brown, dry

> Latex remains white
> Tastes hot
> Spores cream-coloured
> Found in central and northern Europe, rare in the south

Lactarius mammosus has the same odour but it is much weaker and is only detectable once the mushroom has been dried. It grows under spruces in mountainous regions.

Flesh whitish

Gills creamy-white, descending slightly

Alder Milkcap

Lactarius obscuratus (mushrooms with gills)
Cap 1–4 cm   July–October

This *Lactarius* mushroom usually remains very small and, at a glance, is extremely similar to the Deceiver (p. 55) which is often found growing in the same locations. Once alder milkcaps have become so dry that they no longer exude a latex, their flesh is fragile rather than fibrous, making them identifiable as a *Lactarius* species.

Habitat *In boggy alder forests and lowland forests, on the banks of streams lined with alders and in damp hollows in other types of forest, always under alders.*

Cap rim grooved

The preferred host tree is the Common Elder (*Alnus glutinosa*), recognisable by the notched appearance of its leaves.

Cap orange-brown, sometimes with a hint of olive

> Latex remains white
> Tastes almost mild
> Spores whitish
> Patchy distribution throughout Europe, slightly more common in the north and north east

Gills ascending, broad at base

Flesh creamy-orange

Oakbug Milkcap

Lactarius quietus (mushrooms with gills)
Cap 3–8 cm   July–October

Habitat In oak forests and parks, on acidic soils and only under oaks.

> **Latex white, turning cream-coloured**
> **Tastes slightly hot, bitter**
> **Spores creamy-white**
> **Common throughout Europe**

This *Lactarius* mushroom has a strong odour which can only be described as 'insect-like.' Although other mushrooms give off a similar odour, the Oakbug Milkcap is very common and is best characterised by it.

Cap dull fleshy to red-brown, zoned to varying degrees

Stipe same colour as cap

Flesh red-brown towards stipe base

Gills broad at base

The Yellowdrop Milkcap (*L. chrysorrheus*) grows in similar locations and can be identified by the yellow discoloration of its latex. It looks extremely similar to the Saffron Milkcap (p. 207).

Pale Milkcap

Lactarius pallidus (mushrooms with gills)
Cap 5–10 cm   August–October

Habitat In beech forests on neutral to alkaline, relatively dry soils, only under beeches.

> **Latex white, hardly any discoloration**
> **Tastes slightly hot**
> **Spores cream-coloured**
> **Uncommon throughout Europe, absent in the north and east**

The Pale Milkcap usually grows in large numbers and often forms rings or rows. However, the biotopes in which it grows are being seriously affected by acid rain and nitrogen from the air. The sudden disappearance of many mushroom species often becomes apparent long before any damage to plants and trees becomes noticeable.

Lactarius albocarneus has very special requirements and only grows on chalky soils under silver firs. It has the thickest slime layer of all *Lactarius* mushrooms.

Cap flesh-coloured, smooth, greasy

Flesh pale cream-coloured

Gills distant

Stipe same colour as cap

Rufous Milkcap

Lactarius rufus (mushrooms with gills)

Cap 4–8 cm   July–November

Despite its hot taste, people in some regions pick the Rufous Milkcap because it grows in large numbers late in the year. They can be used to make an excellent mushroom goulash if left to soak in water for 24 hours before being pressed and fried.

Lactarius hysginus is a similar colour but has a sticky, dirty-looking cap surface.

Habitat *In coniferous forests on acidic, usually sandy soils, primarily under spruces and pines.*

> Latex white
> Tastes very hot
> Spores pale cream-coloured
> Found throughout Europe

Did you know?

It is difficult to distinguish between the many similar looking red-brown Lactarius *mushrooms. One particular exception is* L. badiosanguineus *which has orange-ochre gills.*

Flesh whitish to pale cream-coloured

Cap has a small hump in the centre

Cap dull red-brown, no zoning

Stipe roughly same colour as cap

Weeping Milkcap

Lactarius volemus (mushrooms with gills)
Cap 6–12 cm   June–October

Habitat *In open deciduous forests, less common in coniferous forests, on neutral to mildly acidic soils.*

> *Odour fish-like after a while*
> *Taste mild, sweetish*
> *Spores pale cream-coloured*
> *Patchy distribution throughout Europe, has been on the decline for many years*

The Weeping Milkcap can be eaten raw with a little salt sprinkled on to its gills or it can be fried. It should be fried as if it were a medium steak, otherwise it becomes dry and chewy. Care should be taken when picking the mushroom to avoid bruising it so it does not lose any of its latex. Caution is also advised when handling the mushroom as its latex causes brown staining which is very difficult to remove from hands and clothes and it also leaves a fishy odour after a while.

The edible and very similar looking *Lactarius rugatus* is the southern European equivalent of the Weeping Milkcap. However, it does not develop a fishy odour and its gills are more distant.

Fruiting bodies solid

Gills become flecked with brown

Did you know?

Although other red-brown Lactarius *mushrooms may not be poisonous, confusion would lead to culinary disappointment! The most similar species is the Tawny Milkcap (p. 219) which looks like a miniature version of the Weeping Milkcap.*

218

Cap rich orange-brown

Cap rim often has a concentric grain

Stipe roughly same colour as cap

Tawny Milkcap

Lactarius fulvissimus (mushrooms with gills)
Cap 3–8 cm   June–October

Experts have been trying to categorise this mushroom into different species for years because its cap colour and habitat are so variable. However, there were always crossovers and exceptions to the characteristics that were to be used to class each different 'species.' As such, these mushrooms are now classed in one species, no matter whether they have dark or light caps with or without yellow rims, or are found in coniferous or deciduous forests.

Cap colour varies considerably depending on moisture and location.

Habitat *In deciduous and coniferous forests on neutral to alkaline soils, also in parks and gardens.*

> **Taste mild to very hot**
> **Spores pale cream-coloured**
> **Found throughout Europe**

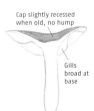

Cap slightly recessed when old, no hump

Gills broad at base

Did you know?

Lactarius rubrocinctus *is a similar species and has a red zone on its stipe tip. Unfortunately, this is not always so apparent. It also tastes quite hot and tastes bitter after cooking.*

Cap orange to chestnut brown

Cap rim has large or small grooves (key characteristic!)

Birch Milkcap
Lactarius tabidus (mushrooms with gills)
Cap 2–6 cm   July–October

Habitat *In damp coniferous forests and in boggy areas, on acidic soils, primarily under birches and oaks.*

> **Tastes slightly hot**
> **Latex white, creamy-yellow when dry**
> **Spores pale cream-coloured**
> **Common throughout Europe**

The Birch Milkcap's appearance is reminiscent of some clitocybes (p. 60) because of its irregular, wavy cap. The discoloration of its latex to cream-yellow is best observed by dabbing a freshly cut section of the mushroom on a paper tissue and waiting for a minute or so.

Cap pinkish-brown with a paler rim

Stipe same colour as cap

Cap slightly recessed when old, irregular

Gills broad at base

Lactarius sphagneti prefers even damper conditions and has a darker, greasy, shiny cap. Its biotope preferences mean that it has become endangered.

Mild Milkcap
Lactarius subdulcis (mushrooms with gills)
Cap 2–6 cm   August–October

Habitat *In beech forests and parks on moderately acidic to alkaline soils, only under beeches.*

> **Taste bitter, astringent**
> **Latex white**
> **Spores pale cream-coloured**
> **Common throughout Europe**

Despite its name, this mushroom tastes bitter and swallowing a piece of it will cause irritation to the back of the throat. The Latin name 'sub-dulcis,' or 'almost mild' is more apt and refers to the fact that it does not taste as hot as some of the other *Lactarius* mushrooms.

Cap dull pinkish-brown, often light olive

Stipe same colour as cap

Flesh pale cream-coloured

Gills broad at base

Lactarius cremor can be distinguished by its almost transparent, whitish latex and its insect-like odour.

Peppery Milkcap

(¶¶)

Lactarius piperatus (mushrooms with gills)

Cap 6–12 cm   July–October

Despite this mushroom's hot taste, many people like to eat it fried or cooked under a grill. It is not to everyone's liking as it still tastes tart to bitter after it is cooked.

Lactarius pargamenus is a further, extremely similar species. Its latex turns green when it dries and turns orange on contact with lime potash.

Habitat In deciduous forests, less common in coniferous forests, prefers neutral to alkaline (clay) soils, sometimes in acidic conditions.

> **Tastes very hot**
> **Latex white, scarce**
> **Spores white**
> **Common throughout Europe, on the decline**

Did you know?

The Fleecy Milkcap (p. 222) cannot be made edible, even after frying it intensively. It can easily be distinguished from the Peppery Milkcap (left) by its more distant gills (right).

Stipe narrows towards base

Gills slender, milky-white

Cap milky white

221

Stipe white

Gills extremely crowded

Fleecy Milkcap
Lactarius vellereus (mushrooms with gills)
Cap 8–25(30) cm   July–October

✗✗

Habitat In coniferous or deciduous forests, prefers neutral to alkaline soils, usually under beeches, spruces and oaks.

> **Taste mild**
> **Latex white, scarce**
> **Spores white**
> **Common throughout Europe**

The size of this mushroom varies considerably. Most specimens have a cap diameter of between 12 and 20 cm. However, giant specimens with cap diameters of 30 cm or more and dwarves with cap diameters of no more than 8 cm are not uncommon. *Lactarius bertillonii* looks identical but has an acrid-tasting latex.

Gills distant

Cap milky white, suede-like

Gills slender, milky white

Stipe short

Stipe white

The rare Willow Milkcap (*L. controversus*) only grows under willows. It is of roughly the same size and stature but has crowded gills and pale pink flecks on its cap.

222

Milk White Brittlegill
Russula delica (mushrooms with gills)
Cap 5–12 cm   June–October

🍴

Habitat In deciduous forests, rarely found in coniferous forests, prefers alkaline, clay soils.

> **Odour fruity, slightly fishy**
> **Spores whitish**
> **Common throughout Europe**

Only the Milk White Brittlegill and the Blackening Brittlegill have intermediate gills, i.e. gills which do not extend from the stipe to the cap rim, but end halfway between the stipe and the cap rim. Other *Russula* mushrooms only occasionally have intermediate gills or have none at all. Although the Milk White Brittlegill is edible, it does not taste particularly good.

Specimens are often found with greenish-blue zone at the stipe tip and sea green gills. They are categorised as var. *chloroides*.

Gills distant with intermediate gills

Cap whitish to cream-coloured, dry

Flesh whitish

Stipe white, short

Blackening Brittlegill

Russula nigricans (mushrooms with gills)

Size 5–12 cm   June–October

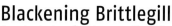

Most mushroom guides unfairly class the edibility of this mushroom as mediocre to inedible. However, young specimens taste excellent when fried together with some bacon and onions. This mushroom is very common and easy to identify by its strikingly thick, widely spaced gills.

Mature, completely black fruiting bodies growing in damp areas are often infested by another mushroom with gills called the Silky Piggyback (*Nyctalis parasitica*).

Habitat In deciduous and coniferous forests, no particular preferences.

> *Taste slightly fruity, like wine barrels*
> *Flesh mild*
> *Spores white*
> *Common throughout Europe*
> *Similar species Crowded Brittlegill*

Flesh reddens (turns black after a few hours)

Cap brown, turning black after some time

223

Gills very distant, thick

Caution!

The gills of the inedible Crowded Brittlegill (R. densifolia) are much more crowded and its flesh has a hot taste. It usually grows in acidic soils in coniferous forests.

Stinking Brittlegill
Russula foetens (mushrooms with gills)
Size 5–12 cm   June–November

Habitat In coniferous and deciduous forests, no particular preferences.

> Odour unpleasant, reminiscent of burning rubber
> Flesh tastes very hot
> Spores cream-coloured
> Common throughout Europe

The name 'Stinking Brittlegill' is an apt one. Its unpleasant odour is usually enough to discourage anyone from picking it. There are, however, many similar species which have a pleasant odour of bitter almonds. Nevertheless, they are all slightly poisonous and taste very hot if eaten raw.

Russula illota has dark dots and dashes on its gill blades which look almost like Morse code.

Cap yellow to ochre-brown, greasy when damp

Cap rim grooved when young

Flesh chambered in stipe

Camembert Brittlegill
Russula amoenolens (mushrooms with gills)
Size 3–8 cm   June–October

Habitat On dry, nutrient-poor, acidic, sandy soils, primarily under oaks.

> Flesh tastes hot
> Stipe rapidly becomes chambered
> Spores pale cream-coloured
> Patchy distribution in Europe

All *Russula* mushrooms with heavily grooved cap rims have a disgusting, hot, rubber-like taste. They always have a strong, unpleasant odour.

The Scallop Brittlegill (*R. pectinatoides*) also grows under oaks on clay soils in parks and bright forests.

Cap yellow to olive-grey, brown

Stipe white

Cap rim heavily grooved

Ochre Brittlegill
Russula ochroleuca (mushrooms with gills)

Size 3–8 cm   June–October

The Ochre Brittlegill is often the only mushroom to be seen in spruce forests in the summer months and occurs in large numbers even when the weather is dry. Although it is edible, its taste varies from being mild to very hot. It is best to avoid the hot and spicy specimens since they taste quite bitter after being cooked. Tasting a small sample from the gills will help in ascertaining this.

The colour of the gills and cap rim on the Ochre Brittlegill contrast sharply, whereas they are one colour on the Geranium Brittlegill.

Habitat *In spruce forests and other coniferous forests on acidic soils, under lone spruces in mixed deciduous forests, very occasionally under beeches.*

> *Stipe turns slightly grey*
> *Spores pale cream-coloured*
> *Common in Europe*
> *Similar species Geranium Brittlegill*

Caution!

Viewed from above, the very hot-tasting Geranium Brittlegill (R. fellea) looks very similar. However, its gills are light ochre and it has a strong, fruity odour. It usually grows under beeches, although is sometimes found in spruce forests.

Flesh whitish, light ochre in the stipe base

   225

Gills white, contrasting with the cap rim

Cap ochre-yellow with some patches of olive

Russet Brittlegill
Russula mustelina (mushrooms with gills)
Size 6–15 cm   June–October

🍴

Habitat *In coniferous forests in mountainous regions, on acidic soils, always under spruces.*

> **Taste nutty**
> **Spores pale cream-coloured**
> **Relatively common in the more mountainous regions of Europe**

Many mushroom collectors throw these mushrooms away after having mistaken them for Ceps. This is very unfortunate since the Russet Brittlegill is one of the best edible mushrooms and many prefer it to the Cep.

Cap yellow to nut brown, smooth

Gills cream-coloured

Flesh white, hard, slightly chambered in the stipe

Russula consobrina is dark brown and is much more common in northern Europe. It has a very hot taste.

Velvet Brittlegill
Russula violeipes (mushrooms with gills)
Size 5–10 cm   June–October

🍴

Habitat *In deciduous forests, less common in coniferous forests, prefers acidic soils.*

> **Cap finely frosted when young**
> **Odour becomes increasingly fishy**
> **Spores cream-coloured**
> **Relatively common in Europe, less common in the south**

The variation in the colour of this mushroom's cap is astonishing. It could be compared to the spectrum of colours seen in blueberry sauce with custard. The rule of thumb is that all *Russula* mushrooms with a fishy odour are edible. However, this may be misleading since typical odours are often absent from young specimens and they are often completely yellow, which makes them harder to identify.

Cap colours are a mixture of yellows and violets

A greenish-yellow variant (var. *citrina*) also exists and has no violet colouring whatsoever.

Gills cream-colored

The stipe often has purple discoloration

The Flirt
Russula vesca (mushrooms with gills)
Size 5–12 cm   June–October

Although all mild tasting russulas are edible, their quality varies. The Flirt is one of the best but unfortunately, it only grows individually. The species is in decline due to the increasing nitrogen-enrichment of soils.

Habitat In deciduous and coniferous forests, prefers nutrient-poor, sandy soils.

> **Taste mild**
> **Spores white**
> **Common in Europe**
> **Similar species the Sickener**

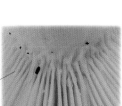

The Greasy Green Brittlegill (*R. heterophylla*) is also edible and its gills are cross-linked where they meet the stipe.

Gills white

Stipe tapered

227

Cap flesh-coloured with ochre-yellow flecks

Cap skin does not reach the rim

Caution!
The cherry to blood red Sickener (p. 229) is well named. It causes severe vomiting if eaten.

Darkening Brittlegill

🍴

Russula vinosa (mushrooms with gills)
Size 5–12 cm   July–October

Habitat In coniferous forests, primarily under spruces, on acidic, relatively damp soils.

> **Cap rim has whitish frosting when young**
> **Spores cream-coloured**
> **Relatively common in Europe, particularly in the north**

The flesh of the Darkening Brittlegill discolours to grey after a few hours and this is particularly apparent in the stipe. Therefore this species is quite easy to identify. However, this characteristic is often only clearly visible on older specimens or specimens that have been lying around for a few hours. There are two further variants of this species, one with an orange cap and one with a yellow cap.

Cap violet, slightly lighter in the centre

Stipe white

The dark discoloration occurs on the cap rim, gill blades and in the stipe.

Flesh turns grey after a few hours

Gills pale cream-coloured

Copper Brittlegill

🍴

Russula decolorans (mushrooms with gills)
Size 5–10 cm   July–October

Habitat In coniferous forests and on the fringes of bogs, usually under pines, on acidic, damp soils.

> **Taste mild**
> **Spores cream-coloured**
> **Common in Europe, particularly in the north**

The species name *decolorans* refers to the fact that the orange cap surface is often discoloured or fades. This cap colour of this species varies from rich orange to pale yellow and sometimes almost white.

Cap usually pale orange

Stipe white

Flesh rapidly turns grey

Gills cream-coloured

The Yellow Swamp Brittlegill (*R. claroflava*) only rows under birches.

Sickener
Russula emetica (mushrooms with gills)
Size 4–8 cm   July–October

The Sickener is the only *Russula* mushroom which, apart from having an unpleasant taste, is actually poisonous. The resinous substances it contains cause severe vomiting in some individuals. Sickeners can be identified by their vibrantly red caps and their pure white stipes and gills.

Habitat In damp coniferous forests, on acidic soils, under spruces, some varieties grow under beeches, birches or pines.

> *Tastes very hot*
> *Spores white*
> *Common in Europe*

Caution!
The Beechwood Sickener (R. mairei, left) has a slight honey-like odour when dried, and the griseascens *variety (right) grows on hill bogs.*

Flesh white

Gills pure white

229

Stipe pure white

Cap cherry red, does not fade

Greencracked Brittlegill

Russula virescens (mushrooms with gills)

Size 5–12 cm   July–October

Habitat In open oak and beech forests, in parks and on heaths, on nutrient-poor, relatively acidic soils.

> Taste mild, nutty
> Spores cream-coloured
> Patchy distribution in Europe

Cracked cap surfaces are usually caused by the effects of the weather. It is, however, a characteristic of this mushroom and the weather has nothing to do with it. Indeed, this feature can be used to identify it once the colour of its cap has faded. Its mild, nutty taste makes it one of the most highly prized edible mushrooms.

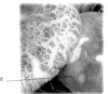

The green colour of its cap is very sensitive to light and fades to ochre-yellow.

Flesh whitish with slight hints of yellow

Gills cream-coloured

Did you know?

The slightly hot-tasting Green Brittle-gill (R. aeruginea) is a very similar colour. Its cap is more of a yellowy-green colour, it does not crack and it only grows under birches and spruces.

Stipe pure white

Cap blue-green, cracked

Charcoal Burner

Russula cyanoxantha (mushrooms with gills)

Size 6–15 cm   June–October

The Charcoal Burner can be identified by its soft, flexible gills; the gills on other *Russula* mushrooms are always fragile. It may owe its unusual name to the variability of its cap colour – it may look purplish or greenish, like the flames of burning charcoal. This is a mild-tasting edible mushroom, which sometimes grows in great profusion.

Habitat In deciduous and coniferous forests, primarily under beeches, prefers acidic soils.

> Taste mild, nutty
> Spores white
> Common in Europe

Caution!

Varieties with green caps may be confused with the Deathcap (p. 116). However, russulas have fragile flesh, no basal bulb, no ring and smooth cap skin which cannot be removed.

Gills pure white

Flesh white

Cap mixture of violet and green

231

Stipe pure white

Tall Russula

Russula paludosa (mushrooms with gills)
Size 5–12 cm   July–October

Habitat In coniferous forests and on the fringes of bogs, usually under pines, on acidic, wet soils.

> Taste mild to hot
> Spores cream-coloured
> Common in central and northern Europe, relatively rare in the south

The taste of the Tall Russula's flesh varies in hotness, like the Ochre Brittlegill for example. Some of the milder ones can be eaten, but the more hot-tasting ones are too unpleasant to be edible.

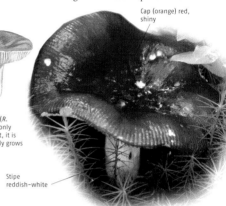

Cap (orange) red, shiny

The cap of the Coral Brittlegill (*R. velenovskyi*) is only shiny when wet, it is smaller and only grows under birches.

Gills rich cream-coloured

Stipe reddish–white

Gilded Brittlegill

Russula aurea (mushrooms with gills)
Size 5–10 cm   June–October

Habitat In deciduous and coniferous forests, particularly under beeches, no soil preferences, only absent from highly acidic soils.

> Taste mild
> Spores buttery yellow
> Patchy distribution in Europe, declining

The Gilded Brittlegill is probably one of the most handsome *Russula* mushrooms. Its intense colours can vary greatly and can include the entire spectrum between red and yellow. Although it tastes very good, it has been in sharp decline for a few decades.

Cap a vibrant mixture of yellows, oranges

Stipe white, becoming yellowish towards base

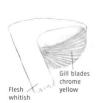

Gill blades chrome yellow

Flesh whitish

Some specimens have no yellow pigmentation and can only be identified with the aid of a microscope.

Purple Brittlegill

Russula atropurpurea (mushrooms with gills)

Size 5–12 cm   July–October

The Purple Brittlegill forms root symbioses almost exclusively with oak trees. Since oak trees are on the decline, this has had a negative effect on Purple Brittlegill numbers. Very occasionally it also grows under other deciduous trees such as beeches, birches and hornbeams.

Habitat In Oak and mixed forests, on neutral to acidic, relatively dry soils.

> **Taste relatively hot**
> **Spores white**
> **Common in Europe, declining**

Cap violet, almost black in the centre

Russula melliolens has more obvious yellow flecks and has an odour of artificial honey when drying.

Stipe white, slightly yellowish

Gills whitish, with yellowish flecks

Flesh whitish

Fragile Brittlegill

Russula fragilis (mushrooms with gills)

Size 3–6 cm   August–November

Like the Purple Brittlegill, this species is part of a group of mushrooms with a mixture of violet, red and green colours, pure white gills and stipes that is closely related to the Sickener (p. 229).

Habitat In deciduous and coniferous forests, primarily under beeches, oaks and spruces, no soil preferences.

> **Tastes very hot**
> **Odour fruity**
> **Spores white**
> **Common in Europe**

Cap violet with a greenish centre

Stipe white, fragile

Russula cavipes only grows under silver firs (*Abies*) and its stipe is typically chambered.

Flesh white

Gills pure white

Russula nauseosa

No common name (mushrooms with gills)

Size 3–7 cm   June–October

Habitat In spruce forests on neutral to alkaline soils, always under spruces.

> **Taste mild**
> **Spores ochre-yellow**
> **Common in Europe**

This relatively small mushroom is one of the earliest occurring *Russula* species. It is particularly easy to spot in the early summer when forests are still practically devoid of any other mushrooms.

Cap dull, pinkish-violet with a hint of green

Stipe white, fragile

Flesh white

Gills creamy-yellow

The similar Purple Swamp Brittlegill (*R. nitida*) grows in boggy woodland with birches.

Yellowing Brittlegill

Russula puellaris (mushrooms with gills)

Size 3–6 cm   July–October

Habitat In spruce forests on acidic, relatively dry soils, always under spruces.

> **Taste mild**
> **Spores cream-coloured**
> **Common in Europe**

Very few *Russula* mushrooms turn such a rich yellow colour as the Yellowing Brittlegill. The other species always grow near deciduous trees. It has a mild taste and, although edible, it is not worth picking because it is small and very fragile.

Russula carpini also turns yellow. It grows on better quality soils under hornbeams.

Cap red-violet, lighter towards the rim

Gills and stipe turn very yellow

Gills creamy-white

Flesh white, developing yellow flecks

Rosy Brittlegill (¶¶)

Russula rosea (mushrooms with gills)
Size 4–10 cm   July–October

The stipe of this mushroom is particularly solid and hard to squash, making it a key feature for identification (so long as it is not riddled with maggots). Although edible, it has a slight taste of turpentine to it and so should only be used in combination with other edible mushrooms.

Russula velutipes does not taste of turpentine, and always has a pure white stipe which is not as solid.

Cap vermilion, matt, often faded

Stipe white, usually with a hint of pink

Habitat In beech forests and parks, consistently under beeches, very occasionally under oaks, on dry soils.

> **Taste mild with a hint of turpentine**
> **Spores rich cream-coloured**
> **Common in Europe**

Flesh white

Gills creamy-white

Bloody Brittlegill ✗

Russula sanguinaria (mushrooms with gills)
Size 4–12 cm   July–October

This mushroom gets its name from the blood red colour of its cap which varies very little compared to those of many other *Russula* species. A further key characteristic are its gills which appear to descend down the stipe.

The similar *Russula rhodopus* grows in acidic soils in spruce forests in the mountains.

Cap blood red, matt

Habitat In open pine forests, on heaths and poor quality grasslands, always under pines, on chalky soils.

> **Tastes hot**
> **Spores cream-coloured**
> **Common in Europe**

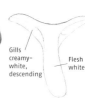

Gills creamy-white, descending

Flesh white

Stipe tinged with blood red

Crab Brittlegill ⏍

Russula xerampelina (mushrooms with gills)

Size 4–12 cm   July–October

Habitat *In spruce and other coniferous forests, on acidic, dry to damp soils, usually under spruces.*

> Odour fishy
> Spores dark yellow
> Common in Europe

Crab Brittlegills are a group of closely related species which gradually develop brown flecks and a fish-like odour. However, Crab Brittlegills make excellent eating since the fishy odour disappears when they are cooked.

Russula schaefferi grows under deciduous trees, particularly under lone birches in coniferous forests.

Gills creamy-yellow

Stipe turning brown towards the base

Did you know?

Russula graveolens *can occasionally be found growing under oaks in deciduous forests and parks. It is rare and should therefore not be picked.*

Cap shiny, carmine

Stipe tinged with bright pink

Burning Brittlegill

Russula badia (mushrooms with gills)

Size 6–15 cm   July–October

This Burning Brittlegill is well named. It is the hottest-tasting *Russula* species of all which becomes apparent after 20–30 seconds of chewing. Eating this mushroom is an unforgettable experience since it leaves behind a burning sensation in the throat which lasts for around half an hour.

Habitat In pine, spruce and other coniferous forests, on acidic, moist to damp, nitrate-poor soils.

> *Taste acrid, burningly hot*
> *Spores light ochre-yellow*
> *Patchy distribution in Europe, on the decline*

Cap claret to mahogany, darker in the centre

Stipe white, often tinged with red

The edible Pine Brittlegill also occasionally has a red cap which makes it impossible to distinguish it from the Burning Brittlegill except by taste.

Gills creamy-yellow

Flesh white

Pine Brittlegill

Russula integra (mushrooms with gills)

Size 6–15 cm   June–October

This mushroom only occurs in coniferous forests. It is common and tastes good but it may be confused with the Burning Brittlegill which has an extremely unpleasant, burning aftertaste. Luckily, the Burning Brittlegill can usually be distinguished by its stipe which is tinged with red.

Habitat In spruce and other coniferous forests, on alkaline to very mildly acidic soils.

> *Taste mild*
> *Spores dark ochre-yellow*
> *Common in Europe*

The colours of this mushroom's cap are very variable and include reds, browns and shades of olive-green.

Cap claret to chestnut brown

Stipe always pure white

Flesh white

Gills ochre-yellow

Olive Brittlegill

Russula olivacea (mushrooms with gills)

Size 6–15 cm   June–October

🍴

Habitat *In beech, oak and hornbeam forests, less common in spruce forests, on alkaline, clay soils, usually under beeches.*

> Taste mild, nutty
> Spores dark yellow
> Common in Europe

The Olive Brittlegill often grows in large numbers if conditions are suitable. It is picked by many people because of its size and nutty taste. Although a recent case of poisoning has been reported, it was almost certainly due to an individual allergic reaction.

The gill blades are a key characteristic for identification since they are usually tinged with pinkish-red where they meet the cap.

Cap sometimes olive-green

Did you know?

The range of colours of Olive Brittlegills is extremely large. The many different colours can be displayed by mushrooms growing in the same location at the same time.

238

Cap claret, grain of rim is concentric

Stipe white, tip usually pinkish-red

Humpback Brittlegill (🍴🍴)

Russula amara (mushrooms with gills)
Size 4–8 cm   July–October

Only the cap skin of the Humpback Brittlegill tastes bitter. If this is removed carefully, this mushroom makes good eating.

Habitat In pine forests and other forests with pine populations, on nutrient-poor, acidic soils or soils with acidic surfaces.

> *Taste mild, cap skin bitter*
> *Spores yolk-coloured*
> *Common in Europe*

Cap claret to bluish-purple

Russula azurea has no hump on its cap and has white gills and spores.

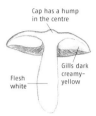

Cap has a hump in the centre

Gills dark creamy-yellow

Flesh white

Stipe white

Iodoform-Scented Russula (🍴🍴)

Russula turci (mushrooms with gills)
Size 4–8 cm   July–October

It is very easy to identify this mushroom because of the medicinal (reminiscent of iodoform) odour that it emits. However, some people are not able to smell this odour quite as clearly as others. In such cases, the frosted appearance of its cap is a further key characteristic for identification.

Habitat In coniferous forests and under coniferous trees in other types of forest, on nutrient-poor, sandy soils.

> *Taste mild*
> *Spores light ochre-yellow*
> *Common in Europe*

Cap red to claret, frosted appearance

Stipe white

Russula amethystea is very similar but the centre of its cap is much darker than the surrounding area and is also recessed.

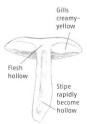

Gills creamy-yellow

Flesh hollow

Stipe rapidly become hollow

Fruity Brittlegill
Russula queletii (mushrooms with gills)
Size 4–10 cm   July–October

Habitat In coniferous forests and under spruces in mixed forests, usually on alkaline soils.

> Tastes very hot
> Spores rich ochre-yellow
> Common in Europe

This mushroom gives off a fruity odour which is particularly reminiscent of gooseberries and is at its strongest in the stipe base. In Germany it is known as the 'Säufernase', or 'drunkard's nose', on account of its stipe which is tinged with reddish-purple.

Russula torulosa is an even deeper shade of reddish-purple and grows under pines.

Flesh white

Gills creamy-yellow

Did you know?

The Primrose Brittlegill (R. sardonia) tastes just as hot and can be distinguished by its bright yellow gills. It only grows under pines, unlike the Fruity Brittlegill.

240

Cap completely blue to reddish-purple

Stipe tinged with violet-red

Golden Brittlegill

Russula risigallina (mushrooms with gills)
Size 3–8 cm   June–October

🍴

Despite this mushroom's name, the cap colour does vary considerably from lemony-yellow to orange to crimson. Even its odour varies a great deal. It can range from being pleasant, like yellow plums, to acidic and vinegary in older specimens.

Habitat *In all kinds of beech forest, in oak and hornbeam forests and parks, absent only from very acidic soils.*

> *Taste mild*
> *Spores deep ochre-yellow*
> *Common in Europe*

Cap orange to yellow

Stipe white

Gills rich yellow

Flesh white

Pure yellow specimens with an acidic odour are sometimes classified as a separate species and are given the name Yellow Russula (*R. acetolens*).

Russula maculata

No common name (mushrooms with gills)
Size 5–12 cm   June–October

✗

The taste of this mushroom is quite variable. The *globispora* variety has large spores, has strong, yellow discoloration and is often mild enough to eat.

Habitat *In Bbeech forests with orchids and wood barley or in oak forests, always on chalky soils.*

> *Tastes hot*
> *Spores deep ochre-yellow*
> *Common in some regions of Europe, rare in the north*

The smaller and rarer *Russula decipiens* grows in similar locations but is usually found under oaks.

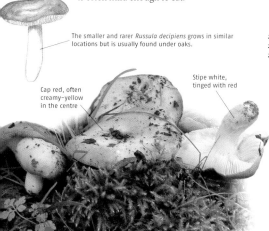

Cap red, often creamy-yellow in the centre

Stipe white, tinged with red

Flesh white

Gills rich yellow

Chanterelle
Cantharellus cibarius (mushrooms with false gills)
Size 3–10 cm   July–November

This is one of the most popular and widely known of all the edible mushrooms. It has a fruity odour (reminiscent of apricots) and a peppery taste and is regarded by many as the most excellent edible mushroom in the world. However, it is protected in some parts of Europe.

Habitat In coniferous forests, occasionally in deciduous forests (under red oaks), primarily on acidic soils.

> Tastes peppery when raw
> Spores yellow
> Common throughout Europe
> Similar species Jack o' Lantern Mushroom

Cantharellus subpruinosus grows on alkaline soils in deciduous forests. It is larger, its cap is a lighter colour and often occurs in early summer.

Flesh becomes paler towards centre

Stipe solid

242

Caution!
The poisonous Jack o' Lantern Mushroom (p. 45) always grows on wood, and is common in southern Europe. Since this mushroom often grows on buried wood and may appear to be growing out of the ground, take great care when picking chanterelles in southern Europe.

Whole mushroom yolk-coloured

False gills thick, forked

Trumpet Chanterelle

Craterellus tubaeformis (mushrooms with false gills)
Size 3–7 cm   July–November

Unlike the Chanterelle, this mushroom has a hollow fruiting body. It makes good eating and often grows in large numbers.

Habitat *In coniferous forests, usually under spruces, always on acidic soils.*

> **False gills beige-grey, forked**
> **Spores yellow**
> **Common throughout Europe**

The similar Golden Chanterelle has a wrinkled, wavy exterior instead of false gills.

Cap brown, slightly scaly

Stipe olive-yellow

Flesh olive-yellow

Stipe hollow

243

Golden Chanterelle

Craterellus aurora (mushrooms with false gills)
Size 3–7 cm   July–November

A basket of Golden Chanterelles left to sit for some time will fill a room with a sweetish, flowery scent. It also has a much more delicate taste than the Trumpet Chanterelle.

Habitat *In coniferous forests, primarily under spruces, on chalky soils, also around hill bogs.*

> **Exterior is pale yellow, wavy and wrinkly**
> **Spores yellow**
> **Patchy distribution throughout Europe, common in some regions**

Cap yellow to brown

Stipe orange-yellow

The rare *Cantharellus ianthinoxanthus* grows on clay and chalky soils.

Flesh apricot

Stipe hollow

Horn of Plenty

Craterellus cornucopioides (mushrooms with false gills)

Size 3–8 cm   August–November

Habitat *In beech forests, on chalky to neutral, clay soils, usually in large numbers.*

> **Fruiting bodies funnel or trumpet-shaped**
> **Spores whitish, then ochre**
> **Patchy distribution throughout Europe, common in some regions**

Despite its slightly unappealing appearance, the Horn of Plenty is a highly sought-after edible mushroom which is also well suited to being dried. Because it has such an intense taste, it is often used as a form of seasoning or in fillings and sauces. Old specimens should be ignored as they have a rubbery texture. Young specimens are fragile by comparison.

The Sinuous Chanterelle (*Pseudocraterellus sinuosus*) looks like a miniature version of the Horn of Plenty and grows in clumps.

Flesh grey, thin

Whole fruiting body hollow

Did you know?

The Ashen Chanterelle (C. cinereus) usually grows alongside the Horn of Plenty. Although it has pronounced false gills, it is often picked at the same time without being recognised. Like all mushrooms with false gills, it is edible.

244

Cap wavy, brown-black

Exterior ash to blackish-grey, wavy and wrinkled

Pig's Ear

Gomphus clavatus (mushrooms with false gills)

Size 3–8 cm   July–October

The Pig's Ear is often picked in regions where it is still common. Its fruiting bodies have firm flesh and are very rarely attacked by maggots. However, it is a protected species in parts of Europe where it is in decline and should only be picked for personal use.

The spinning top-like shape is less apparent on young specimens and they are usually a deep shade of violet.

Habitat In Beech and coniferous forests, on chalky to neutral, clay soils, usually grows in rows.

> *Fruiting bodies spinning top-shaped*
> *Spores ochre*
> *Relatively common in Alpine regions, otherwise rare*

Did you know?

Young Lilac Oysterling (Panus conchatus) specimens look remarkably similar. However, they grow on wood and have actual gills. Although they are not poisonous, they quickly become tough and inedible.

Flesh white, fibrous

Fruiting bodies full-fleshed

245

Exterior violet, wavy and wrinkled

Upper surface rapidly fades to ochre

Giant Club

Clavariadelphus pistillaris (coral fungi)
Height 10–20 cm   August–November

♨

Habitat In beech forests, always on alkaline to neutral soils.

> **Taste bitter**
> **Spores ochre**
> **Patchy distribution throughout Europe, less common towards the north**

This fungus has an absolutely unique shape. However, this club-like shape only develops after some time and young specimens are roughly the same width from top to bottom. If the conditions are right, hundreds of specimens of this fungus can be found growing together.

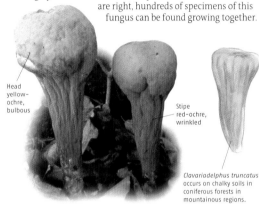

— Fruiting bodies full-fleshed

— Flesh pale ochre-yellow, cotton wool-like

Head yellow-ochre, bulbous

Stipe red-ochre, wrinkled

Clavariadelphus truncatus occurs on chalky soils in coniferous forests in mountainous regions.

Pipe Club

Macrotyphula fistulosa (coral fungi)
Height 10–30 cm   September–December

♨

Habitat In all forest types, on various soils apart from highly acidic soils, on buried wood, often under birches.

> **Taste bitter**
> **Spores ochre**
> **Patchy distribution throughout Europe**

Despite its height, the Pipe Club is easily overlooked since the thin fruiting bodies barely penetrate the thick layer of plant debris present on many forest floors. They often appear after the first frost.

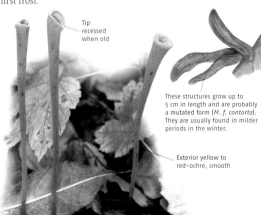

Tip recessed when old

These structures grow up to 5 cm in length and are probably a mutated form (*M. f. contorta*). They are usually found in milder periods in the winter.

Exterior yellow to red-ochre, smooth

Tip rounded when young

Fruiting body hollow

White Spindles

Clavaria fragilis (coral fungi)
Height 4–8 cm   July–November

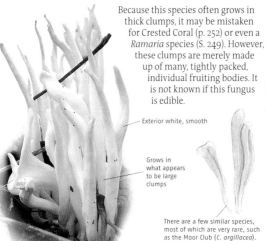

Because this species often grows in thick clumps, it may be mistaken for Crested Coral (p. 252) or even a *Ramaria* species (S. 249). However, these clumps are merely made up of many, tightly packed, individual fruiting bodies. It is not known if this fungus is edible.

Habitat In forests and on meadows, on various soils apart from highly acidic soils, prefers relatively nutrient-poor soils.

> **Taste insipid**
> **Fruiting body highly fragile**
> **Patchy distribution throughout Europe**

Exterior white, smooth

Grows in what appears to be large clumps

Flesh white

Fruiting bodies worm-like

There are a few similar species, most of which are very rare, such as the Moor Club (*C. argillacea*).

Yellow Club

Clavulinopsis helveola (coral fungi)
Height 2–5 cm   July–November

Clavulinopsis species, hygrocybes (p. 46) and a large number of entolomas (p. 109) all thrive on unfertilised grazing land. Such biotopes are in steady decline which means that these species have become endangered.

Habitat In extensively used meadows with short grass, no soil preferences, never on nitrogen-enriched soils.

> **Fruiting bodies fragile**
> **Spores pale ochre**
> **Rare to patchy distribution throughout Europe**

Exterior completely yellow, smooth

Meadow Coral (*Ramariopsis corniculata*, below) smells of flour and has branchlets, while *Ramariopsis pulchella* (above) is a pretty shade of purple.

Flesh yellow

Fruiting bodies worm-like, with stipes

Wood Cauliflower

Sparassis crispa (coral fungi)
Size 20–50 cm   July–November

🍴

Habitat In pine forests or mixed forests with pine populations, on sandy, nutrient-poor soils, very occasionally occurs on larches or Douglas firs.

> Fruiting body fragile
> Spores pale ochre
> Common to patchy distribution throughout Europe

The Wood Cauliflower is a highly sought-after, large and easily identifiable edible fungus. However, the effort required to clean it may put a slight dampener on things! While growing, the fungus accumulates sand, earth, twigs and other debris, so it is best to cut it into slices and clean each one individually under running water.

The Cauliflower Mushroom's branchlets are paler and their rims are not turned in.

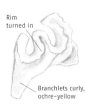

Rim turned in

Branchlets curly, ochre-yellow

Did you know?

The Cauliflower Mushroom (S. laminosa) grows on silver firs and spruces and occasionally also on beeches or oaks. Although it is also edible, many people say it does not taste as good as the Wood Cauliflower.

Fruiting body sponge-like

Rosso Coral
Ramaria botrytis (coral fungi)
Size 8–15 cm   July–October

Ramaria species were once very popular edible fungi. Nowadays they are all rare and, as such, they should not be picked. In

addition to this, all *Ramaria* species cause laxative effects to varying degrees which should be enough to discourage most people from picking them.

The fruiting bodies of *Ramaria fennica* var. *fumigata* are completely violet when young.

Habitat *In beech, oak and hornbeam forests, on alkaline, clay soils, also under spruces in mountainous regions.*

> *Flesh white*
> *Spores yellow-ochre*
> *Rare throughout Europe, slightly commoner in some mountainous regions*
> *Similar species Colic Coral*

Caution!
The branchlet tips of the Colic Coral (p. 251) are pale pink when young. It is one of the more common Ramaria *species and grows in deciduous and coniferous forests. If eaten, it causes severe and painful food poisoning with colic-like symptoms.*

Branchlets with many forks

Branchlets white when young

Branchlet tips purple-red

Stalk white

Yellow-Tipped Coral

Ramaria formosa (coral fungi)

Size 8–20 cm   July–October

Habitat *In beech, oak and hornbeam forests, also in coniferous forests in the mountains, on alkaline, clay soils.*

> **Flesh white**
> **Spores yellow-ochre**

When young, this fungus can be identified by its white stalk, salmon-pink branchlets and yellow branchlet tips. As with all *Ramaria* species, however, it turns completely ochre-yellow with age, making it very hard to identify.

Branchlet tips yellow

Branchlets salmon pink when young

Branchlet tips forked

Apex between branchlets always acute

Probably the prettiest native species is the Rose Coral (*R. subbotrytis*) whose branchlets are a vibrant pinkish-red colour when young.

Golden Coral

Ramaria largentii (coral fungi)

Size 10–20 cm   July–October

Habitat *In forests with spruces and silver firs, on alkaline, clay soils, only in elevated locations.*

> **Flesh white**
> **Spores yellow-ochre**
> **Rare throughout Europe, slightly commoner in some mountainous regions**

The rule of thumb in many older mushroom guides is that any golden-yellow *Ramaria* species with no salmon-pink tinges are edible. However, dozens of new *Ramaria* species have been documented in the last 20 years and very little is known about their edibility. As such, it is best to ignore the advice given on *Ramaria* species in older mushroom guides.

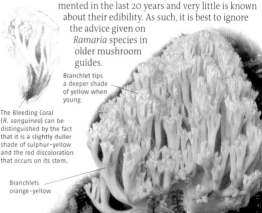

Branchlet tips a deeper shade of yellow when young

The Bleeding Coral (*R. sanguinea*) can be distinguished by the fact that it is a slightly duller shade of sulphur-yellow and the red discoloration that occurs on its stem.

Branchlets orange-yellow

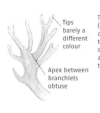

Tips barely a different colour

Apex between branchlets obtuse

Colic Coral

Ramaria pallida (coral fungi)
Size 10–20 cm   July–October

The name of this fungus does not sound particularly inviting and rightly so. It causes stomach pains and severe vomiting and diarrhoea. It is one of the most common of the large *Ramaria* species.

Habitat In forests with spruces and silver firs, on alkaline, clay soils, only in elevated locations.

> **Flesh white**
> **Spores yellow-ochre**
> **Patchy distribution throughout Europe, common in some mountainous regions**

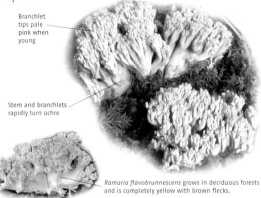

Branchlet tips pale pink when young

Stem and branchlets rapidly turn ochre

Tips barely a different colour

Apex between branchlets relatively acute

Ramaria flavobrunnescens grows in deciduous forests and is completely yellow with brown flecks.

Upright Coral

Ramaria stricta (coral fungi)
Size 4–8 cm   July–October

This fungus gets its name from the fact that its branchlets are all straight and vertical. Unlike the large *Ramaria* species, it decomposes rotting deciduous wood rather than forming root symbioses with trees.

Habitat In deciduous and mixed forests, on alkaline or mineral-rich soils, always on rotting deciduous wood.

> **Flesh relatively elastic**
> **Spores yellow-ochre**
> **Common throughout Europe**

Branchlets crowded, straight and vertical

Whole fruiting body is ochre

The much more delicate *Pterula multifida* has a very strong ink-like odour.

Tips lemon-coloured when young

Apex between branchlets U-shaped

Greening Coral

Ramaria abietina (coral fungi)
Size 2–6 cm   July–October

Habitat In coniferous forests, primarily under spruces, always among fallen needles, on acidic to slightly alkaline soils.

> Grows in compact groups
> Spores yellow-ochre
> Common to patchy distribution throughout Europe

The Greening Coral is part of a group of similar, small, ochre-yellow *Ramaria* species that grow among fallen spruce needles. They are too delicate to be picked for eating and are rumoured to have laxative effects.

The almost identical *Ramaria flaccida* grows in the same locations but has no discoloration.

Whole fruiting body olive-ochre

Green discoloration towards stem

Tips and branchlets turn green

Apex between branchlets U-shaped

Crested Coral

Clavulina coralloides (coral fungi)
Size 2–8 cm   July–October

Habitat In deciduous and coniferous forests, no soil preferences, among fallen needles or on defoliated areas.

> Flesh fragile
> Spores white
> Common throughout Europe

Even though it may look similar to the *Ramaria* species, the Crested Coral is not a close relative. This becomes apparent on closer inspection of the spores and other characteristics. Although it is edible, it is small and has little taste.

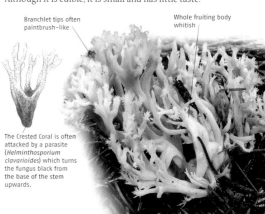

Branchlet tips often paintbrush-like

Whole fruiting body whitish

Branchlets heavily forked

The Crested Coral is often attacked by a parasite (*Helminthosporium clavarioides*) which turns the fungus black from the base of the stem upwards.

Tips also creamy-white

Wood Hedgehog

Hydnum repandum (tooth fungi)

Size 4–10(15) cm   July–October

¶¶

The Wood Hedgehog, known as the 'Pied de Mouton' (sheep's foot) in France, tastes good and is very easy to identify. Older specimens taste slightly bitter, so it is better to pick only those whose teeth do not fall off on contact.

Habitat In deciduous and coniferous forests, among fallen spruce needles or beech leaves, frequently on alkaline soils.

> Flesh yellows slightly
> Spores white
> Common throughout Europe

Did you know?

The Terracotta Hedgehog (H. rufescens, left), which grows in mountain pine forests, and the White Hedgehog (H. albidum), found on southern chalky soils, are both edible.

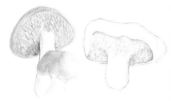

Flesh yellowish-white

Teeth on underside of cap removable

Cap cream-coloured to pale orange-ochre

Stipe white, usually off-centre

Shingled Hedgehog

Sarcodon imbricatum (tooth fungi)

Size 8–20 cm   July–October

🍴

Habitat In coniferous forests, usually under spruces, on alkaline soils.

> Odour intensely aromatic when dry
> Spores brown
> Patchy distribution throughout Europe, rare in parts, common in mountainous regions
> Similar species Bitter Hedgehog

The Shingled Hedgehog usually grows in large rings and rows, making it easy for collectors to select the youngest and best-tasting fruiting bodies. Older specimens usually taste bitter and are best when mixed with mince to make mushroom beef burgers.

The rare *Boletopsis grisea* has very small pores instead of teeth. It grows in nutrient-poor soils in pine forests.

Flesh pale brownish-grey

Teeth pale grey-brown, descending

Caution!

The Bitter Hedgehog (*S. scabrosus*) has a very unpleasant taste. It has flat, grid-like cap scales and a grey-green stipe base.

254

Cap brown with upturned, prominent scales

Stipe whitish

Devil's Tooth

Hydnellum peckii (tooth fungi)
Size 4–8 cm   July–October

✕ 🍴

As with most ground-dwelling tooth fungi (apart from the Wood Hedgehog) the Devil's Tooth is a reliable indicator of semi-natural, nutrient-poor biotopes. Many variants of this species are usually found growing together in the same locations. Almost all of them are seriously endangered in most European countries.

Habitat In coniferous forests, usually under spruces, on alkaline soils, rare in deciduous forests.

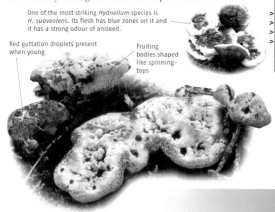

One of the most striking *Hydnellum* species is *H. suaveolens*. Its flesh has blue zones on it and it has a strong odour of aniseed.

Red guttation droplets present when young

Fruiting bodies shaped like spinning-tops

> Tastes very hot
> Flesh tough like cork
> Spores brown
> Rare throughout Europe, slightly more common in some mountainous regions

Flesh red-brown with concentric zoning

Teeth fine, descending far down stipe

Sheep Polypore

Albatrellus ovinus (tooth fungi)
Size 4–8 cm   July–October

(🍴)

Although not strictly a tooth fungus, the pores on the Sheep Polypore can become very angular and tooth-like with age. It is frequently picked in Alpine regions where it is still relatively common. Although it is best suited to being pickled, it is also very tasty when eaten as an accompaniment.

Habitat In coniferous forests in mountainous regions, primarily under spruces, on relatively alkaline to acidic soils, sensitive to nitrates.

Cap white, often tinged with greyish-purple

The Goat's Foot (*A. cristatus*) can be identified by its olive to yellow-green cap.

> Flesh tough like cork
> Spores white
> Rare throughout most of Europe, common in some mountainous regions

Bruised areas turn yellow

Pores very small

Flesh white, firm

Bearded Tooth

Hericium erinaceus (tooth fungi)
Size 8–20(25) cm   July–October

Habitat *In various types of deciduous forests with populations of old trees, primarily on old beeches.*

> **Spores white**
> **Rare throughout Europe**

The Bearded Tooth is the least common of the four *Hericium* species. Its bulbous fruiting bodies make it easy to identify. Because it tastes good, it has been cultivated for some time and is available from some specialist greengrocers.

Fruiting body round, creamy-white

Flesh cream-white

The Coral Tooth (*H. coralloides*) grows on fallen beech trees and has coral-like fruiting bodies which feel like rubber.

Teeth flexible, crowded

Teeth up to 5cm long

256

Earthfan

Thelephora terrestris (crust fungi)
Size 3–20 cm   Perennial

Habitat *In various types of coniferous forest, on relatively acidic, nutrient-poor, sandy soils, often grows in masses in tree nurseries.*

> **Spores brown**
> **Fruiting bodies flat or with caps**
> **Common throughout Europe**

The shape and size of this fungus varies greatly. Depending on the substrate, it can grow as a flat layer or it can sometimes form caps or brackets. It is one of the first species to form root symbioses with young spruces and is also used for the artificial mycorrhization of saplings.

Thelephora palmata has coral-like, forked, upright fruiting bodies which have a very unpleasant odour like rotting cabbage.

Growth zone whitish

Underside covered with small nubs

Upper surface dark brown, fibrous

Fruiting bodies have irregular lobes

Dry Rot

Serpula lacrymans (crust fungi)
Size 10–100 cm   Perennial

Dry Rot only requires moisture in the initial stages to thrive. Mature fruiting bodies are able to produce water by themselves which is what makes it such a persistent threat to timber. Thanks to modern timber impregnation techniques, it has now become relatively rare and it is often only found in poorly maintained, older buildings.

Habitat On all kinds of timber inside buildings, almost never occurs outside buildings.

> **Spores brown**
> **White mycelium, like cotton wool**
> **Relatively uncommon in central Europe**

The smaller, thinner Wild Dry Rot (*S. himantioides*) grows on coniferous trees. It is less aggressive and has a pink mycelium.

Fruiting layer with lobed folds, orange-brown

Did you know?

The blight caused by Dry Rot makes timber disintegrate into many small, brown fragments. White rot, on the other hand, causes timber to become soft and spongy, although it maintains its structure.

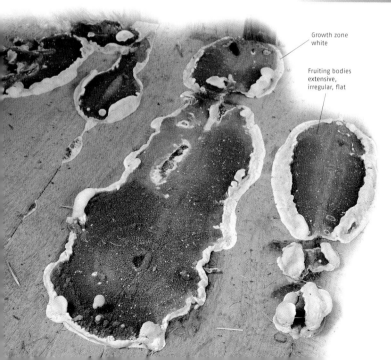

Growth zone white

Fruiting bodies extensive, irregular, flat

Peniophora quercina

No common name (crust fungi)
Size 3–30 cm   Perennial

Habitat *On dead oak branches, usually those which are still attached to the tree, no particular biotope preferences.*

> Rim turns up when dried
> Fruiting bodies up to 1mm thick
> Common throughout Europe

Crust fungi are a group of fungi that decompose wood and are often form layers that are not particularly easy to spot. They can be web-like or leathery, thin or thick, smooth or uneven and are usually white, cream-coloured or ochre. Space dictates that only a few of the most common species can be described in this book.

The Rosy Crust (*P. incarnata*) binds with wood even when it is dry. It then appears as though some pink paint has been applied to the wood.

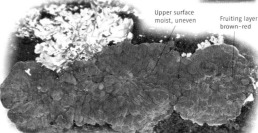

Upper surface moist, uneven

Fruiting layer brown-red

Surface cracks when dry

Underside black

Waxy Crust

Vuilleminia comedens (crust fungi)
Size 10–100 cm   Perennial

Habitat *Usually on oak branches, no particular biotope preferences.*

> Upper surface moist, waxy
> Fruiting body only 0.1 mm thick
> Common throughout Europe

The Waxy Crust is very common. It grows under the bark of dead branches which eventually tears the bark open. Although branches affected by the Waxy Crust can be found in every deciduous forest, it is almost impossible to see the fruiting bodies, especially when the weather is dry.

Bark rolled back from edge of fungus

Almost invisible when dry, whitish

The Cobalt Crust (*Terana caerulea*) is much easier to spot. It occurs north of the Alps in warm locations.

Surface is iridescent when moist

Hairy Curtain Crust

Stereum hirsutum (crust fungi)
Size 2–10 cm   Perennial

This is one of the first fungi to appear after a tree has fallen. Its presence indicates that the tree has just entered the first stages of decomposition, whereas other wood-dwelling fungi, such as the Rusty Porecrust (p. 262) only grow on wood that has already been rotting for some time.

Habitat On various types of deciduous wood, particularly on oaks, no particular biotope preferences.

Underside orange-yellow, smooth

> *Colour does not change when rubbed*
> *Fruiting bodies thin, tough*
> *Very common throughout Europe*

Some crust fungi turn red when rubbed, such as the very common Bleeding Broadleaf Crust (*S. rugosum*).

Darker zoning

Rim wavy, frizzy

Upper surface hairy

Wrinkled Crust

Phlebia merismoides (crust fungi)
Size 5–50 cm   Perennial

As with many crust fungi, the Wrinkled Crust is pale, flat and hard to spot when it is dry. It is much easier to spot when the weather is wet. As such, many of them can be seen during mild winter periods when the fruiting bodies are swollen and orange.

Habitat On various types of deciduous wood, no particular biotope preferences.

Upper surface with irregular folds

> *Consistency jelly-like, gristly*
> *Fruiting bodies up to 2 mm thick*
> *Common throughout Europe*

The creamy-white *Mycenastrum corium* has a similar upper surface and which feels like suede.

No wrinkles near rim

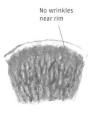

Bright orange to salmon pink

Tiger's Eye

Coltricia perennis (bracket fungi)
Size 3–10 cm   July–October

Habitat On dry, sandy, nutrient-poor soils, primarily in pine forests with lichen populations.

> Weathering only occurs gradually
> Fruiting bodies leathery, tough
> Common in some parts of Europe, in decline

The appearance of Tiger's Eye fruiting bodies vary from specimen to specimen. The variation in the width and number of bands and colours is huge. This is why florists often use them to decorate bouquets and wreaths. Old fruiting bodies from the previous year can still be seen alongside newly grown specimens.

Upper surface has variable zones

Many shades of brown

Flesh brown, no zoning

Unlike the similar Devil's Tooth (p. 255), which has teeth on its underside, the Tiger's Eye has pores.

Silvery Porecrust

Inonotus nodulosus (bracket fungi)
Size 10–40 cm   July–October

Habitat In all types of forest, primarily beech forests, always on dead beeches that have fallen or are still standing.

> Flesh whitish
> Fruiting bodies corky, hard
> Common throughout Europe but not found north of southern Sweden

This bracket fungus forms large layers on substrates. They consist of fused, individual fruiting bodies and have irregularly distributed caps which are 2-3 cm wide. The stretched pore layer is iridescent in certain light conditions, hence the name given to this species.

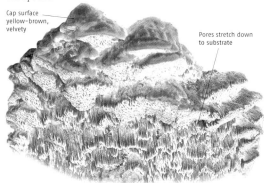

Cap surface yellow-brown, velvety

Pores stretch down to substrate

Pore layer silvery

Shaggy Bracket
Inonotus hispidus (bracket fungi)
Size 6–20 cm   June–October

The Shaggy Bracket is a parasite which attacks living trees. The destruction of its host is gradual, even lasting decades in some cases. The remaining black clumps of old fruiting bodies can be seen on trees all year round.

Another great bracket fungus is the Oak Bracket (*I. dryadeus*) which only occurs on very old oak trees.

Habitat In all types of forest, primarily on ashes, often on apple trees outside forest environments.

> *Fresh fruiting bodies heavy, spongy*
> *Bruised areas turn black-brown*
> *Almost absent in northern Europe, otherwise common*

Did you know?
There is a great difference in the appearance of young (left) and older specimens (right). Older specimens are harder, and more clearly defined with solid rusty brown caps.

Upper surface bristly on the growth zone

Flesh brown

Cap surface fox-coloured

Pores yellow-brown, iridescent, water droplets often present

Robust Bracket

Phellinus robustus (bracket fungi)

Size 6–15 cm   Perennial

Habitat *In parks, open oak forests and on old, lone oaks, always on the trunks of living trees.*

> **Fruiting bodies bracket-shaped**
> **Pores turn dark brown when bruised**
> **Common throughout Europe, absent north of central Sweden**

This is probably the hardest of all the tree-dwelling fungi. Indeed, it is so hard, it can only be removed from trees with the aid of a saw. Oak trees affected by it do not topple during storms, but rather, they break at the part of the tree where the fruiting bodies are growing.

The Willow Bracket (*P. trivialis*) grows on old coppiced willows and has a very defined cap rim.

Cap rim rounded

Cap surface blue–grey

Flesh dark brown

Multiple pore layers

Rusty Porecrust

Phellinus ferruginosus (bracket fungi)

Size 10–100 cm   Perennial

Habitat *In various types of forest, on forest boundaries, in parks, always on rotting, fallen trees.*

> **Fruiting bodies corky, hard**
> **Pores very small**
> **Common throughout Europe**

Not all *Phellinus* species have bracket-shaped fruiting bodies. Some form layers over the substrate like the crust fungi. The Rusty Porecrust is one of the most common.

Fruiting bodies extensive, rusty brown

Rim zone lighter

Pores irregular

The Pine Bracket (*P. Pinus*) grows on living pine trees.

Beefsteak Fungus
Fistulina hepatica (bracket fungi)
Size 10–30 cm   July–October

(❦)

Although this fungus can be eaten when young and has a delicious-sounding name, it has to be soaked in water beforehand to remove the tannic acid it contains. It can then be fried like a steak, though it is not to everyone's taste.

Habitat In open oak forests, parks, always on living oaks, prefers warmer conditions.

> Pores are not fused together
> Spores white
> Common in some parts of Europe, otherwise patchy

Young Beefsteak Fungi are round and cushion-like and look nothing like older specimens.

Pores pale pink

Did you know?
The consistency of this fungus is actually like that of meat. The fungus even 'bleeds' in that it exudes a lot of red fluid when pressed.

263

Stipe lateral, basic

Fruiting bodies broad, fan-shaped, brown-red

Conifer Blueing Bracket

Spongiporus caesius (bracket fungi)
Size 3–8 cm   Perennial

Habitat In all types of forest, primarily in spruce forests, always on rotting coniferous wood, no soil preference.

> **Flesh corky, hard**
> **Blue colour often fades**
> **Common throughout Europe**

This fungus contains a large volume of fluid even when the weather is dry. All of this fluid can be pressed out of the fungus, leaving it as light as a piece of polystyrene.

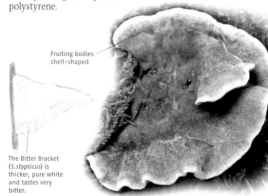

Fruiting bodies shell-shaped

Flesh pale bluish

Single pore layer, bluish

The Bitter Bracket (*S.stypticus*) is thicker, pure white and tastes very bitter.

Root Rot

Heterobasidion annosum (bracket fungi)
Size 6–30 cm   Perennial

Habitat On dead and living deciduous and coniferous trees, primarily on nutrient-rich soils.

> **Fruiting bodies have caps or are completely flat**
> **Odour strong, acidic**
> **Common throughout Europe**

Root Rot is a much feared tree parasite. It causes red rot in spruce forests which turns the inside of the wood brownish-red. As the name suggests, most of its fruiting bodies are formed in the roots of trees.

Pore layer creamy-white

Root Rot is not always a parasite. For example, this specimen is living on a spruce cone.

Rim zone white

Pores very small

Upper surface grey-brown, hard

Birch Polypore

Piptoporus betulinus (bracket fungi)
Size 6–20 cm   June–December

The Birch Polypore was used by people in ancient times and ice mummy 'Ötzi' had a specimen in his possession when he died. However, it is unknown whether it was used for strong teas or as some kind of medicine to stem wounds.

Habitat *On standing and fallen, dead birch trees, no biotope preferences.*

The similar Oak Polypore (*Buglossoporus quercinus*) only grows on the trunks of old oak trees. Its upper surface is bristly.

> **Pore layer creamy-white**
> **Fruiting bodies soft when young**
> **Common throughout Europe**

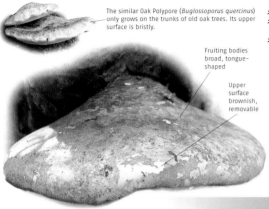

Fruiting bodies broad, tongue-shaped

Upper surface brownish, removable

Flesh white

Single pore layer

Artists' Bracket

Ganoderma lipsiense (bracket fungi)
Size 10–40 cm   Perennial

The pure white underside of this fungus turns dark brown on contact, meaning that it is possible to use a twig to write or draw on the pore layer. This is how the fungus gets its name.

Habitat *On deciduous tree stumps or fallen, rotting deciduous wood, no particular biotope preferences.*

The Lacquered Bracket (*G. lucidum*) has a shiny, lacquer-like layer on its cap and is used in Asian medicine.

> **Pore layer creamy-white**
> **Fruiting bodies soft when young**
> **Common throughout Europe**

Upper surface brownish, hard

White pore layer instantly turns dark brown on contact

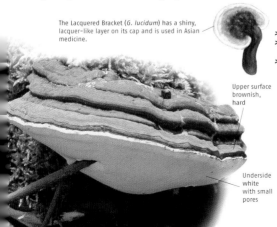

Underside white with small pores

Bay Polypore

Polyporus badius (bracket fungi)

Size 10–40 cm   April–September

Habitat In lowland and other forests, in warmer areas, always on dead deciduous wood.

> Cap irregularly shell-shaped
> Fruiting bodies corky, tough
> Patchy distribution throughout Europe, absent towards the north

The Bay Polypore is one species that is benefiting from the average increase in temperature. Whereas it was once restricted to the warmer conditions found in valleys, it is now often found growing at altitudes of up to 450 metres. This species has spread quite considerably.

Polyporus melanopus is similar and appears as though it is growing on the earth. It often develops multiple caps on a single stipe.

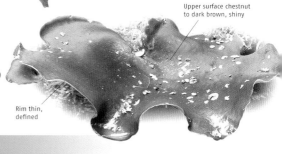

Upper surface chestnut to dark brown, shiny

Pores whitish, very small

Stipe short, black

Rim thin, defined

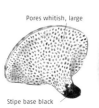

Dryad's Saddle

Polyporus squamosus (bracket fungi)

Size 20–40 cm   April–July

Habitat In lowland forests, avenues and on lone deciduous trees or stumps, less common on fallen trees.

> Stipe lateral, very short
> Strong floury/cucumber-like odour
> Common throughout Europe

Although young specimens can be eaten, they do not taste particularly good. Sometimes it is used in decoctions for mushroom soups, although it tastes nowhere near as good as the Tuberous Polypore.

Pores whitish, large

The Tuberous Polypore (*P. tuberaster*) has a pleasant mushroomy odour. It has a centralised stipe, relatively prominent cap scales and grows on beech branches.

Cap ochre-yellow

Stipe base black

Scales brown, not prominent

Fringed Polypore

Polyporus ciliatus (bracket fungi)
Size 5–12 cm   April–July

Unlike a few other *Polyporus* species with stipes, this fungus is leathery and tough even when it is young and so cannot be eaten. Old fruiting bodies only weather gradually and can often still be seen in late autumn.

Habitat *In lowland forests, avenues and on lone deciduous trees or stumps, less common on fallen trees.*

The Winter Polypore (*P. brumalis*) can be distinguished by its much larger pores.

> **Stipe surface like snakeskin**
> **Pores only visible under a microscope**
> **Common throughout Europe**

Cap dark brown, smooth

Stipe thin, brown

Pores whitish, tiny

Elegant Polypore

Polyporus varius (bracket fungi)
Size 1–7 cm   April–October

Even though its cap colour varies greatly, this fungus can easily be identified by its jet black stipe base. It is much smaller than the slightly similar Dryad's Saddle (p. 266) and its flesh quickly becomes very tough.

Habitat *In all types of beech forest, on fallen branches.*

Pores whitish, relatively large

The Umbrella Polypore (*P. umbellatus*) is easy to identify by its many branching caps. It can be eaten when young.

> **Cap rim has a fine fringe**
> **Pores irregular, polygonal**
> **Common throughout Europe**

Cap brown to ochre-yellow

Stipe short, often off-centre

Stipe base jet black

Chicken of the Woods (⑂⑂)

Laetiporus sulphureus (bracket fungi)
Size 15–30 cm   April–September

Habitat *In lowland forests, avenues and on lone deciduous trees or fallen trees, occasionally also on coniferous trees (yews).*

> Flesh yellow, juicy
> Pores only visible with the aid of a magnifying glass
> Common throughout Europe
> Similar species Cinnamon Bracket

This fungus is a tree parasite and it often forms carpets of fruiting bodies on tree trunks which can be many metres long. However, only young specimens taste good and even then, it depends on how they are cooked. One method it to cook it like chicken fricassee, although its slightly acidic taste does not appeal to everyone. It is, nevertheless, still popular because it occurs so early in the year.

The Giant Polypore (*Meripilus giganteus*) is a parasite on Beech trees. It is more of an ochre-yellow colour and turns black when bruised. It tastes good when young.

Cap rim turned in, sulphur yellow

Pores yellow

Caution!
Although it is the same shape, the Cinnamon Bracket (p. 269) is much smaller and a completely different colour, but has been confused with the Chicken of the Woods. It is now known to be highly poisonous.

268

Caps fan-shaped, stalkless

Fruiting bodies completely sulphur yellow

Cinnamon Bracket

Hapalopilus nidulans (bracket fungi)
Size 5–15 cm   July–October

This species is highly poisonous because of the large quantities of polyporic acid it contains. This acid also turns a deep shade of violet when it comes into contact with soap, which makes it a popular for dying wool. No other bracket fungi are known to be poisonous.

Habitat Primarily in deciduous forests, on fallen, dead deciduous wood, usually on beech.

The much less common *Hapalopilus croceus* grows on old oaks and is bright orange–yellow.

Fruiting bodies completely cinnamon–coloured

Caps fan–shaped, stalkless

> Flesh cinnamon-coloured
> Pores only visible with the aid of a magnifying glass
> Common in most parts of Europe, absent in the north

Turns violet on contact with soap

Dyer's Mazegill

Phaeolus schweinizii (bracket fungi)
Size 10–25 cm   July–October

This large fungus is usually found on the ground. It is a vibrant shade of yellow-brown and it has a soft, corky texture when fresh. It becomes darker and harder as it gets older and eventually turns completely black. Old specimens from the previous year are often found next to newly grown fungi.

Habitat Primarily in spruce forests, appears to be growing out of the ground although it is actually attached to spruce roots or stumps.

The Wood Bolete (*Pulveroboletus lignicola*) is sometimes found growing on the same roots as Dyer's Mazegill.

Upper surface yellow–brown, finely felted

> Pores small, slightly maze-like
> Fruiting bodies shaped like spinning tops
> Common throughout Europe

Bruised areas turn brown immediately

Rim bulging

Smoky Bracket

Bjerkandera adusta (bracket fungi)

Size 5–50 cm   Perennial

Habitat *In all types of forest, on fallen, rotting deciduous wood, less common on coniferous wood.*

> Flesh beige-brown
> Fruiting bodies corky, tough
> Common throughout Europe

As with many wood-dwelling fungi, the shape of this species depends on where it is growing. Two-dimensional fruiting bodies are formed if growing on the underside of the substrate. Small caps are formed if growing laterally on wood. Specimens growing on the upper surface of the substrate have small stipes as well as caps.

Lophoria spadicea is a similar colour but does not have any pores.

Pores very small, grey

Dark line between pores and cap flesh

Upper surface, grey-brown, slightly bristly/felted

Pore layer smoky grey

Lumpy Bracket

Trametes gibbosa (bracket fungi)

Size 7–20 cm   Perennial

Habitat *In all types of forest, on dead deciduous wood that is still hard, primarily on beech stumps.*

> Flesh creamy-white
> Fruiting bodies corky, hard
> Common throughout Europe

This fungus gets its name from the lumpy area where it is attached to the tree. This area is usually green on older specimens due to algae growth. The older, whitish-green specimens are easier to recognise since very young specimens are bulbous and do not display many of the key characteristics required for identification.

The Hairy Bracket (*T. hirsuta*) grows in similar locations. It has round pores and its upper surface is bristly.

Upper surface whitish, lumpy

Fruiting bodies bracket-shaped

Pores characteristically oblong, comma-shaped

Underside whitish

Turkeytail

Trametes versicolor (bracket fungi)

Size 5–10 cm   Perennial

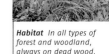

The Turkeytail's fruiting bodies are very durable which makes them ideal for dry flower arrangements or for handicrafts. However, they are often attacked by insects and anyone wishing to use one for decorative purposes should put it in the freezer for a few days to kill off any insects and their eggs.

Old fruiting bodies are often covered by algae which makes them look green.

Habitat In all types of forest and woodland, always on dead wood, no biotope preferences.

> Flesh creamy-white
> Fruiting bodies corky, hard
> Very common throughout Europe

Did you know?

There are other Trametes *species which do not have the same pretty shades of blue. The most similar species is the* T. multicolor *which, despite its name, is actually ochre.*

Underside creamy-white

Rim slightly bristly

271

Upper surface has blue, brown and white zones

While some zones are hairy, others are not

Blushing Bracket

Daedaleopsis confragosa (bracket fungi)
Size 5–15 cm   Perennial

Habitat *In damp woodlands, usually on the banks of streams or ponds, on dead deciduous wood, particularly willow and birch.*

> Flesh creamy-white
> Fruiting bodies corky, hard
> Common throughout Europe

Pores oblong

Underside turns pale pink when bruised

Many bracket fungi are difficult to identify, but the pale pink colour of the Blushing Bracket makes it easy to identify. If a specimen is left to dry indoors for one or two days, the entire underside turns pinkish-red.

The *tricolor* variety has gills on its underside and is a deep brown-red. Sometimes both varieties are found growing on the same branch.

Upper surface brownish-pink

Rim white

Split Porecrust

Schizopora paradoxa (bracket fungi)
Size 10–100 cm   Perennial

Habitat *On all types of dead deciduous wood, less common on coniferous wood, no biotope preferences.*

> Flesh creamy-white
> Fruiting bodies very difficult to remove, hard
> Very common throughout Europe

Underside has rows of tooth-like prickles

This uneven, prickly fungus is very common and takes many forms. The length and breadth of the prickles and the colour vary considerably. It can develop very long fruiting bodies, depending on the substrate.

The rare *Dentipellis fragilis* has even longer prickles which can be up to 5 cm long.

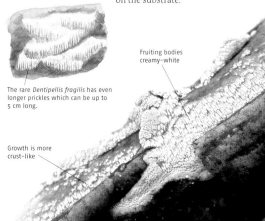

Fruiting bodies creamy-white

Growth is more crust-like

Purplepore Bracket

Trichaptum abietinum (bracket fungi)

Size 1–5 cm   Perennial

Although the individual fruiting bodies of this fungus are small, they grow in very close proximity to each other and can often cover areas of over a metre in length. However, only flat fruiting bodies are formed on the underside and upper surface of the wood.

Habitat In coniferous forests, on dead coniferous wood, particularly on spruce and fir.

> Flesh thin, leathery
> Fruiting bodies very difficult to remove
> Very common throughout Europe

Upper surface of cap rims defined

The Bleeding Conifer Crust (*Stereum sanguinolentum*) is often found in the same locations and can be identified by its smooth, reddening upper surface

Underside tinged with violet

Underside has irregularly twisted pores

273

Cinnabar Bracket

Pycnoporus cinnabarinus (bracket fungi)

Size 3–10 cm   Perennial

This fungus was relatively rare up until around 50 years ago. It may have something to do with the fact that dried wood used to be collected from forests, thereby leaving the fungus less substrate on which to grow. Today, most debris from trees is left to rot in forests resulting in ideal conditions for this fungus to thrive.

Habitat In open locations in forests, on dead deciduous wood, usually on beech, prefers dry conditions.

> Flesh cinnabar red
> Fruiting bodies corky, hard
> Common throughout Europe

Upper surface cinnabar red, slightly felted

Fruiting bodies bracket-shaped

Although the Fuzzy Orange Polypore (*Pycnoporellus fulgens*) is similar, it is a much brighter shade of orange and is not so hard. It grows on coniferous wood.

Underside completely cinnabar red

Pores round, almost regular

Hoof Fungus

Fomes fomentarius (bracket fungi)

Size 10–50 cm   Perennial

Habitat *In forests and woodlands, on thick, dead deciduous tree trunks, usually on beech and birch.*

> *Odour very acidic*
> *Fruiting bodies very hard*
> *Very common throughout Europe*

The Hoof Fungus has been used by people for centuries. For example, it was once used to transport embers since the hollowed-out fruiting bodies would smoulder for days on end instead of burning. Another practice involved obtaining a leather-like material from the mycellial core of the fungus.

Fruiting bodies growing at an angle of 90°, as often seen on fallen trees.

Fibrous, brown mycellial core

Flesh brown

Multiple pore layers

Did you know?

Craftwork with the Hoof Fungus used to be a relatively common practice in Germany. It involved making items such as hats or bags from the leather-like material obtained from the mycellial core. It has now almost completely died out.

Upper surface grey

Bulging rim zone

Red Banded Polypore

Fomitopsis pinicola (bracket fungi)
Size 10–40 cm   Perennial

No other bracket fungus inhabits so many different tree species. Over 30 deciduous species and 10 coniferous species are known to play host to this fungus. However, the colour of the fungus varies considerably with age and it takes many years of experience to be able to identify it positively every time.

Habitat On almost all types of tree in various types of forest and woodland.

> Odour very acidic
> Fruiting bodies very hard
> Common throughout Europe

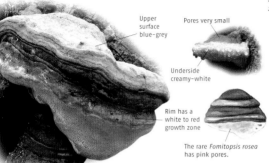

Upper surface blue–grey

Pores very small

Underside creamy–white

Rim has a white to red growth zone

The rare *Fomitopsis rosea* has pink pores.

Pores round, almost regular

Underside completely creamy–white

Oak Mazegill

Daedalea quercina (bracket fungi)
Size 10–40 cm   Perennial

The Oak Mazegill and the Robust Bracket (p. 262) are the two hardest bracket fungi in Europe. Both this and its maze-like underside make it easy to identify, even though it is very occasionally flat and only has very slight cap rims.

Habitat In all types of forest, always on rotting but still intact oak stumps.

> Odour slightly acidic
> Fruiting bodies very hard
> Common in all parts of Europe apart from the north

The intricate, maze-like pore layer is characteristic of this species.

Upper surface grey–brown

Rim has a white growth zone

Flesh beige-brown

Pore layer light beige

Conifer Mazegill

Gloeophyllum sepiarium (bracket fungi)

Size 5–20 cm   Perennial

Habitat *On thick, fallen coniferous branches and trunks, often also on timber.*

> *Odour slightly acidic*
> *Fruiting bodies very hard*
> *Very common throughout Europe*

Almost everyone has seen a Conifer Mazegill at some point as it grows mainly on poorly protected timber. Common places to find it are on fence posts, wooden balconies and railway sleepers. It is not particularly aggressive, but it can cause damage if left unchecked for a few years.

Growth zone bright orange when fresh

Upper surface orange-brown

Underside has orange-brown gills

Gills cross-linked

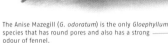

The Anise Mazegill (*G. odoratum*) is the only *Gloephyllum* species that has round pores and also has a strong odour of fennel.

Common Porecrust

Schizophyllum commune (bracket fungi)

Size 5–20 cm   Perennial

Habitat *On newly felled deciduous trees, usually beeches, tolerant of open, dry conditions.*

> *Flesh creamy-white*
> *Fruiting bodies thin, tough*
> *Very common throughout Europe*

The Common Porecrust is hard to categorise because it has longitudinally split gills and it is unknown as to which other species it might be closely related. The fungus can expand its gills to protect itself against bright sunlight and is therefore capable of surviving in very sunny locations.

Both halves of each gill can expand outwards to cover the entire fruiting layer.

Rim white, shaggy

Gills spilt longitudinally

Fruiting bodies attached without stipes

Underside brown to violet-grey

Yellow Stagshorn (¶)

Calocera viscosa (jelly fungi)
Size 3–10 cm   June–December

Although not poisonous, this texture of this fungus is like rubber and it has no taste whatsoever. Some people use it to garnish salads because of its pretty colour and it is completely harmless.

Habitat In coniferous forests and mixed forests, always on dead, very rotten coniferous woods.

Fruiting bodies coral-like, with branchlets

> **Flesh orange-yellow**
> **Fruiting bodies very rubbery**
> **Very common throughout Europe**

The Small Stagshorn (*C. cornea*) is much smaller, has no branchlets and grows on deciduous wood.

Fruiting bodies yellow-orange

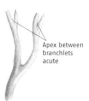

Apex between branchlets acute

Common Jellyspot (✗)

Dacrymyces stillatus (jelly fungi)
Size 0.5–1 cm   Perennial

Although the individual fruiting bodies of this fungus are very small, masses of them grow in such close proximity to each other that they merge. As such, they form orange-yellow layers on wood which are particularly striking when the weather is wet.

Habitat Always on dead, rotten deciduous or coniferous wood, no biotope preferences.

Fruiting bodies yellow

> **Flesh yellow to orange**
> **Fruiting bodies as hard as horn when dry**
> **Very common throughout Europe**

Fruiting bodies button-like, jelly-like

The larger Jelly Fungus (*Femsjonia peziziformis*) can be distinguished by the fact that it has two colours.

Individual fruiting bodies merge

Jelly Ear
Auricularia auricularia-judae (jelly fungi)
Size 2–10 cm   Perennial

🍴

Habitat In forests, coppices and on forest boundaries, primarily on dead elder branches, occasionally on beech and other deciduous wood.

> Flesh jelly-like
> Fruiting bodies as hard as horn when dry
> Very common throughout Europe

This fungus and similar Asian species are an important constituent of Chinese cuisine because of their jelly-like texture. This species is called *muh-err* in China which means 'cloud ear.' In Western shops, they are often given the rather misleading name 'China Morel.'

The fruiting bodies of the Tripe Fungus (*A. mesenterica*) are crust-like rather than ear-shaped.

Fruiting bodies almost cup-like when young

Did you know?

Auriculariopsis ampla grows on dead poplar and willow branches. It looks like a miniature version of the Jelly Ear but it is not eaten.

278

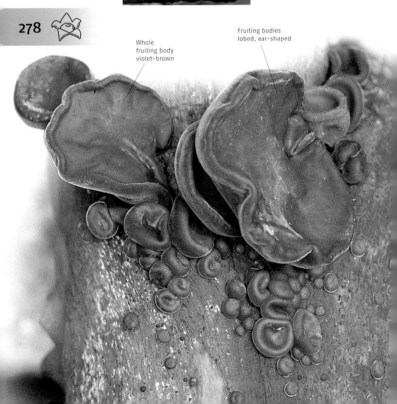

Whole fruiting body violet-brown

Fruiting bodies lobed, ear-shaped

Black Witch's Butter

Exidia plana (jelly fungi)
Size 10–100 cm   Perennial

Individual fruiting bodies can still be distinguished on very young specimens but they soon merge and cover extensive areas.

Habitat *Always on dead deciduous wood, primarily on oak, no particular biotope preferences.*

> **Flesh jelly-like**
> **Fruiting bodies turn very hard when dry**
> **Common throughout Europe**

Fruiting bodies merge to form irregular, crust-like layers

Whole fruiting body black

Exidia cartilaginea forms white crusts and only grows on lime wood.

Individual fruiting bodies merge with each other

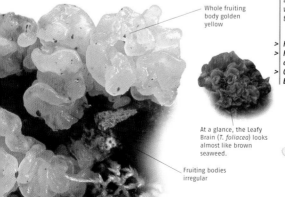

279

Yellow Brain

Tremella mesenterica (jelly fungi)
Size 2–5 cm   Perennial

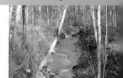

It is not hard to see where this fungus got its name from. However, when the weather is dry, the Yellow Brain becomes hard and shrivels so much that it is barely recognisable.

Habitat *In various biotopes with high humidity, always on dead deciduous branches, usually those which are still attached to the tree.*

> **Flesh jelly-like**
> **Fruiting bodies as hard as horn when dry**
> **Common throughout Europe**

Whole fruiting body golden yellow

Fruiting bodies brain-like

At a glance, the Leafy Brain (*T. foliacea*) looks almost like brown seaweed.

Fruiting bodies irregular

Apricot Jelly Fungus

Tremiscus helvelloides (jelly fungi)
Size 3–7 cm   July–November

🍴

Habitat *In coniferous forests on chalky soils, often beside paths with chalk gravel, even if the base soil is acidic.*

> *Flesh jelly-like*
> *Fruiting bodies as hard as horn when dry*
> *Uncommon in Europe, patchy distribution in some regions*

The Apricot Jelly Fungus is one of very few fungi that can be eaten raw. It can, for example, be used in fruiting salads or put in aspic with vegetables. However, it tastes of very little and has a texture similar to that of wine-gums, which does not appeal to everyone.

Some *Otidea* species also have similar-shaped fruiting bodies.

Fruiting bodies similar in shape to paper bags

Did you know?

Fungi from other families also form similar-shaped fruiting bodies, such as Hohenbuehelia geogenium. *Although it is edible, it is rare and should not be picked.*

280

Fruiting bodies grow in groups

Whole fruiting body salmon pink to cinnabar red

Jelly Tooth

Pseudohydnum gelatinosum (jelly fungi)

Size 2–5 cm   July–November

🍴

This fungus is also used as an edible decoration on salads and other cold dishes. The Jelly Tooth is either brown or white and neither colour is found on the same tree stump.

Habitat In coniferous forests, usually at altitude, always on rotting coniferous tree stumps.

> Flesh jelly-like, elastic
> Fruiting bodies as hard as horn when dry
> Patchy distribution throughout Europe, common in some regions

Fruiting bodies tongue-shaped

The Earpick Fungus is as hard as cork and only grows on spruce cones.

Stipe short, lateral

Underside has jelly-like teeth

Devil's Fingers

Clathrus archeri (stinkhorns)

Size 5–12 cm   July–November

☠

This fungus was imported in sheep's wool from Australia and was first discovered in Europe in the western Vosges in around 1920. It spread rapidly throughout Europe which was easy to track because of its striking appearance. Today, it is still quite common in central Europe, but largely absent from the north and east.

Habitat In forests and coppices, on meadows and grasslands, no biotope preferences.

> Odour of carrion, unpleasant
> White mycelium threads at base
> Common in most parts of central Europe, rare in the north and east

The Red Cage (*C. ruber*) is very common in the Mediterranean region.

4–7 red 'fingers' with light olive-coloured spores

The crowded 'witch's eggs' (immature fruiting bodies) of this species are reminiscent of bird eggs. They have a jelly-like exterior.

The red 'fingers' are even visible inside the witch's egg

Stinkhorn (⑪)

Phallus impudicus (stinkhorns)
Height 12–20 cm   June–November

Habitat In forests and coppices, no biotope preferences, although slightly more common on acidic soils.

> Fruiting body grows out of a witch's egg
> White mycellium threads at base
> Common throughout Europe, as far north as southern Finland

The fruiting body can be recognised inside the witch's egg

Exterior of witch's egg jelly-like

Mature Stinkhorns are unmistakable because of their unique shape and the very unpleasant odour emitted by the olive-coloured head. The Stinkhorn is inedible when mature but it can be eaten when still inside the 'witch's egg' (immature fruiting body). If eaten raw, it has a strong, radish-like taste. It is best to cut the witch's egg into slices and fry them until crispy.

The smaller, orange Dog Stinkhorn (*Mutinus caninus*) is harder to find.

Did you know?
The spores of this fungus are spread by insects which are attracted by the carrion-like smell emitted by the spores. It only takes one or two days for insects to devour all of the spores, leaving nothing but a white, chambered head.

Head coated with foul-smelling, olive-coloured spores

Stipe white, fragile, porous

Remnants of the witch's egg

Rosy Earthstar

Geastrum rufescens (puffballs)
Size 4–8 cm   July–November

Earthstars are perhaps the most unusual looking of all fungi and are particularly reminiscent of fictional spaceships. However, the elevated position of the ball is a very effective way of ensuring that a maximum number of spores enter the air when released.

Habitat *In forests and coppices, particularly in spruce forests, on chalky soils.*

> **Spores released when ball is squeezed**
> **Spores olive-brown**
> **Common to patchy distribution in Europe, very rare in the north**

Earthstars grow out of an underground bulb and only appear above ground after some time.

No stipe under head

5-7 fleshy, stilt-like 'arms'

Opening irregular, fringy

Head bulbous

Rayed Earthstar

Geastrum quadrifidum (puffballs)
Size 3–6 cm   July–November

The fruiting bodies of earthstars and particularly those of this species, only weather gradually and often remain intact throughout the winter. As such, it is possible to find earthstars throughout the year, although fresh specimens can only be found in summer and autumn.

Habitat *In forests and coppices, primarily in spruce forests, on chalky soils.*

> **Spores released when ball is squeezed**
> **Spores olive-brown**
> **Common to patchy distribution in Europe**

Head has a stipe

4 stilt-like 'arms'

The Sandy Stiltball (*Battarraea phalloides*) releases its spores in a similar way but has a long stipe instead of stilts.

Opening cone-shaped

Rest of exterior between lobes

Grey Puffball

Bovista plumbea (puffballs)

Size 3–8 cm   July–November

Habitat *On moderately fertilised grasslands of all types.*

> Spores released when ball is squeezed
> Spores olive-brown
> Common in Europe

Whereas fresh Grey Puffballs are relatively heavy, mature fruiting bodies are very light once the outer skin has flaked off. The wind blows these fruiting bodies across grassland and they release spores over a wide area in the process.

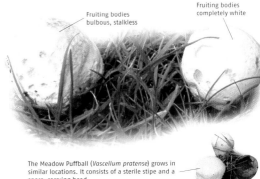

Fruiting bodies bulbous, stalkless

Fruiting bodies completely white

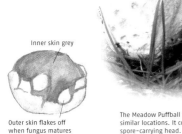

Inner skin grey

Outer skin flakes off when fungus matures

The Meadow Puffball (*Vascellum pratense*) grows in similar locations. It consists of a sterile stipe and a spore-carrying head.

Pestle Puffball

Handkea excipuliformis (puffballs)

Size 3–8 cm   July–November

Habitat *In deciduous and coniferous forests, no particular soil preferences.*

> Spores released when ball is squeezed
> Spores olive-brown
> Common in Europe

The rule of thumb for puffballs is that they are all edible as long as they are white on the inside. When they are too old, the insides are an olive-brown colour due to the large amount of mature spores. However, even young specimens do not appeal to everyone. They are best when cut into slices and fried.

Fruiting bodies club-shaped or sack-like

Fruiting bodies creamy-white when young

Inside of ball gradually turns olive-brown

Stipe remains creamy-brown

The sterile stipe often remains in place for many years, whereas all that remains of the rest of the fungus is the collapsed shell.

Giant Puffball
Calvatia gigantea (puffballs)
Size 20–50 cm   July–November

This fungus is unmistakable because of its incredible size, with large specimens weighing up to 15 kilos. As with all puffballs, it can be eaten as long as it is white inside. It is best when cut into thick slices and fried. It does not taste good when steamed.

Habitat In orchards and on fertilised grasslands, also in coppices, always in nitrate-rich locations, especially on sludge.

Did you know?
The Mosaic Puffball (*Handkea utriformis*) is also edible and can be up to 20cm across. The trophy-shaped fruiting bodies (right) are carried across grasslands by the wind.

> Spores released when ball is squeezed
> Spores olive-brown
> Patchy distribution in Europe

Inside of ball turns olive-brown with age

Outer skin flakes off with age

Inside white when young

Fruiting bodies, bulbous, large

Common Puffball

Lycoperdon perlatum (puffballs)
Size 4–7 cm   June–December

This puffball can be identified by the small, removable warts on its outer skin. After these have fallen off, they leave behind polygonal pits which give the exterior of the puffball a fungus-like appearance. It can be eaten as long as it is white inside. However, it should be fried and eaten on its own as a separate dish.

The Dusky Puffball (*L. nigrescens*) can be distinguished by its dark warts.

Habitat *In coniferous and deciduous forests of all types, among fallen leaves or needles, no soil preferences.*

> **Spores released when ball is squeezed**
> **Spores olive-brown**
> **Very common in Europe**
> **Poisonous similar – species young Fly Agaric specimens**

Inside of ball turns olive-brown

Stipe foam-like

Caution!

Young Fly Agarics can look remarkably similar (left). Once they are cut open, however, the red cap skin can be observed in the form of an orange-red line (right).

Fruiting bodies shaped like inverted pears

Covered with removable, white warts

Stump Puffball

(🍴)

Lycoperdon pyriforme (puffballs)

Size 3–6 cm June–December

Although the Stump Puffball is edible when young, it has an unpleasant taste and cannot be recommended. It is also the only puffball that grows on wood.

Habitat *In deciduous and coniferous forests of all types, always on rotting wood, no soil preferences.*

> **Rooting threads white, noticeable**
> **Spores olive-brown**
> **Very common throughout Europe**

The rare Flaky Puffball (*L. mammiforme*) can be distinguished by its large, flat scales on its surface.

Exterior smooth

Fruiting bodies club-shaped

Inside of ball turns olive

Fruiting bodies club-shaped

Spiny Puffball

(🍴)

Lycoperdon echinatum (puffballs)

Size 3–6 cm July–November

Unlike any of the other puffballs, this species has very long, securely fixed spines all over its outer surface. Indeed, these spines are so difficult to remove that the there is no way this species can be eaten.

Habitat *In beech forests, primarily on alkaline, clay soils.*

> **Spores released when ball is squeezed**
> **Spores olive-brown**
> **Patchy distribution in Europe**

Spines long, soft

Spiny puffballs lose their spines as they get older leaving a mosaic of polygonal pits.

Fruiting bodies completely brown

Inside of ball turns olive

Exterior completely covered with spines

Common Earthball

Scleroderma citrinum (puffballs)
Size 5–15 cm July–December

Habitat In coniferous forests, less common in deciduous forests, always on acidic, relatively nutrient-poor soils.

> **Fruiting bodies burst open unevenly**
> **Spores olive-brown**
> **Very common in Europe**

Earthballs are the only puffball-type fungi which are poisonous if eaten. However, they are easy to identify because they are violet on the inside, even when young.

The Scaly Earthball (*S. verrucosum*) is smaller, a deeper shade of brown and has a thinner outer skin.

Fruiting bodies round, bulbous

Exterior has rough scales

Inside violet-black

Outer skin very thick

Dyeball

Pisolithus arrhizus (puffballs)
Size 5–20 cm July–November

Habitat In biotopes with pioneer vegetation, often on slag heaps, always on nutrient-poor, sandy soils.

> **Fruiting bodies turn powdery and collapse**
> **Spores reddish-brown**
> **Relatively uncommon in most of Europe, common in some regions**

The Dyeball is treated as though it were a truffle in the regions where it is most common. Although its flavour is nothing like that of real truffles and it looks quite unappetising, it is still a prized edible fungus. It should be noted, however, that this fungus turns all other food a deep blackish-brown.

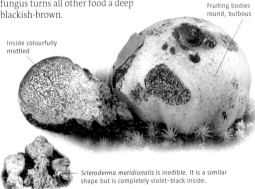

Fruiting bodies round, bulbous

Inside colourfully mottled

Inside chambered, iridescent

Stipe completely brown

Scleroderma meridionalis is inedible. It is a similar shape but is completely violet-black inside.

Cowberry Redleaf

Exobasidium vaccinii (sac fungi)
Size 0.5–1 cm   July–November

All *Exobasidium* species are parasites which usually inhabit berry bushes or rhododendrons. They attack the leaves or even entire saplings, which then become red and swollen in places. Despite this, the effects of these fungi are not life-threatening.

Habitat *In damp coniferous forests and boggy areas, on nutrient-poor, sandy soils, always on the leaves of cowberry bushes (Vaccinium vitis-idaea).*

> **Fruiting layer inside leaf**
> **Exterior of swellings white when mature**
> **Common in Europe**

Inside colourfully mottled

Exobasidium vacinii-uliginosi grows on bog Blueberry bushes. It affects entire shoots rather than leaves.

Red-yellow mark on upper surface of leaf

Causes red swellings on the underside

Ergot

Claviceps purpurea (sac fungi)
Size 1–3 cm   July–November

Before seed cleaning was introduced, Ergot was responsible for mass poisoning which affected entire regions. The fungus caused circulatory dysfunction in its victims which started with unbearable irritation of the skin and eventually led to entire limbs dying off. Nowadays, the poison contained within Ergot is actually used in medicine.

Habitat *In grain fields, on grasslands with high grass, no soil preferences.*

> **Fruiting bodies purple-violet**
> **Heads have a pustulated surface**
> **Common in Europe, has become rare in some regions**

Sclerota black, curved

Stem occupied by multiple sclerota

Corn Smut (*Ustilago maydis*) is another parasite which is much-feared by farmers. It is sometimes even eaten in other countries.

Multiple fruiting bodies develop in spring

Yellow Morel
Morchella esculenta (sac fungi)
Size 10–20 cm   April–May (June)

Habitat In lowland forests and trees lining the banks of streams, almost always under ash trees, sometimes in orchards, on chalky soils.

> Flesh waxy, gristly in the stipe
> Spores cream-coloured
> Patchy distribution in Europe
> Similar species Gyromitra species

Morels are among the most highly prized edible fungi and are especially delicious when cooked in a creamy sauce as an accompaniment to fillet steak. Finding morels presents a new challenge each year as they are particularly hard to identify.

Morels can have various different colours.

Dried morels have a particularly intense aroma.

Fruiting body hollow

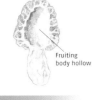

Caution!

Gyromitra *species* (p. 291), such as the Snow Morel (Gyromitra gigas, *left*) are poisonous and must not be confused with the Yellow Morel (right) or the Black Morel (middle).

Cap web-like, ochre-yellow

Stipe white

Black Morel

Morchella conica (sac fungi)
Size 8–15 cm   March–June

The Black Morel is often found growing on mulched beets beside farm buildings and on grassland. They normally grow in large clumps with hundreds of fruiting bodies. It is protected in some parts of Europe.

Habitat In mossy spruce and fir forests, on wood piles and on bark mulch on chalky soils.

> **Flesh waxy, gristly in the stipe**
> **Spores cream-coloured**
> **Common to patchy distribution in Europe**

Cap web-like, oblong, grey-black

Stipe creamy-white

The cap rim of the Semifree Morel (*M. gigas*) is not attached to the stipe which can be seen clearly in the cross-section. It is edible but does not taste particularly good.

Fruiting body hollow

False Morel

Gyromitra esculenta (sac fungi)
Size 8–15 cm   April–June

The False Morel contains gyromitrin, a poison which attacks the liver, but which is not heat-resistant. If this fungus is cooked or dried for long enough, the poison dissipates and so it is sold as an edible fungus in some countries. However, eating this fungus will always be risky since it is difficult to determine the point at which the poison has been neutralised.

Habitat In pine forests, on nutrient-poor, non chalky, sandy soils.

> **Flesh waxy, gristly in the stipe**
> **Spores cream-coloured**
> **Patchy distribution in Europe**

The Pouched False Morel (*G. infula*) can be distinguished by the unique shape of its cap.

Cap brain-like

Stipe creamy-white

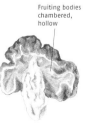

Fruiting bodies chambered, hollow

Pig's Ears
Gyromitra ancilis (sac fungi)
Size 3–10 cm   April–June

🍴

Habitat *In coniferous forests, always on very rotten tree debris, usually from spruces, occasionally on bark mulch.*

> Flesh waxy, fragile
> Odour indistinctly mushroomy
> Patchy distribution in Europe

This fungus is hard to spot since its fruiting bodies are almost flush with the wood they occupy. Unlike the similar Bleach Cup, which has a similar aroma to the morels, Pig's Ears are small and do not taste particularly good.

Fruiting layer red-brown

Almost stipe-like where attached to wood

Underside whitish

Upper surface irregular, wrinkled

The similar Bleach Cup (*Disciotis venosa*) grows on the ground and has a distinct odour of chlorine. Despite this, it tastes very good.

Vinegar Cup
Helvella acetabulum (sac fungi)
Size 3–15 cm   April–June

🍴

Habitat *In deciduous forests, at the edges of paths in deciduous and coniferous forests, on alkaline soils.*

> Flesh waxy, fragile
> Fruiting bodies trophy-shaped
> Patchy distribution in Europe

This size of this species varies considerably. The stipe is often also hard to identify since it can be very short or completely underground. As such, it can be very difficult to identify this fungus, despite its appearance.

Interior grey-brown

Exterior a lighter shade of brown

Stipe 'limbs' extend far up the cup

Stipe white, with prominent 'ribs'

The Elastic Saddle (*H. elastica*) has no 'ribs' on its stipe and a saddle-like cap.

White Saddle (❨❨❩)

Helvella crispa (sac fungi)
Size 5–20 cm   August–November

Although the White Saddle does taste of much, the texture of its flesh makes it ideal for Asian cuisine. However, caution must be exercised since this fungus is poisonous if not cooked thoroughly.

Helvella queletii has a thinner stipe and a regular, saddle-shaped cap.

Habitat *In deciduous forests, on the edges of paths and forest boundaries, usually on moderately nutrient-rich soils.*

> *Flesh waxy, gristly in the stipe*
> *Odour mushroomy*
> *Common in Europe*

Did you know?
Apart from being grey-black, the Elfin Saddle (H. lacunosa) is practically a mirror image of the White Saddle. It usually grows among the fallen leaves in deciduous forests which makes it hard to spot. It can be eaten if thoroughly cooked.

Cap flesh thin

Stipe ribbed and chambered

293

Cap lobed or saddle-like

Whole fruiting body creamy-white to beige

Violet Crowncup

Sarcosphaera crassa (sac fungi)
Size 5–15 cm   June–August

Habitat In coniferous forests and at the edges of paths, usually under pines, primarily on chalky soils.

> Flesh waxy, fragile
> Exterior turns slightly yellow
> Rare to patchy distribution in Europe

The Violet Crowncup is the only cup-shaped fungus that is known to be poisonous. There are many other similar, violet species which do not grow out of the ground and only occasionally have fruiting bodies which break open in star shapes. The Violet Crowncup is also always larger and has thicker flesh.

Did you know?

Pure white albino specimens are occasionally found. These are the result of genetics rather than the effects of the weather and grow in the same locations year after year.

Young fruiting bodies grow out of the ground

Interior violet

Exterior off-white

Bay Cup
Peziza badia (sac fungi)
Size 5–15 cm   July–November

The Bay Cup grows along paths on sandy, acidic soils in coniferous forests and is sometimes found in large numbers. However, it is rarely eaten since it does not taste good. It is also very fragile and it would be hard to keep it intact in transit.

Habitat In coniferous forests and on the edges of paths, on acidic, sandy, relatively dry soils, usually under spruces.

The flesh of the Yellowing Cup (*P. succosa*) exudes a watery, yellow fluid, making it easy to identify.

> Flesh waxy, fragile
> Odour insignificant
> Common in Europe
> Similar species Violet Crowncup

Caution!
The Violet Crowncup (p. 294) can be distinguished by its colour and grows in completely different locations under pines on chalky soils. It also grows out of the ground.

Flesh brownish

Fruiting bodies often have short stipes

295

Exterior brownish-red

Interior olive-brown

Hare's Ear

🍴

Otidea onotica (sac fungi)
Size 3–7 cm   July–November

Habitat In deciduous forests, particularly under beeches, less common in coniferous forests, on alkaline, clay soils.

> Flesh thin, fragile
> Grows in groups and clumps
> Patchy distribution in Europe

There are a number of *Otidea* species and they can all be identified by the fact that they resemble various animals' ears. Although they are edible, they are relatively rare and should not be picked.

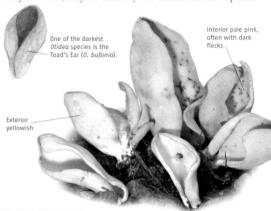

One of the darkest *Otidea* species is the Toad's Ear (*O. bufonia*).

Interior pale pink, often with dark flecks

Exterior yellowish

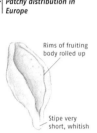

Rims of fruiting body rolled up

Stipe very short, whitish

296

Toothed Cup

✂

Tarzetta cupularis (sac fungi)
Size 2–4 cm   May–July (September)

Habitat In deciduous forests, on embankments, on the banks of streams and on the edges of paths, on defoliated, clay soils.

> Flesh odourless
> Grows in groups
> Common in Europe

Little is known about the edibility of this fungus, which has very small fruiting bodies. It is therefore best not to pick it.

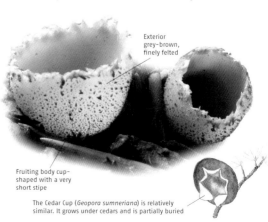

Exterior grey-brown, finely felted

Rim of fruiting body notched

Flesh light beige

Fruiting body cup-shaped with a very short stipe

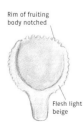

The Cedar Cup (*Geopora sumneriana*) is relatively similar. It grows under cedars and is partially buried

Glazed Cup
Humaria hemisphaerica (sac fungi)
Size 1–2 cm   May–November

The exterior of the Glazed Cup is covered with hairs which cling to the fungus and are almost like wool. They are too small to be eaten.

The Glazed Cup is often attacked by another fungus when mature. It forms a white layer across the inside of its host.

Interior grey-beige

Exterior covered with brownish hairs

Habitat *Primarily on defoliated, clay soils, often on embankments or landslips.*

> **Fruiting bodies hemispheric, cup-shaped**
> **No stipe**
> **Common throughout Europe**

Brownish fringe on rim

Flesh whitish

Common Eyelash
Scutellinia scutellata (sac fungi)
Size 1–2 cm   May–November

A magnifying glass is needed in order to see the hairs on this fungus clearly. These black, very pointed hairs actually look quite menacing at large magnifications, although they are so soft and thin that they cannot penetrate the skin.

Habitat *Primarily on rotten deciduous and coniferous wood, some varieties also grow on clay soils.*

> **Fruiting bodies flat, cup-shaped**
> **No stipe**
> **Common throughout Europe**

Interior bright orange

Exterior covered with thick hair

Many cup-shaped fungi have hairy exteriors, such as the tiny *Lasiobolus ciliatus* which has transparent hairs.

Hairs brown–black, pointed

Hairs length varies

Orange Peel Fungus ⚔️

Aleuria aurantia (sac fungi)
Size 2–7 cm   August–November

Habitat *Along compacted forest paths, beside ditches with little plant growth in them and on grassy areas, rarely in deep forests.*

> *Fruiting bodies irregular, lobed*
> *Flesh orange, fragile*
> *Common throughout Europe*

This is one of the few cup-shaped fungi that are known to be edible. Although it is almost tasteless, it can be used to decorate puddings, salads or other cold dishes.

Exterior turns whitish when dried

Exterior bright orange

Base is often almost stipe-like

Small, young specimens have a regular, cup-like shape.

Interior bright orange

Golden Cup ⚔️

Caloscypha fulgens (sac fungi)
Size 2–5 cm   March–May

Habitat *In spruce or silver fir forests on chalky soils, also among elder trees and other deciduous trees.*

> *Fruiting bodies irregular, cup-like*
> *Flesh orange, fragile*
> *Rare throughout Europe, only occurs sporadically*

Often, this wonderful spring species suddenly appears in large numbers after not being seen for years or even decades. The reason behind this is unknown and little is known about the edibility of this fungus. In any case, it is rare and should not be picked.

Interior bright orange

Exterior turns a dirty, bluish-green colour

Exterior matt ochre-orange

The Ebony Cup (*Pseudoplectania nigrella*) occurs at the same time on rotting coniferous tree stumps.

Scarlet Elfcup

Sarcoscypha austriaca (sac fungi)
Size 3–6 cm   (December) January–March

This brightly coloured fungus occurs early in the year after the thaw. It has been discovered that tiny fruiting bodies are formed in late autumn which continue to develop in mild winter periods between frosts. As such, the fruiting bodies sometimes only reach maturity after many months.

The dark, brownish-black Devil's Urn (*Urnula craterium*) also occurs early in the year.

Habitat In humus-rich, damp deciduous forests and beside trees lining river banks, always on fallen deciduous wood.

> Flesh thin, creamy white
> Fruiting bodies corky, hard
> Very common throughout Europe

Did you know?

Yellow or white albino variants are found occasionally. This is down to genetics rather than the effects of the weather since these variants grow in the same locations year after year.

Exterior almost white when dry

Interior bright red

Fruiting bodies trophy-shaped

Black Truffle

Tuber melanosporum (sac fungi)
Size 2–8 cm November–March

Habitat In deciduous forests or under lone trees, in chalky soils, primarily oaks and hazel.

> Fruiting bodies bulbous, grow underground
> Odour becomes increasingly strong with age
> Rare in Europe, found mainly in the western Mediterranean region

Because Black Truffles sell for such high prices, it is not uncommon for some sellers to fraudulently increase their weight by pressing stones or earth into them. Another tactic is selling less desirable truffles or even other types of fungus as Black Truffles.

The Indian Truffle (*T. indicum*) is often fraudulently sold as it costs less than 10% of the price of Black Truffles. The way to tell the difference is by looking at the spore patterns. The Black Truffle has spiky spores (left) and the Indian Truffle has netted or burred looking spores (right).

Exterior black, uneven

The brownish parts inside the truffle increase in size with age.

Fruiting bodies almost black inside, criss-crossed with thin, white threads

Summer Truffle

Tuber aestivum (sac fungi)
Size 2–8 cm September–November

Habitat On forest boundaries or under lone trees, on chalky soils, primarily under beeches, oaks and hazel.

> Fruiting bodies bulbous, grow underground
> Odour becomes increasingly strong with age
> Patchy distribution in southern Europe, rare north of the Alps

The Summer Truffle is the only kind of black truffle which is also occasionally found in central Europe. It is sometimes used to flavour pate, sausages and other foods. It is a heavily protected species in some European countries where picking it is forbidden, even if it is found growing in your own garden.

The surface if real black truffles is hard and covered with pyramidal warts.

Exterior black, uneven

Fruiting bodies almost black inside, criss-crossed with thin, white threads

Alba Truffle

Tuber magnatum (sac fungi)

Size 2–15 cm   November–March

The Alba Truffle is the most highly sought-after of all truffles and is even more expensive than the Black Truffle. Prices can be in the region of £4,200 per kilo and one record-breaking truffle weighing over a kilo was even sold for £35,700! It can only be found in central and northern Italy in regions such as Lombardy, Piedmont and Umbria. So far, all attempts to cultivate Alba Truffles have failed.

The inside of most species of fungi that grow underground is not mottled, such as *Melanogaster broomeianus*.

Habitat In young deciduous forests, on chalky, flat soils, primarily under oaks and hazel.

> Fruiting bodies potato-like, grow underground
> Odour becomes increasingly strong with age, similar to garlic
> Only found in Italy, rare
> Similar species White Truffle

Fruiting bodies criss-crossed with thin, lighter-coloured threads inside

301

Caution!

The White Truffle (Choiromyces maeandriformis) grows in other European countries, but it doesn't taste particularly good and is poisonous if eaten raw.

Exterior off-white to beige, smooth

Jellybaby

Leotia lubrica (sac fungi)

Size 3–6 cm   July–October

Habitat *In deciduous forests on relatively nutrient-rich soils, primarily among fallen beech leaves.*

> Fruiting bodies rubbery, jelly-like
> Patchy distribution throughout Europe, common in some regions

Many mushroom guidebooks used to class this species as edible. It had to be cooked in a pot with a lid since the jelly-like fruiting bodies would pop and jump like popcorn. Today, some experts doubt the edibility of the Jellybaby and so it is best avoided.

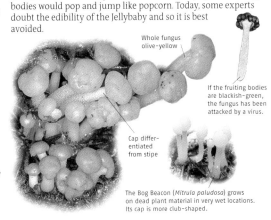

Whole fungus olive-yellow

If the fruiting bodies are blackish-green, the fungus has been attacked by a virus.

Scales almost same colour as stipe

Cap differentiated from stipe

The Bog Beacon (*Mitrula paludosa*) grows on dead plant material in very wet locations. Its cap is more club-shaped.

Hairy Earthtongue

Trichoglossum hirsutum (sac fungi)

Size 2–5 cm   July–October

Habitat *On nutrient-poor, damp grasslands and around boggy areas, intolerant of nitrates.*

> Fruiting bodies reminiscent of liquorice
> Flesh pale creamy-grey
> Rare to patchy distribution in central and northern Europe, in serious decline

The Hairy Earthtongue is adapted to nutrient-poor biotopes and cannot survive in locations that have been artificially fertilised. Even one application of fertiliser to Hairy Earthtongue's habitat will cause it to disappear almost immediately, just like many hygrocybes (p. 46) and coral fungi (p. 247).

The rare Green Earthtongue (*Microglossum viride*) grows on nutrient-poor, acidic soils on damp river banks, or under large beeches.

Tip irregular, head or club-like

Fruiting bodies have prominent hairs

Stipe longer than tip, black

Anemone Cup

Dumontinia tuberosa (sac fungi)
Size 0.5–2 cm   April–May

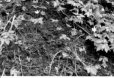

There are many parasitical cup-shaped fungi which inhabit various plants, such as grass, berry bushes or flowers. Many of these fungi develop a sclerota which is a bulbous structure made up of fungal hyphae and host plant tissue. This can survive the winter and new fruiting bodies grow from it in spring.

Habitat In deciduous forests on clay soils, a parasite on the roots of the anemone (Anemone nemorosa).

> **Fruiting bodies waxy, soft**
> **Flesh watery brown**
> **Common throughout Europe**

The Alder Goblet (*Ciboria caucus*) grows on willow catkins in the early spring.

Multiple fruiting bodies usually grow out of one sclerota.

Centre wrinkled, constricted

Fruiting bodies brown, cup-shaped

Fruiting bodies grow directly from the sclerota

Sclerota bulbous, black, white on the inside

Purple Jellydisc

Ascocoryne sarcoides (sac fungi)
Size 0.5–2 cm   November–March

Remarkably, the watery, very soft fruiting bodies of this fungus turn as hard as fingernails when dried and break up when being cut. It is a very easy fungus to identify because of its colour.

Habitat In all types of deciduous forest, on moderately rotten deciduous wood, usually beech wood.

> **Fruiting bodies jelly-like**
> **Common throughout Europe**

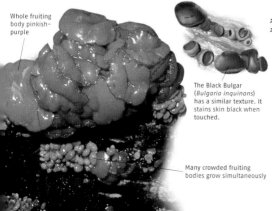

Whole fruiting body pinkish-purple

The Black Bulgar (*Bulgaria inquinans*) has a similar texture. It stains skin black when touched.

Many crowded fruiting bodies grow simultaneously

Fruiting bodies like spinning-tops, watery and jelly-like inside

Spring Pin
Cudoniella clavus (sac fungi)
Size 0.5–1 cm   March–July

Habitat In fast-flowing streams and rivers, on submerged or partially submerged, hard deciduous wood.

> Fruiting bodies jelly-like
> Patchy distribution in Europe's mountainous regions

Fungi can literally be found everywhere. It is therefore unsurprising that this species grows on branches and other parts of trees that have fallen into rivers and streams. It spends some of its life growing underwater. It only grows on wood in fast-flowing, clean water and its presence can even be used to determine the quality of the water.

Caps roundish, differentiated from stipe

Stipe long and thin

Whole fruiting body milky white

The Water Club (*Vibrissea truncorum*) also grows in water.

Green Elfcup
Chlorosplenium aeruginascens (sac fungi)
Size 0.2–0.5 cm   June–October

Habitat In deciduous forests of all types, on fallen, dead deciduous wood.

> Fruiting bodies waxy, soft
> Common throughout central Europe

The Green Elfcup's mycellium colours the wood it inhabits a wonderful shade of turquoise. Since the wood is not softened by the fungus, it is often used for inlays or other ornamental purposes. It is certainly much easier to find the coloured wood than it is to find actual Green Elfcup fruiting bodies.

Wood coloured by the Green Elfcup

Fruiting bodies smooth, cup-shaped

Whole fruiting body turquoise

Stipe same colour

Snaketongue Truffleclub

Cordyceps ophioglossoides (sac fungi)

Size 4–7 cm   July–October

This fungus is a parasite on Deer Truffles (*Elaphomyces granulatus*) which grow underground. Since it grows above ground, it indicates where the otherwise well-hidden Deer Truffles are growing. Unfortunately, Deer Truffles are inedible for humans and are only eaten by deer and other animals.

Habitat In damp coniferous forests, on acidic soils, usually in spruce forests with blueberries, always on Deer Truffles.

> Fruiting bodies corky
> Patchy distribution throughout Europe

Cordyceps gracilis is often found in early summer.

The rooting threads between this fungus and the deer truffle are easily torn.

Did you know?

Almost all other Cordyceps *species are parasites on insects and their larvae, such as* C. entomorrhiza *on ground beetles. It is often necessary to dig out the host before identification of the fungus is possible.*

305

Fruiting bodies club-shaped, almost black

Base and rooting threads yellow

Sycamore Tarspot

Rhytisma acerinum (sac fungi)
Size 1–2 cm   Perennial

Habitat *On sycamore leaves, no particular biotope preferences.*

> **Upper surface of fruiting bodies rough, soft inside**
> **Very common throughout Europe**

This fungus can probably be found on every sycamore tree and the black, tar-like spots it develops on the leaves are easy to spot. These spots continue to develop throughout the early summer and become thicker. The exterior hardens and closes up when dry. When it is wet, this opens up to expose the soft fruiting layer.

Individual fruiting bodies irregular, maze-like, open when weather is wet

Similar species, such as the Tar Spot (*R. salicina*), grow on rhododendrons, azaleas and willow leaves.

Fruiting bodies appear as black spots

Coral Spot

Nectria cinnabarina (sac fungi)
Size 0.2–0.3 cm   Perennial

Habitat *On freshly felled deciduous wood, sometimes on living deciduous trees.*

> **Exterior of fruiting bodies rough**
> **Very common throughout Europe**

The Coral Spot grows on the bark of living trees and it can cause them damage. It is the first fungus to develop on freshly felled wood, no matter whether this includes brushwood or thick tree trunks.

Pink at first, then red

Fruiting bodies tiny, crowded

Individual fruiting bodies red, round, with a small point

The Yellow Cushion Hypocrea (*H. gelatinosa*) has green spores which is a totally unique phenomenon in the world of fungi.

Beech Woodwart

Hypoxylon fragiforme (sac fungi)
Size 1–2 cm   Perennial

✗

This species is one of the first fungi to develop on dead beech wood. It can often be seen beside forest tracks growing on the trunks of felled beech trees waiting for transportation.

Habitat *On dead beech wood, no particular biotope preferences.*

> *Fruiting bodies rough, hard*
> *Very common throughout Europe*

Upper surface warty

The much larger King Alfred's Cake (*Daldinia concentrica*) is black and has concentric zones inside it.

Fruiting bodies bulbous, rusty brown

Many round holes inside fruiting bodies

Candlesnuff Fungus

Xylaria hypoxylon (sac fungi)
Size 2–5 cm   Perennial

✗

This antler-shaped fungus is possibly the most common fungus visible to the naked eye in central Europe and can be found on almost all types of wood. Although it grows between spring and autumn, the fruiting bodies live for a long time and can be found in winter.

Habitat *On moderately rotten wood of all types, no particular biotope preferences.*

> *Flesh white, tough, corky*
> *Very common throughout Europe*

Tips white, powdery

The Beechmast Candlesnuff (*X. carpophila*) is also common and grows on beech cupules among fallen leaves. It has fewer branches and is thin and thread-like.

Fruiting bodies black at base

Fruiting bodies usually reminiscent of antlers

Index of Species

Index of Species

Index of Species

All illustrations by Tanja Bšhning. All photographs by Andreas Gminder, except those listed in the following.

Key (see pages 4-5)
B = Biotope, M = Main Image, I = Info Box, A = Additional Image
Position: l = left, m = middle, r = right, t = top, b = bottom

Ayer: 45A; Barth: 207bA; Bineau: 45M, 142bM; Bšhning: 18B, 18M, 19Im, 23B, 26bB, 27B, 27M, 27Im, 30bB, 30bM, 31B, 32tB, 43M, 47bB, 66tB, 69M, 76M, 80bM, 84bB, 87I, 88tB, 90B, 94I, 95bB, 98M, 99tM, 99b all, 102tA, 108tB, 109bM, 109bA, 110tB, 110bB, 112tM, 113tM, 113tB, 113bA, 115tA, 115bA, 120I, 122A, 123M, 129B, 133B, 138A, 142tM, 147tM, 148bA, 152M, 153B, 153A, 154bB, 158tA, 159bA, 167I, 171tA, 178B, 178I, 182M, 185tM, 207bB, 209B, 212tB, 213bB, 215tB, 215bB, 216bB, 217M, 220b all, 226tM, 226bM, 231M, 234tM, 237tA, 239bM, 247tM, 249B, 256tA, 259bB, 260tB, 261M, 263A, 265t all, 269bM, 270tA, 271A, 272tB, 273tA, 274M, 275tA, 278I, 283tM, 284bM, 286A, 288bM 297tA, 302tA, 303tA, 304tM, 304bM, 306I, 307bM, 307bA; Bollmann: 18I, 19Ir, 20tM, 20bM, 21M, 21A, 22I, 23M, 23I, 24tM, 24bM, 24bA, 25tM, 25bM, 25bA, 26tM, 26tA, 26bM, 26bA, 27Ilr, 28M, 28A, 29II, 32tM, 32bM, 33tM, 33bM, 33bA, 34bM, 35bM, 37tM, 37tA, 37bM, 37bA, 38I, 40M, 41tM, 41bM, 41bA, 43I, 44A, 46tM, 46bM, 47tM, 47tA, 47bM, 48tM, 48bM, 48bA, 49I, 50tM, 50bM, 51bM, 52tM, 52bM, 52bA, 53M, 53I, 54tM, 56bA, 58I, 59tM, 59bM, 60tA, 61bM, 62M, 62A, 63M, 63A, 64M, 64I, 64A, 65M, 65I, 66tA, 66bM, 67M, 68tM, 68bM, 69I, 69A, 70M, 70I, 71tM, 71bM, 71bA, 72bA, 74I, 75tM, 75tA, 75bM, 75bA, 77tM, 78I, 79bM, 80tM, 81bM, 81bA, 82tM, 82tA, 82bM, 82bA, 83tM, 83tA, 84tA, 85bM, 86bM, 88tM, 89b all, 90M, 92bM, 93t all, 93bM, 93bB, 95tM, 95tA, 95bM, 97tM, 98I, 99tA, 101M, 101I, 102bM, 102bA, 103tM, 104M, 105M, 105I, 105A, 107M, 107I, 107A, 108tM, 108tA, 109tA, 110tM, 111M, 111I, 114tM, 114bM, 114bA, 115tM, 115bM, 116M, 116I, 117M, 118A, 119M, 119A, 120M, 120A, 121M, 122I, 123I, 124M, 124I, 124A, 125tA, 125bM, 125bA, 126I, 127tM, 127tA, 127bM, 127bA, 129M, 129I, 130M, 130A, 131tM, 131tA, 132M, 132I, 132A, 133M, 133I, 133A, 134tM, 134bM, 136tM, 136bM, 137bA, 138M, 138I, 139M, 140M, 140I, 143I, 148tM, 148tA, 149bA, 151tM, 151bM, 152A, 154tM, 155M, 156bM, 156bA, 157bM, 159tM, 160M, 161bA, 162M, 162I, 163bM, 164M, 164A, 165M, 165I, 166M, 167M, 168M, 169tM, 169bA, 170M, 170I, 171tM, 172bM, 173I, 174tM, 176I, 177tM, 177tA, 177bA, 179tM, 179bM, 180tM, 180bM, 181M, 181I, 184A, 185bM, 187M, 187I, 188M, 189tM, 189bM, 191M, 191I, 192M, 192I, 193tM, 193bA, 194M, 195bM, 196M, 196A, 197bA, 198M, 198I, 199tM, 199bM, 199bA, 200tM, 200tA, 200bM, 201M, 201I, 202tM, 202bM, 203tM, 203tA, 203bM, 203bA, 204M, 206I, 206A, 207tA, 207bM, 208M, 208I, 209M, 209I, 209A, 210tM, 201bM, 211tM, 211tA, 211bM, 211bA, 212tM, 212bM, 212bA, 213tM, 213bM, 213bA, 214tA, 214bM, 215tM, 215bM, 216tA, 216bM, 217I, 217A, 218M, 219M, 219I, 219A, 220tM, 220tA, 221M, 221I, 222tM, 223A, 224tM, 225M, 225I, 227tM, 228tM, 229A, 230M, 230A, 231I, 231A, 232tM, 232bM, 233tA, 235tM, 235bM, 235bA, 236I, 237tM, 237bM, 238M, 238I, 239bA, 240M, 240I, 242M, 242A, 243tM, 243bA, 244M, 244I, 245M, 245I, 246tM, 246bM, 247bA, 248M, 249M, 249I, 250tM, 250bM, 251tM, 251bM, 253M, 254M, 255tM, 255tA, 255bM, 257M, 258tM, 259tM, 259tA, 259bM, 260tA, 260bM, 260bA, 261B, 261I, 261A, 262tM, 262bM, 264tM, 264bA, 265bM, 266bM, 267tM, 268I, 269bB, 270bA, 271M, 271I, 272tA, 272bM, 273tM, 273bM, 273bA, 276tA, 277tA, 278M, 279bM, 279bA, 280M, 281tM, 281bM, 281bA, 282M, 282A, 284tM, 284bA, 285M, 285I, 286M, 286I, 287tM, 287tA, 287bM, 287bA, 288tM, 288bA, 290M, 290I, 290A, 291tM, 291tA, 291bM, 292tM, 292bM, 293M, 293I, 294M, 294I, 295I, 297tM, 297bM, 298tM, 298bM, 298bA, 299M, 299I, 300tM, 300bM, 301I, 302tM, 302bM, 303tA, 303bA, 304tA, 305bM, 306M; - Cheype: 44I; Consiglio: 73bM, 175tM; Deneyer: 61tM, 172tM, 182I, 186bM, 196I, 205bM, 239tM, 252tA, 256bM, 278A, 296tM; Emgenbroich: 289tM; Fernandez: 144I; Ferry: 258bM; Fischer: 28I; Floriani: 193bM; Gebert: 73tM; Ghyselinck: 150tM, 150bM, 230I; Hermosilla: 45I; Keller: 39bA; Kunze: 91bB, 91bM, 289tA; Laurant: 301M; Lehr: 85tM, 137bM, 149bM; Maurice: 20bA; Morgner: 274I; MÏller: 56M, 56A, 72tM, 78M, 79tM, 83bM, 86tM, 93bA, 96M, 145A, 152I, 153I, 158bM, 159bM, 160I, 162A, 163tM, 168A, 169bM, 171bM, 177bM, 182A, 185tA, 190M, 190I, 190A, 191A, 243bA, 244A, 247bM, 248I, 267bA, 268A, 276bM, 280II, 289bM, 289bA, 296bM, 298tA, 303bM; Nogu re: 130I, 131bM; Pflaum: 100tM; Pruss: 74M; Schmid: 51tM; Schmitz: 29M, 34tA, 35tM, 36M, 54bM, 55tM, 55bM, 60tM, 60bM, 66tM, 91tM, 142tA, 157bA, 283bM, 292tA, 297bA, 305bM; Schott: 141I, 143A, 197bM; Schreiner: 29Ir, 38M, 39tM, 39bM; Sklorz: 270tM; Vandercastle: 175bM, 241tA; Vidonne: 164I, 256M; Wallner: 250tA; Wilhelm: 238bA, 242I; Zajonc: 188I

BLACK'S NATURE GUIDES

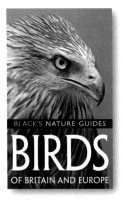

BIRDS
OF BRITAIN AND EUROPE

ISBN 978 1 4081 0155 1

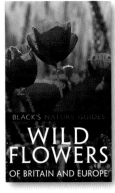

WILD FLOWERS
OF BRITAIN AND EUROPE

ISBN 978 1 4081 0153 7

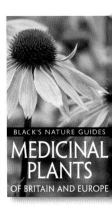

MEDICINAL PLANTS
OF BRITAIN AND EUROPE

ISBN 978 1 4081 0154 4

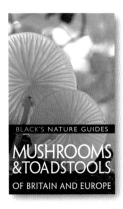

MUSHROOMS & TOADSTOOLS
OF BRITAIN AND EUROPE

ISBN 978 1 4081 0156 8

TREES
OF BRITAIN AND EUROPE

ISBN 978 1 4081 0152 0

The new Black's nature guides – compact, concise and comprehens

www.acblack.com

Discover nature
with A&C Black

ISBN 978 07136 8666 1

ISBN 978 07136 7237 4

ISBN 978 07136 7560 3

RSPB
HANDBOOK OF
BRITISH
BIRDS

PETER HOLDEN AND TIM CLEEVES 2nd Edition

AMAZING BIRDS
A TREASURY OF FACTS AND TRIVIA

ROGER J. LEDERER

ISBN 978 07136 8666 1

THE
SECRET LIVES OF
GARDEN BIRDS
Dominic Couzens Illustrated by Peter Partington

ISBN 978 07136 6616 8

www.acblack.com

Authors

Andreas Gminder has been heavily involved with the world of fungi since 1990 when he became a German Mycological Society adviser. He enjoys an international reputation, with around 40 publications in his native Germany and abroad. He has lived in the city of Jena since 2003 and offers courses for mushroom enthusiasts and mycologists in the nearby Thuringian Forest (www.pilzkurse.de).

Tanja Böhning has been self-employed as an artist since 2004. She fell in love with the world of mushrooms while studying in Jena in 1996 and subsequently changed her course to Biology. She has been an adviser for the German Mycological Society and the Thuringian Mycological Society since 2002 (www.naturaquarelle.de).

Includes 1,264 photographs and illustrations (see acknowledgements on p. 317)

Photograph on p. 2: Grisette. Photographs on p. 4 (top to bottom): Bay Bolete, *Rhodocybe gemina*, Fragile Brittlegill. Photographs on p. 5 (top to bottom): Rose Coral, Giant Puffball, Golden Cup. Photograph on pages 16–17: Sheathed Woodtuft (Hans E. Laux).

Published 2008 by A&C Black Publishers Ltd, 38 Soho Square, London W1D 3HB

www.acblack.com

First published 2007 by Franckh-Kosmos Verlags GmbH & Co. KG, Stuttgart, Germany

Copyright © 2008 Franckh-Kosmos Verlags GmbH & Co. KG

ISBN 978-1-4081-0156-8

A CIP catalogue record for this book is available from the British Library

All rights reserved. No part of this publication may be reproduced or used in any form or by any means – photographic, electronic or mechanical, including photocopying, recording, taping or information storage or retrieval systems – without permission of the publishers.

This book is produced using paper that is made from wood grown in managed sustainable forests. It is natural, renewable and recyclable. The logging and manufacturing processes conform to the environmental regulations of the country of origin.

Authors: Andreas Gminder and Tanja Böhning
Commissioning Editor: Nigel Redman
Project editor: Jim Martin

Translation by Eoghan G. Cameron (in association with Artes Translations)
Design by Fluke Art, Cornwall

Printed in Italy

10 9 8 7 6 5 4 3 2 1

Cover photograph: Porcelain Fungus © Adrian Davies/Alamy

Important Note to Reader
Using a mushroom guide is not a substitute for experience. It is best to have any mushrooms you pick examined and identified by an expert. If you are in any doubt as to the species of mushroom you have picked, do not, under any circumstances, eat it. Neither the publisher nor the authors can accept responsibility for the misidentification of mushrooms by anyone using this book or the consequences thereof. As a general rule, mushrooms should never be eaten raw. Where used in this book, the term 'edible' is taken to mean that the mushroom has undergone some form of cooking, such as frying or boiling.